Tyrant

Book 1

The Secret of the Scroll

by

DJ Harrison

Published in Great Britain by Open Circle Publishing in 2021

ISBN 978-1-909607-14-9

Open Circle Publishing
49-51 St Thomas's Road
Chorley
Lancashire
PR7 1JE

For Henry, Poppy, Georgia, and Charlie

1

The faint thud as an unfortunate bird dropped lifelessly onto the roof dragged Lone's consciousness back to her body. She was naked, filthy, hungry, and thirsty. Her physical discomfort was a testament to the number of days she'd been squatting on the floor of her hut.

For two long and arduous years, she'd been subjecting herself to the same torturous regime. Spells, incantations, prayers, and rituals followed by long periods sitting on the floor and projecting her entreaties into the earth beneath. She was searching for the vanished deity who had abandoned all her kind. *Gods don't die*, she kept telling herself, *my god still exists*. She felt the vestige of divine power within herself as a living legacy and a promise of what would come if she succeeded in attracting her god's attention.

At last, something had responded. She'd felt faint echoes. In reply, her spirit had descended deeper into oblivion than ever before until the tiny thread of humanity that tethered it to her body had been stretched almost to breaking point.

The contents of a bowl of tepid water disappeared in one desperate gulp. Breathing deeply, she reinforced the wards of protection that surrounded her to prevent anyone from approaching. Should any of the citizens of Bounty observe her present state, they would immediately conclude that she was a witch and drag her off to be hanged. Worse than the threat of discovery was the prospect that being disturbed could destroy many months of painstaking work.

Sustained by her intake of fluid, she returned to dredge the depths of darkness. It was like fishing in deep mud below a black river. Evidence of a presence was limited to half-imagined ripples, but she knew something was there. It wasn't her god, she could be sure of that, but it was something she could use. Something from another realm that would serve her purpose in this world.

She ignored the pleadings of her physical body and sank deeper. Whatever was down there had recognised her probing. What she was feeling wasn't the automatic thrash of a semi-animate beast, but a clear conscious flash of understanding. The first glimmer she'd encountered in all the long years of trying. It tasted like curiosity piqued. Smelt like the attraction of a composed mind to a new experience. A mind unlike hers, but one that weighed possibilities and pondered on outcomes.

If this was fishing, she was dangling herself on the end of the line. It felt to her more like being tethered to a stake in a predator-filled jungle. Attracting attention, difficult and time-consuming as it had been, was only the prelude. Her excitement fed energy into her system and she recognised that the really dangerous part of her task was beginning.

It was as if she'd observed a bubble rising from the ooze to leave an iridescent slick, betraying what lay below. It wasn't much, but it was more than she'd experienced before.

Incantations rolled around her mind in complex rhythms. Invitations, promises, temptations. She paraded her naked vulnerability to the denizen of the dark sludge. Begged. Pleaded. Promised pleasure. Abundant, never-ceasing ecstasy. Fleshy delights that only a human could offer.

Whatever it was, it came closer. Ripples disturbed the deep levels of her consciousness. Voices began to sound in her mind.

More incantations. Bargains to be struck. You scratch my back. I'll do whatever it is that you desire. I'll invent delights that you haven't even thought of. This is your chance. Join me in my world and I'll give it all to you.

But first, the pact.

The binding.

A small agreement, but a necessary one.

Something and nothing.

It responded. Tasted the offered inducements. Accepted the bargain.

She felt its unworldly power, and she exulted.

***

As she strode through Bounty, she wondered how she'd managed to remain so long in this isolated town without going completely mad. It had been her work, of course. Long hours of tedium flecked with intense danger had seen her through. Contact with the residents had been kept to the minimum required for survival.

Now she had tethered her demon and could unleash it on the unsuspecting King. But first, she would have to travel to the capital and find her husband and fellow conspirator. Travelling alone was out of the question, though. A woman without a man to protect her was asking for trouble in this misogynistic world.

Two mercenaries swaggered past her, brandishing over-sized weapons. The man dragging the heavy two-handed sword paused to look at her. She watched his eyes as they traversed the length of her body. Her stomach twisted as he licked his lips and raised a sweaty hand to paw at her chest.

You don't want to do that. Lone whispered into his mind while reaching inside him and squeezing. His mouth opened wordlessly as he fought for breath. She tried hard to resist the impulse to crush his windpipe, squash his heart into pulp, and leave him writhing in the agonising death his callous disrespect deserved. It was a close thing, but she succeeded in restraining herself by reasoning that his companion was likely to need the same treatment and then the good citizens of Bounty would have even more reason to proclaim her a witch. That would inconvenience her greatly. She'd have to fight her way out, kill more people, and risk being pursued on her way back to civilisation. Her work here was done. Better to leave quietly, but to do that, she needed male company without which she would stand out like a tall poppy in a field of stubble.

These two morons had seemed her only option until the big stranger wandered into town.

'That's Tyrant,' one of the women whispered, eliciting an exaggerated intake of breath from the others.

'Tyrant?' Lone asked.

The woman gave her a surprised look. 'He's from Gort. He's famous. Kills people if they so much as look at him. They've tried to hang him lots of times but they never succeeded.'

The swordsman's colour changed from purple to red as she released her hold on his throat. His eyes turned away and Lone followed them towards the large, unkempt fellow heading their way. The swordsman gripped his weapon tightly and his partner gave him a look of encouragement.

That man has taken your money. Now you have the chance to take it back.

Lone shot the idea into the man's mind, then walked away to mingle with a group of women, heavily laden with vegetables, who had paused to take in the impending confrontation.

Lone watched the big man as he ambled towards the mercenaries. If he were a mighty warrior, he didn't look the part. More like an oversized vagabond with little purpose and fewer possessions. A man to avoid, perhaps, but only because there could be no possible advantage to any form of engagement. The suggestion she'd made to her two thugs would be powerful enough, though, and bloody conflict was inevitable.

2

The two men blocking Tyrant's path looked as if they meant it. One was fat and grubby, dressed in smelly rags and cradling a longsword in need of a good clean. His scrawny companion carried a long-handled pike with a wicked hook at the pointy end.

Tyrant gave them a hard stare. They both glowered back at him.

Tyrant tried a smile and spread his hands to show they were free of any dangerous weapons. The men gripped their ironmongery tighter and bared their teeth.

Tyrant tried a step backwards. They advanced.

'Hold on,' Tyrant said, 'what are we trying to achieve here?'

Two puzzled looks gradually dissolved as the words were digested. 'You,' the pikeman said enigmatically.

'Me?' Tyrant said. 'Me what? Be more specific.'

'We've come for you,' Pikeman explained.

'So you know who I am, then?'

Tyrant's question seemed to tax their brains because they looked at each other as if seeking guidance. 'You've got our money and we want it back.' Pikeman came up with an answer as if he'd plucked it out of the air.

'All I have are the clothes I stand in and a crust of bread in my pocket. You're welcome to that if you want it. I'm afraid it's more mould than bread, but you might be able to scrape it clean.'

The puzzled look returned and the men took another step closer.

'Hold on,' Tyrant said. 'Before you do anything rash, you should know that I'm Tyrant.'

'We don't care what your name is,' Pikeman said. His companion nodded as if to lend additional weight to the remark.

'Then you should. I've got nothing worth stealing and you're only going to get yourselves hurt.'

'Don't see how.' Pikeman smirked. 'We've got a pike and a sword. It's you that's going to get hurt.'

'I don't need a sword,' Tyrant said. 'I have my reputation. That's enough. Now get lost.'

Tyrant took a deep breath. This was the trouble with the more remote reaches of the kingdom. Back in Gort, everyone knew him and, apart from an occasional drunken brawl, he was given a wide berth. 'As for the weapons you carry, let me give you the benefit of my experience. A pike can be really useful if you're being attacked by a man on a horse. That was what they were designed for. Prodding horses. Once you've skewered the horse, though, it becomes something of a liability. Think about it. Whoever's on the horse isn't going to be happy, is he? On the contrary, he's not going to take kindly to you prodding a hole in his beloved steed. When there's no horse involved, a pike is worse than useless. Too long, too unwieldy. I don't know why you bother dragging it around with you.'

The potential altercation had attracted quite a crowd, with more onlookers arriving every minute. Tyrant found himself addressing not only the men confronting him but also a gaggle of unwashed faces. Unwashed apart from one. There was a woman standing front and centre whose dark eyes were ablaze with excitement, presumably at the prospect of Pikeman trying his luck. He found himself fascinated by her face. It was not only clean but unblemished. No pox marks, no boils, no pimples, not even the obligatory wart to add distinction. Her cheeks were full, smooth, and free of slap marks and bruises. It was a wonder how she'd managed to get through to middle age without any marks to denote the passage of time. She was unusual, extremely attractive and, Tyrant searched for a more appropriate epithet and came up with the perfect one: Dangerous.

'Get on with it,' a gruff voice shouted from the back, though his impatience didn't appear to be shared by the majority of the assembly who seemed content to stand silently and let the tension build.

'Before we do that,' Tyrant said, 'I need to say something about that big sword your friend is dragging around. If I'm honest, it's no more use than your pike. It's too heavy by far. You'd be hard put to hit anything more mobile than a tree. Look, lads, there's no shame in backing down when you realise that you're already beaten. After all, I am Tyrant. Many have put me to the test; most of them younger, fitter and better equipped than you. I don't need to add to my already awesome reputation. Let's call it a draw and go our separate ways.'

For a moment, Tyrant felt that his wise calming words were having the desired effect, then his eyes were inevitably drawn back to the dark-haired woman who returned his gaze with what felt like mild amusement. The crowd began to voice their mounting frustration. They'd turned up to watch a fight and weren't leaving until they'd seen one.

As if in response, Pikeman swung his weapon in a wide arc then thrust it savagely in Tyrant's direction.

Tyrant grabbed the pike with his left hand and pulled it towards him. Pikeman, clinging on to his weapon, practically launched himself onto Tyrant's right fist which, judging from the pain it caused to his hand, connected with enough force to fell a horse. Grabbing the semi-conscious pikeman by the scruff of his neck, Tyrant twisted him around so that his body provided protection from his accomplice, who had raised his enormous sword above his head and was about to strike.

The possession of the pike was being barely contested, its owner having lost interest on receipt of that blow to the face. Tyrant swung the unwieldy object and struck the swordsman's shoulder. This upset the swordsman's already precarious balance and he toppled backwards, sword still in the raised position. Having deposited Pikeman in a heap on top of his fallen ally, Tyrant stood on the sword hand until it obligingly released its grip.

'There you are. Now do you understand what I've been trying to tell you? These are hard and dangerous times. Try something like this again and you're going to end up dead. Most men in my position would have killed you to improve their reputation. You're fortunate that I already have more than enough of a reputation to protect me against all but the very stupid; a classification that you have to admit is appropriate for you two.'

He picked up the sword and hefted it. The pommel was loose, and the blade was notched and rusty. It was ridiculously heavy, even for his strong arms to wield. He brought it down hard onto the pike and it broke into two pieces while the wooden pole remained intact. Swordsman's face clouded with a look that might have been disappointment but ought to have been embarrassment.

Discarding what was left of the sword, he ignored the voices demanding blood and pushed his way through the crowd.

***

As he sat in the tavern, nursing the weak grog that was all the few coppers in his pockets would stretch to, Tyrant contemplated his next move. With no money left for food or lodgings, his options were sorely limited. Stay where he was and sleep in the filth amongst a collection of drunken thieves, or move on and find some accommodating piece of bracken well away from noise and trouble. There had been recent rain and more was sure to come during the night, but being damp was a small price to pay for peace and quiet. If he stayed here, he risked someone else trying their luck now that they'd seen the kindness he'd shown those two. On reflection, he should have at least roughed them up, broken a few bones, and left them in a sorry state as a disincentive to others. That's what a reputation was all about, after all. It was a dog-eat-dog world, and he needed to be recognised as a man who swallowed rottweilers whole and had wolves for breakfast. There were plenty who would, at the first sign of weakness, take the opportunity to smash his head in, beat his brains out, slice off his genitals, and generally mess him around. Better not to have to deal with all that waving around of swords and axes; better to have a reputation. He resolved to be less merciful next time.

Having spent a long time wistfully staring at his empty tankard contemplating the soft wetness of bracken, he was surprised when a feminine hand deposited a large foaming ale on the table in front of him. He pushed it away. 'I didn't order this,' he said.

'No, but I did. I'm Lone and I was impressed by your performance today.'

It was the unblemished face from the fight crowd attached to the body of a woman far too attractive for a place like this. Her eyes were intense and made him feel nervous. 'I still can't accept it,' he said, not entirely convincing himself.

'Why not?' her voice was even and authoritative. There was no hint of nervousness, even though she was a woman alone in a cacophony of drunken males.

'Because then I'd owe you for it and you'd have to be paid back. I'm not vain. I'm on the wrong side of thirty; I have no possessions, no money, and no prospects. That rather rules out a romantic motive, doesn't it? So you want something from me and, in my experience, that will lead to trouble I can do without. So, thank you very much but no thanks.' The smell of the fresh beer was singing in his nostrils, his mouth was anticipating the delicious taste, and his digestive system had already adjusted itself in readiness.

'You've got that right,' she laughed. 'I'm a married woman, anyway.'

'So where's your husband?'

'Gort, the capital city. Where the King resides.'

'I know Gort; I was there only a few weeks ago. Horrible place, full of rabble come in from the countryside in search of an easy life. You would do well to stay away.'

'I have to go there to be reunited with him, surely you can understand that?'

'Not really,' Tyrant said, still sniffing the beer. 'He should be the one to come to you. That's if he's still interested. How long has he been gone?'

'Two years.'

'Sounds to me like he's abandoned you and doesn't want you back.'

'It was my decision to come here without him. I had things I needed to do. Now, it's time to return and I want you to accompany me.' She gently pushed the tankard even further under his nose.

'Out of the question,' Tyrant said, wondering if this long conversation was justification for drinking this woman's ale without incurring some form of obligation. It was, after all, a sort of calling card. An introductory ploy to get his attention. If he didn't drink it, they wouldn't give her a refund. A quick look into her eyes convinced him and he took a large swig. 'I'm not going that way.'

'But you could,' she said in a husky whisper that set his body tingling. 'I'd make it worth your while.'

'You have nothing that I want, lady,' Tyrant said, wiping his foamy mouth with his sleeve.

She waved her hand. It was a small, insignificant sort of wave. More of a slight flick of the wrist than a full-blown gesture. A man in a grimy apron hurried over with another tankard of beer and set it down on the table without a word. Tyrant moved his empty one aside and contemplated the new arrival. A shiver ran down his spine which he tried to remove by taking a swig. Weariness began to seep through his body and he wondered if he had enough energy to get himself up to the woods for the night. Maybe he could rest his head on the table for a few moments so that he could recover.

'Come with me,' she said.

He drained his tankard and followed dutifully. His legs were happy to walk beside her, but his head wanted to stay in the tavern.

***

Her home was a rough-looking hut on the edge of town, but inside it was fragrant and welcoming. There were herbs and spices in the air and a feeling of warmth and comfort. The most striking feature, though, was that it was clean. The rush matting underfoot was mud free – an amazing achievement.

Tyrant decided that one night's accommodation, even when added to the beers, would not commit him to anything. He'd made it perfectly clear that he wasn't going anywhere with her and still she'd invited him back to the warm dryness of her home. It had been her choice, freely given. As he fell asleep on the soft dry matting, he tried to keep those thoughts uppermost, but without success. Instead, there was a much wiser version of him telling him to get up and run away. That nothing good would come of an association with this woman. That there was something very dangerous about her. That he was going to get himself killed because of two beers and shelter for the night.

3

Ambrose trudged up the hill towards the citadel perched menacingly in the epicentre of the city. The sight of the King's fortified residence evoked dread in his guts, as it was undoubtedly designed to do. Nobody living in Gort could fail to be cowed by the overpowering menace the palace and its monstrous tower exerted.

Underfoot, the mud of the streets, made sloppy by the same drizzle that soaked his face, slowly became transformed by stone as he approached the inner wall and the great gate that controlled entrance to the garrison and the fortress. Cobbles, slippery and ankle-twisting, rose out of the mire becoming whole slabs of smooth stone as he approached the soldiers, who were controlling the straggling procession of humanity and goods awaiting permission to enter through the archway gated with wood and iron.

Beneath his cloak, the scroll wrapped tightly in weathered pigskin was protected from the rain and hidden from prying eyes. In comparison with the ancient treasure he'd repeatedly hauled back from the North, a series of intricate drawings wasn't likely to impress the King, but it was all that he had left and he was hoping it might be enough to save him. The King's patronage was a fickle thing that his livelihood and possibly continued existence depended on. Over the years, his forays into the inhospitable land in the far North had yielded enough in the way of artefacts to convince the King to fund his work. Now, however, everything that remained was rolled up tightly under his cloak.

The guard spied him in the line, nodded slightly in his direction, and ushered him through the gate. Recognition was a two-edged sword that brought both privilege and peril. There was a price to pay for being close to the King and that involved keeping him content. A scroll wasn't the kind of thing to interest him at the best of times, but it was all he had. It would have to serve as his only shield against the King's displeasure.

This most recent expedition had been a disaster. Half his men had disappeared into the cave system, never to return. There had been an outbreak of an unknown disease that caused weakness, hair loss, pustulating sores, and a slow, agonising death. Four of the party had died, and the rest had fled south before he'd any chance to obtain the sort of items that the King required. The scroll he clutched had been discovered several years ago, but it was all he could find to try to justify the expense and loss of this expedition. Careful study over the years had convinced him that it contained powerful secrets. The memory of the terrible affliction that he'd so narrowly avoided made him determined never to return to the bad lands of the far North. The King, however, had an insatiable appetite for artefacts and wasn't at all concerned about the loss of life involved in their pursuit.

As he walked across the smooth flagstones that paved the large open square in front of the palace, Ambrose's thoughts turned away from his immediate predicament and towards his son. Ant was fifteen and becoming more difficult to control. The boy bristled with disobedience and resentment. There was a growing irritation between them that wasn't helped by having to leave the boy to his own devices for long periods now that he'd finally dispensed with the services of his housekeeper.

Getting out of Gort, away from the King and his demands, was the only solution that would safeguard them both. The King wouldn't allow it, that was certain, and defying the King had only one outcome, which involved hanging from the end of a rope. The possibility of one final expedition from which he wouldn't return was the only way. There was a large lake to the North well before the wastelands began that he'd earmarked as a possible place to live away from the sight of the King. He wished he'd taken Ant on the previous expedition and never returned. Coming back empty-handed like this meant his opportunity to evade the King's long arm might have passed him by.

As the guard opened the door to admit him, the churning in his guts reminded him that getting out of the King's chamber alive might be his most pressing problem. The look on the King's face did nothing to reassure him.

The monarch's jowls quivered as he expressed his displeasure, accentuating his points by prodding Ambrose's face with a pudgy finger. Spittle spattered, he held himself as still as possible, waiting for the verbal onslaught to subside. 'Do you know how much your pathetic little jaunt has cost me? And for what? Tell me. Go on. Show me the items you promised me. Where are they? How do you propose to recompense all my trouble? What do you have to offer that might justify your miserable existence?'

The King's chamber was lined by armed guards and tapestries depicting horrible scenes of slaughter. The big round table was weighed down by dishes piled with foodstuffs and the detritus of discarded and spat out pieces. The room smelt of over-ripe fruit, old fish, and flatulence.

Ambrose knew from experience not to try to interrupt the King, to keep looking at him and stand his ground despite the uncomfortable proximity of that fat distended angry face. The King's breath was sweetly foul, as if there were carcasses rotting in his oesophagus. More prodding, more drizzle in his face, more ranting. The words that assailed him flowed unrecognised past his ears as he watched the fat face grow redder until it glowed purple. The King suddenly stopped shouting and gasped for breath, clutching his chest with both hands. Two burly servants rushed to assist and carry him to a couch where he lay wheezing as an unhealthy pallor returned to his features.

Ambrose's own breath returned. He gasped in concert with his King while feeling his legs threatening to give way and deposit him onto the straw matted floor. Gradually, the King recovered to the extent that he could half sit and once again stare menacingly. Ambrose took this as his prompt to try to recover the situation, if that were still possible. The knowledge that at least he'd not already been marched off to the gallows provided faint consolation. That possibility was by no means excluded, even if the initial tirade had been endured.

'Your majesty,' Ambrose bowed deeply, 'your expedition may have been disappointing in its outcome, yet it yielded some important information. The artefacts we previously discovered may have been all that existed. I am of the opinion that our diligent search failed because there is nothing more to find. You may well have every magical item that exists already secured in your vaults. I would humbly remind you that our previous expeditions were a great success. Your power and the security of your domain have been immeasurably enhanced by our work.'

The King blinked and gave a slight shake of the head as if he were finding comprehension difficult. 'Explain yourself,' he responded with a voice approaching his rasping normality.

'We ventured further north into the wastelands than ever before and found an extensive system of underground caverns. I sent out parties to explore these and to look for artefacts. The whole situation appeared to be very promising at first. Then men failed to return. They just vanished, as did the ones sent to search for them. We lost twelve like this. Then some men came back reporting strange caverns where it was as light as day because of a glow coming from the walls. Unfortunately, these men fell ill, beset by a terrible wasting disease. Their hair fell out, they vomited blood, and they died in horrible pain over a period of several days. I gave orders that the glowing caves were to be avoided, but my words weren't heeded and more men went missing or died horribly. In the end, despite our gallant efforts, we found no useful items. Still, we searched diligently until our food supplies ran low and we were forced to make the long journey back to Gort.'

'Without anything to show for my troubles other than half my men dead or missing,' the King said.

'That is the unfortunate truth, your majesty. We tried and failed this time, but I have plans for the next expedition that will hopefully remedy the situation and determine once and for all if any valuable items remain hidden.' Ambrose found himself breathing more easily now that the King had adopted a more passive posture and was no longer spitting in his face. How long this would last was dependent on his being allowed to continue to reassure the monarch without inflaming his redoubtable temper.

'You are sure that all these caves were empty?' the King asked.

'Absolutely, sire. They were completely devoid of any items. Just caves, dark and musty and stretching for ever. The valuables I recovered for you on previous expeditions were always in small discrete caverns. We found no more of these unconnected caves as we travelled further north. Further forays will concentrate on the smaller caves where there is more chance of success.'

The King heaved himself into an upright sitting position with obvious effort. His face was blotchy pink and the excess flesh under his chin quivered and rippled with his laboured breathing. 'That's not good enough and you know it. Months away, all that expense and you have the effrontery to come back empty-handed. You don't seem to understand why I employ you.' Staggering to his feet, the King slapped the table with the flat of his right hand, sending a shockwave through Ambrose's system.

Ambrose felt his body stiffening in response and his chest tightened uncomfortably. Sudden dryness in this throat made his voice cracked and hoarse. Any semblance of composure had evaporated in the face of the renewed onslaught. 'We did discover something of great significance.' His words dried up and he brought out the scroll from the folds of his cloak, laid it on the messy table, and unrolled it from its pigskin protection, trying not to sully it with detritus.

'Paper? I have no use for scribblings. You must understand that there are unseen forces at work to dethrone me. I'm under constant threat of attack from witches and demons. I require items with which to defend myself, not rolls of parchment.'

'There is something recorded here that I believe will provide a great deal of protection to you. It appears to be a device that will allow you to survey the length and breadth of your kingdom. To anticipate any attack. To be prepared for anything.' Ambrose placed his finger on the ancient document to indicate the intricate pattern that he believed held the key to whatever the device might be.

'You believe? Aren't you sure? These scrawls could be anything or nothing. What makes you believe they will be useful?'

'Sire, I have been studying this particular scroll very carefully. The inscriptions around the pattern indicate farsightedness and great power. If it works, this may be more effective than any of the artefacts you already have. You will become unassailable.'

'You have no idea what I'm faced with.' The King's voice was calmer now, his eyes no longer boring into Ambrose's face but casting around the tabletop as if in search of a dainty morsel. 'There are forces you cannot comprehend out there waiting for me to lower my guard.' He wiped his greasy mouth with his sleeve as his eyes, already pig-small, narrowed even further. 'Perhaps this thing might allow me to see them more clearly. What do you propose?'

'We should construct one of these devices in the tower where it will command a view over the whole of Gort and surrounding land.'

The King stuffed a handful of meat into his mouth and began to chew slowly. Ambrose was forced to wait for a response until the mastication had been completed and a goblet of wine guzzled to help the food down the royal gullet. 'Very well. Have it ready for when I return from my vineyards. And it better be good. For your sake.'

4

Ambrose stood looking out of the tower. He really liked being all the way up here with the whole city beneath him. The tiny figures scurrying around below had no idea that they were being overlooked, and he enjoyed the feeling of power that knowledge gave him. The gentle scent of wood smoke drifted around him, tinged occasionally with the not-so-gentle stench of human ordure. The clatter of iron on iron and the clunk of stone being worked echoed around the elaborate semi-spherical roof.

He looked back at the stonemasons, who were chipping away as if their lives depended on it. Maybe the promise made by the foreman to throw the one deemed to be the slowest from the tower and watch him bounce from rooftop to rooftop was having the desired effect. The King would be returning in two days' time and he would be expecting his artefact to be ready and working.

The disturbing figure of Malachi, the King's chief adviser, appeared at the top of the stairs like a black ghost. The cloak and hood revealed only the tip of a prominent nose, yet he could feel those dreadful eyes boring into his being. It was as if the man had little need for conversation, instead preferring to suck thoughts directly from his brain. Ambrose shuddered involuntarily as he felt a constriction in his throat, as if invisible fingers were gently throttling him.

Long periods away from court had made his encounters with Malachi mercifully few and far between. In truth, their paths had rarely needed to cross and Malachi had shown only a fleeting interest in him. Until now.

Perhaps the prospect of losing influence had caused him to make the long climb up the spiral stone steps to reach the heady heights of this seldom-used space at the top of the world. Ambrose smiled inwardly at the thought. Anything that upset this awful man and loosened his undoubted hold on the King had to be a positive thing. The imagined grip on his throat tightened as Malachi spoke. 'What's going on here?'

'An installation,' Ambrose replied. 'By order of the King. We are reproducing an ancient pattern which we believe will enhance His Majesty's security. It will, I hope, enable him to oversee the realm more easily and warn of any impending threat, thus keeping all his loyal citizens safer.'

'You believe? You don't know?' Malachi emerged sufficiently into the light for the sun's rays to be reflected on the hooded eyes.

'As the King's archaeologist, it is my expert opinion that my discovery is a valuable addition to the resources the King has at his disposal.'

'Where did you find this inscription?'

Ambrose knew he didn't have to explain himself to this man. Nor should he reveal secrets that should be kept between him and the King. Yet something about the way the question was asked compelled him to struggle for an answer. 'In the wastelands, far to the north.'

'Is this what the King sent you to find?' Malachi took a step nearer.

'No, of course not,' Ambrose found himself blurting out more than he wanted. 'The King has no need for scrolls. I took this for my own study.'

'The items you bring back for the King. Describe them to me.'

'No, I can't do that. The King has insisted that I keep that information strictly between him and me.'

'Only you and the King and two dozen soldiers who carried the things south plus the men who guard the secret store and advisers such as myself who have examined these artefacts on the King's behalf. Don't flatter yourself, Ambrose. You're just a journeyman in all this. Someone who is sent off into the wilderness from time to time. You have no idea what it is you're bringing back.'

Ambrose felt the heat in his face as he responded. 'I know more than anyone else about these things. They are relics of an ancient civilisation. Weapons of war.'

'Weapons of war indeed. Very powerful ones which, if they ended up in the wrong hands, could alter the balance of power in the kingdom. That's why the King jealously guards them. This is very different, though. It reeks of magic. You must be well aware that the King abhors anything to do with witchcraft, sorcery, or demons. The penalty for dabbling in the occult is a swift death at the end of a rope. That's where you're headed if you persist in this foolish enterprise. Mark my words, this is a magical pattern. It's unlikely to function without the necessary arcane expertise and that, my friend, is going to be your only saving grace. Swallow your pride, cease this fruitless and dangerous endeavour, and admit to the King that you've made a mistake.' Malachi turned and walked away, the sound of his footsteps slowly fading as he disappeared down the steps.

A terrible uncertainty gripped Ambrose. It was true that he had no guarantee that the device would perform the way he expected or that it would work at all. Malachi's words left him with a hollow space in his chest and struggling to breathe. Was he trying to help? Unlikely, given the man's nature and reputation for missing no opportunity to ingratiate himself with the King.

There was the irritating grit of truth in what Malachi had said, though. The King was, without doubt, violently averse to any form of magic. Yet he'd happily accepted the mysterious objects brought back from the North whose function was completely beyond comprehension. Surely, this device was no different in essence from the boxes made from strange substances and the metal tubes they contained? Both had been derived from the same geographical source, hadn't they? Wasn't he merely constructing just such an artefact from scratch, using the ancient instructions left on the cave wall for him to find?

Possibly. Possibly not. Artefacts were hard, metallic, and could be weighed in the hand. If he were honest with himself, this pattern did smack of wizardry, and this made him nervous. The King had granted him leave to go ahead without examining the scroll or questioning how the thing might work. Where did he draw the line between ancient technology and magic? One was acceptable, welcome even. The other punishable by death.

All forms of spirituality had long since been forbidden. The temple had been pulled down. Worship of any deity had been banned. Witches, wizards, and priests had been systematically rooted out and hanged. The merest suggestion of divine inspiration or demonic possession was enough to get you killed.

This, however, might be his last option to persuade the King that he should be allowed another expedition so he could escape with Ant to relative safety. If the device failed to work, he would be in mortal danger. If it was deemed by His Majesty to be magical, his fate would be brutally swift. Malachi's grain of doubt was scratching away at his confidence.

The percussive harmony of the chisels kept up a constant beat. The pattern was being gouged from the stone along the chalk lines he'd set out. It was simple yet beautiful. A circle within a circle adorned with arcs. Lines forming hexagrams. Intricate yet uncomplicated.

Ambrose recovered his composure. At the very least, it was a pleasing inscription for the King to initially admire then forget about. It wouldn't work. Of course it wouldn't. If it needed magic, he had no magic with which to coax it into life. And that was for the best. Once his ruler's initial disappointment had subsided, provided that it hadn't been ruthlessly violent, he'd persuade him to send him back north in search of more artefacts and perhaps an answer to the riddle of the pattern. Breathing out long and luxuriously, Ambrose came back to a place of calm in his body. He'd try. He'd fail. The King would forgive him. As long as the device didn't work, he'd survive this difficult time.

5

Ant was feeling exhilaration and sorrow in roughly equal measures as he strode proudly towards the citadel at his father's side. This visit to the palace and his father's place of work was a childhood dream come true.

His father had provided new clothes for the occasion, which helped him feel older and more confident than his fifteen years might warrant. As they approached the gate, he dragged his feet, leaving showers of sparks from his new iron-shod boots in his wake. The soldiers stood back and nodded deferentially, making Ant wish his friends had been present to witness his passage.

This visit could have been an even more wonderful birthday present had he been able to share it with Mona. Even after all this time, when he thought of her, the pain in his abdomen spread throughout the hole in him that her absence had chiselled out. She was his mother. Not his birth mother, but the only mother he'd ever experienced. He'd grown up in her soft embrace.

He longed for the evenings when she'd laid his head across her lap and he'd watched the dancing flames as she told him stories of days long ago when gods were worshipped and, in return, shepherded their human flock. This had been their custom for many years whenever Ambrose was absent. Her hand would grip the pendant she habitually wore whenever she mentioned her goddess: Persephone. 'One day, her eyes will once again turn towards Gort and she will return to restore her temple,' she'd say, then bow her head in prayer. Ant would join in on the basis that whatever Mona desired, he desperately wanted to provide.

But now she was gone. Banished by his unfeeling father in an act of supreme cruelty. Despite his father's dire warnings, Ant was determined to find her and bring her back to him. In order to do that, he needed to be free of Ambrose and he could only achieve freedom if he could support both himself and Mona. This visit was a first step inside the source of power and wealth that would allow him his heart's desire.

Meanwhile, the hollow pain subsisted even in his mounting excitement as his boots clattered across the cobbles that led uphill to the towering majesty of the palace itself. Part way across the enormous square flanked by stone, Ant's eyes were unable to wrest themselves from the grisly sight of the gallows ahead of them. Thankfully, there were no bodies swinging gently in the cold morning breeze, but even the structure itself, with its three nooses dangling in wait, gave him a feeling of utter dread.

It was a great relief when his father led him inside the building and into a long corridor scattered with grim-faced soldiers who gave him cold looks as they passed. Ant shivered, despite it being considerably warmer inside. There was a hostile feel to this place. Perhaps this was merely because it was unfamiliar and he'd get used to it when the King employed him. Because that was what he needed to happen. He had to step out of the shadow of his father, who had steadfastly refused to let him become part of his work. That left Ant with only one option: to make his own way in life, and that meant becoming a member of the court.

'Not far now,' Ambrose said, as they passed through a doorway and found themselves at the foot of a spiral staircase.

They climbed until Ant's calves cried out in pain and his legs were threatening to give way. Despite the squirt of brightness they projected onto the central stone column, the slit windows were too far apart to properly light the way, and Ant had to concentrate hard on his feet to avoid stumbling in the dark. Falling would mean being battered by hard stone all the way to the bottom, where he'd lie in bloody fragments. Holding the outer wall with his left hand, he trod carefully on the widest part of the stair that only just accommodated the full length of his foot. The higher he got, the more nervous he felt, and the occasional glimpse of the world beneath through the impossibly bright windows made his stomach churn.

Ambrose, in contrast, strode inexorably upwards, never pausing to draw breath and making Ant strain to keep up. His legs hurt so badly that he was about to give up and take a rest when a brighter patch of light beckoned him further and the end of the staircase was revealed. With tottering legs, he emerged onto the top of the tower. Stone columns supported a substantial roof, but there were no walls to hide the view of the city below. Ant's head swam with giddiness and fatigue and he sunk to the ground and sat clinging to the stone slabs to steady his whirling senses.

'Come on,' Ambrose said, 'take in the view. You can see the whole of Gort from here. Some might say the whole of the kingdom if your eyes are sharp enough.'

Dutifully, Ant scrambled to his feet and joined his father in leaning on the low wall that surrounded the tower summit. Despite his queasiness, Ant was determined to show his father he was taking it all in his stride. Ambrose was constantly accusing him of being soft and laying the blame on Mona for coddling him for so long. Getting rid of her had been his father's attempt to toughen him up and make him a man, or so he said. The sheer injustice of it stung him to tears that he could barely hold back even now.

'It's very impressive,' Ant said.

'Imagine how many stonemasons it took to build this,' Ambrose said. 'Yet the King comes here very rarely.'

'Why is that?' Ant asked. If this were his tower, he'd come here every day. Once he'd grown used to the height, which he was slowly beginning to do.

'Your young legs were hard pressed to climb this far. The King is hardly in a fit state to do that without assistance and the confines of the staircase make it difficult to carry him. Still, he's promised to come up here to see my latest project when it's complete.'

Ambrose stood in the centre of the space and indicated the intricate pattern that was being chiselled into the stone. He pulled a scroll from beneath his cloak and unrolled it on the ground. 'This is what I'm having inscribed,' he said. 'It's an ancient device that will greatly increase the King's power and influence.'

'If it works, which I doubt,' a voice suddenly intruded into their conversation and Ant looked up to see a tall man in a black cloak with its hood hiding everything but the tip of a long, thin nose.

'Malachi,' Ambrose said. 'I didn't expect to find you up here.'

'I made a special trip just for you,' Malachi said. 'I heard you'd brought your boy here and thought it only polite to greet him.'

'There was no need for that,' Ambrose said. 'My son is no concern of yours. I promised to show him the palace and this will be the one and only time he comes here. I'd thank you for leaving the boy alone. He's young and harmless.'

Ant squirmed at the description his father was giving. There was a cloud of suspicion hanging between the two men that threatened to thicken into outright enmity. Malachi's eyes were sparks of reflected light from the darkness of his hood and they caught him up and held him fast. Ant lost his breath for a moment, almost as if it had been taken from him, then returned as an act of kindness. That wasn't possible, but it certainly felt as if it had happened. Malachi evoked feelings of awe and respect that bypassed his mind and were delivered directly into his body.

'Let the boy speak for himself,' Malachi said. 'Tell me, young man, what is your greatest ambition in life?'

Ant knew that telling him that he wanted more than anything to find Mona and live with her forever had to remain unsaid, yet he felt compelled to tell Malachi despite the damage it would do to his relationship with his father. Struggling against the impulse, he managed to blurt out something less damaging. 'I want to be an archaeologist like my father,' he said. 'Become a trusted adviser to the King,' he added and wished he'd not.

'It remains to be seen how much trust will be left after your father's latest folly,' Malachi said.

'It's not a folly.' Ambrose rose to his full height and faced the hooded figure. 'It's a powerful device that will allow our King to view far distant areas of his kingdom and greatly increase his power.'

'What makes you think that?' Malachi asked with a chuckle in his voice.

'I have this ancient scroll.' Ambrose bent over and stabbed the parchment with his finger. 'It's perfectly clear to someone as experienced as I am.'

'This writing,' Malachi said, 'what does it say?'

'It's a lost language in an unfamiliar script,' Ambrose replied.

'So you don't know what it says?'

Ant could feel the heat radiating from his father as the exchange progressed. Didn't he understand that Malachi was baiting him? Trying to demean him in front of his son? Why was Ambrose being so defensive when it was he who had the knowledge and Malachi was merely a bystander?

'I don't need the script,' Ambrose said. 'The drawings are clear enough.'

Ant stared at the scroll. There were several diagrams. One showed the pattern in plain view, another depicted wavy lines emanating from a black line. Inside the wavy lines were what looked like eyes to Ant, but they could have been squiggles and dots.

'I hope for your sake you're right,' Malachi said. 'Though I fear that your son is going to sit disappointed, waiting for you to return home one day soon. When that happens, he can come to me and I'll take care of him. It's the least I can do for a friend and a colleague who has incurred the wrath of our King.'

'You'll do no such thing.' Ambrose was shouting and waving his arms about. Ant was used to seeing him angry, but this was a new level of incandescence. 'Leave my son alone, you despicable monster. I'll not have him fall under your evil influence. I'd rather die than let you have him.'

'That, my friend,' Malachi said, 'may not be a choice within your power to make. As far as your scroll is concerned, I reckon your son has a better idea of what it means than you do. I've already warned you about this foolhardiness. Better to stop now, make your peace with the King and save yourself from disaster.'

With that, Malachi turned and made his way to the stairs. When he was gone, Ant felt a lightness return to his chest as if someone had been standing on it and had now removed his foot. Ambrose stood red-faced with his fists clenched, staring at the stairwell.

'That is the most evil man in the world,' Ambrose said. 'I wish I'd not given into your childish pleadings and brought you here. He should never have been allowed to know even that you exist, let alone see you with his own eyes. Now you've put us both in danger. I know him. He'll use you against me, mark my words. You must swear on your dead mother never to have anything more to do with that awful man. Go on.'

'It's not up to me, though, is it? I can't be expected to make a solemn promise that isn't mine to keep. What should I do if Malachi approaches me? What could I do? He's a powerful man; even I can see that after such a short acquaintance. There's nothing either of us could do to resist him.'

Ambrose hissed through his teeth and gave Ant such a look of scorn that he almost wilted like a broken flower. Instead, he focussed on the scroll and tried to decipher the drawings. As he stared at them, his vision began to swim. It was as if the pictures came to life. The swirls started moving upwards and the eyes became larger as they seemed to come nearer. Then he realised that it wasn't only eyes he was looking at. Behind the eyes was a presence, a disturbing shadow that seemed to be solidifying inside the half-drawn lines. For an instant, his heart stopped and he felt very cold. Then it restarted with a bump, and the scroll returned to flat immobility with the eyes hardly visible.

Ant took a breath and began to form the words of warning that his encounter with the scroll required. His father's eyes warned him to hold his counsel. Anything he said now would appear to be an echo of Malachi's taunts. It would be better to wait until his father was in a calmer frame of mind.

6

'Witches have teeth.'

Ant struggled to understand the point of what Pepper was saying. The statement had been delivered as if it was an astounding revelation.

'Everybody has teeth,' Col said, narrowly beating Ant to the obvious riposte.

'I'm not talking about teeth up here.' Pepper pointed to his mouth. 'I'm telling you they have teeth down there.' He pointed in the vague direction of his stomach and grinned awkwardly.

'Down where, exactly?' Ant asked.

Pepper's face adopted the colour of the morning sky. 'You know…' his voice trailed off into inaudible muttering.

'I don't know,' Ant said. 'That's why I'm asking. What precise part of a witch's body possesses these additional teeth?'

'It's her you-know-what,' Pepper blurted. 'Her front bottom. There I've said it. You made me. Now are you satisfied?'

'You mean her vagina,' Col said.

'Call it what you like, it's the same thing. I don't like saying bergina 'cos it's rude.' Pepper paused as if waiting to receive the appropriate reaction to his momentous news.

'That can't be right,' Ant said, struggling with the whole process of imagining the inner working of a woman's private parts that he'd never even glimpsed. He'd often tried to picture them in his mind's eye based on information gained from vague impressions glimpsed when the wind blew clothing tight into that area. 'Who told you that?'

'It was my dad and his mates. They were talking one evening and thought I had gone to sleep. But I was listening to every word. That's how I found out. My dad should know; he's had to arrest plenty of witches.'

'But why would they?' Col asked, as his large amiable face creased into a gentle smile.

'Cos they're witches. That's what they have. Teeth down there, inside their, well, bodies. Between their legs. They were talking about it. Saying that any man who tried to have a witch would lose his willy. They'd bite it clean off, and he'd bleed to death in an instant.'

'Then they shouldn't even try doing that sort of thing to a witch,' Col said. 'It would be their own fault if it happened. Serve 'em right.'

'Ah, but that's not the point. How do you know if you're doing it with a witch until it's too late?' Pepper said.

'You could try asking,' Ant laughed. 'Anyway, if she wanted you to do what you're doing, then she'd have no reason to bite you with her vagina and everything would be OK. Be polite. And gentle. Then there's not going to be a problem with any woman, not even with a witch.'

'Until they rid the land of witches, I'll not feel safe having sex with a woman,' Pepper said. 'I'm not risking having my willy bitten off.'

'That sounds like a wise move.' Ant laughed. 'Though I think we all might think differently if ever the opportunity arose, witch or not.'

'My willy is in more danger of freezing off,' Col said. 'It's getting cold at nights around here.'

'Then we'll get you a nice blanket,' Pepper said. 'Leave it to me and Ant. We'll nip down to the market and see what we can get.'

'I'm not getting hanged for stealing a blanket,' Ant protested as equal measures of terror and excitement rippled through his body.

'It won't come to that,' Pepper replied. 'Anyway, if they did catch you, we'd rescue you. Wouldn't we, Col?'

Col raised both hands in a gesture that could have been agreement with Pepper or despair at the prospect of losing a friend to the hangman.

'I'm sure you mean well, but how could two boys manage to overcome a whole army of men?' Ant asked.

'Cunning. We'd outwit them, wouldn't we, Col?' Pepper looked again at their placid friend for support but received only a shrug. 'Anyway, it won't come to that. Even if they did catch you, I bet they wouldn't hang you. Just give you a telling off and a smack on the head. It's only real criminals that get hanged. A bit of stealing doesn't matter. Everyone steals stuff. They wouldn't hang you for that,' Pepper said.

'Little Billy got hanged,' Col said.

'For stealing?'

'Naw, for being possessed by a demon, they said. Hanged the poor lad up there in the castle.'

'He can't have been more than six,' Ant said.

'Six or not, they said he was possessed on account of the way he spoke. Said it were the demon talking,' Col said.

'He's always talked funny,' Pepper said, 'ever since he was a baby. Only his brother could tell what he was saying.'

'They hanged him too. For fighting. Tried to stop them taking Little Billy.'

'That's crazy; why would they kill two children like that?' Ant asked.

'It's the King. He can't abide anything to do with demons. Apparently, the very notion makes him crazy,' Col said. 'If there's even the slightest hint of witchcraft, magic, or demons, you get hanged right away. It's the law.'

'Then we should get ourselves another king,' Ant said.

'You can't say that,' Pepper said. 'It's treason and that's worse than stealing. If they hear you say that you get hanged for sure.'

'I don't care,' Ant said. 'Any king that hangs children deserves all the treason in the world.'

Pepper picked up the tattered remains of Col's only blanket and began to unravel it. 'See?' he said. 'It's rubbish. Wouldn't keep a baby warm, never mind a big lad like Col. Just a pile of old wool.'

'It is now you've unravelled it,' Ant said. 'If he needs a blanket, I'll get one from home. My father has lots of them for his expeditions to the cold wastelands in the North.'

'That's stealing just the same,' Pepper said. 'Not only that, but it will be obvious who did it. You're bound to get into trouble. It's safer to get one from the market. Anyway, I bet your father's are old and tatty. Col deserves a nice new one, don't you, Col? Me and Ant will get you something special, won't we?'

A heaving mass of unwashed humanity swilled between stalls. Ant moved slowly with the flow. A trestle piled with green and brown dyed woollen blankets appeared to his right and he placed a tentative hand to feel the soft warmth. These were perfect. Thick and comfortable, made from sheep's wool that would keep his friend warm during even the harshest winter. He reached out to touch.

Ant's heart raced as he saw the familiar face appear briefly on the far side of the stall. Then she was gone. It was her. Mona. His mother, though his father hated him calling her that. Just that glimpse had filled his soul with happiness and hope. She was still here. One day soon they would be reunited. Just as soon as he was able to earn enough to keep them both.

Suddenly, his head filled with pain and stars. A lightning fist knocked him down in the dirt beneath shuffling feet. He rose, trying to clear his head, and came face to face with a stocky man with a ruddy face. 'Get your thieving hands off my blankets,' he bellowed, spittle into Ant's face.

'I was only looking at it,' Ant said as he struggled to his feet.

'You look with your eyes,' said the stallholder, 'not your thieving hands.'

'How much are they?' Ant asked, jangling the few coins in his pocket.

Blanket man's face changed. 'You got money?'

'My father has given me funds to purchase a new coverlet, if that's what you mean. If this is how you treat a customer, then I wouldn't buy from you even if your goods were decent quality. Which they're not.' Ant turned his back.

'Wait,' blanket man said. 'I might have been a bit hasty. There's thieves everywhere.'

'Do I look like a thief?' Ant turned to face his accuser.

The portly jaw dropped a notch instead of answering. Ant's head was still ringing but the pain didn't prevent him from enjoying the man's discomfiture. 'Forget it,' Ant said, 'I'll go elsewhere.'

A blanket was thrust into his arms. 'Feel the weight and quality of this,' blanket man said. 'You'll not get anything nearly as good from anywhere else. My reputation speaks for itself. The King himself sleeps swaddled in my blankets.'

'I very much doubt that. My father is close to the King. If you want, I could take this for His Majesty to try. Then you would be truly famous and people would be clamouring for your wares.'

The man's brow wrinkled. 'Do you think I'm dumb enough to fall for a trick like that?'

Resisting the obvious answer, Ant held tight to the blanket and began to back away. 'If the King hears you've been making false claims about his sleeping arrangements, you'll be in big trouble. One blanket is a small price to pay to gain the King's endorsement and avoid the hangman's noose.'

Blanket man followed him, reached out a calloused hand, and gripped the edge of his blanket. Ant held on tight. He was inching further and further away from the stall. Uncertainty clouded the man's face. A swirl of bodies surrounded them, drawn by a potential confrontation.

Blanket man's eyes suddenly blazed with anger as he prised his property from Ant's grasp. Ant let go and melted away into the crowd.

***

He found his friends sitting atop the temple ruins where they had an eagle's eye view of the cacophony and confusion of Gort's main marketplace. Vendors were yelling, donkeys braying, carts clattering past, and chickens fluttering. Col had a purple blanket wrapped around him even though it was midday and the sun was warming the jumble of stones.

Pepper greeted him with a wide grin. 'Could have taken two if I'd had a mind to.'

'Thanks,' Col said, 'that was nicely done.'

'It's good practice for being a soldier,' Pepper said.

'I don't see why you're so intent on being a soldier,' Ant said, scratching intricate patterns in the dust with a piece of wood.

'It's a good life and I'll be defending my King.'

'What's so good about marching all over the place until you find someone who wants to kill you?'

'It's not like that. It's the comradeship. Anyway, there's not been a proper war for years. It's more of a policing role nowadays.'

'Is that what your dad says?' Col sat slightly apart from the other two, his eyes fixed on the hustle of the marketplace.

'Yes, and he should know. He's the highest-ranking soldier in the army,' Pepper replied.

'He's a sergeant,' Ant said. 'That's not the highest rank.'

'It is for a soldier. The higher ones are officers, not soldiers. You have to be able to read and write to be an officer.'

'If you were a soldier, you'd have to arrest us and take us to be hanged,' Col said.

'I'd never do that,' Pepper said.

'You'd have to,' Ant said. 'We've been stealing, haven't we?'

'You'd have to arrest yourself as well 'cos it was you that actually took the blanket, wasn't it?' Col said.

'Anyway,' Pepper said, 'I'm still going to be a soldier. Though I promise not to arrest either of you, whatever you might do.'

'That's a relief,' Ant said, his heart lifting as Col joined in the laughter.

'If it weren't for the army, we'd all be living in fear. They'd be all sorts of thieves and ruffians walking the streets, terrorising us all,' Pepper continued. 'Borders have to be guarded, otherwise there's no knowing who might come into our land and start stealing our things.' Ant could see that the talk about Little Billy had upset him.

'But they can't stop people coming. And they don't. Anyway, it's not possible to guard a border. You'd need more soldiers than there are people. Also, you can't tell when our kingdom stops and some other country starts,' Ant said.

'That's because it all rightfully belongs to the King. There is no end to his empire. That's what the army does. Keeps the King's land as his own and stops anyone trying to claim it from him.'

'If the whole world belongs to the King, then there can be no border to guard and no need for an army,' Col said and laughed.

'My father says that there are lots of other countries with loads of different kings. The world is much bigger than we think it is,' Ant said.

'And your father would know, would he?' Pepper snorted.

'Yes, actually he would,' Ant said.

'How does he know?' Col asked.

'He's an archaeologist.'

'Oh yes. I remember,' Col said. 'I just couldn't remember the name for it.'

'A waste of time, if you ask me,' Pepper said. 'And a waste of talent. Your dad can read, so he could be an officer. An officer in the King's army. Now that's a proper job, ordering soldiers around. They'd give him a sword. That's what you should do, Ant. Don't waste your time like your father does.'

'My father's work is important,' Ant protested, his frustration growing.

'Digging up old bits of stone doesn't sound important to me. There's no point to it. It's a complete waste of time. Anyone could do it.' Pepper scraped back the dirt at his feet. 'Oh, Look. I've discovered a stone. I'm an archepoligist.'

'It's not just stones. He discovers powerful things that have been lost. That's why the King employs him.'

'Like what?' Pepper asked.

'Lots of things. Old weapons and the like. Secret things that only he and the King know about.'

'Then how do you know about them if they're so secret?' Col asked.

'My father sometimes tells me stuff that I can't possibly tell you about or the King would have me hanged for sure,' Ant said.

'We'll not tell, will we, Col?'

Ant looked around the broken, empty building. He had to show Pepper whose dad had the more important job. 'You're not allowed to even breathe a word of this. It's a deadly secret.'

'Our lips are sealed,' Col said.

'My father discovered something on an expedition to the far North, way beyond the edge of the wastelands. He says it was made long ago by a very ancient and wise civilisation.'

'What is it?' Pepper asked, prodding the ground with a stick.

'It's a parchment containing powerful secrets that even the King doesn't know.'

'A piece of paper?' Pepper's words were mocking. 'What's the use of a piece of paper?'

'There are things written on it. Important things.' Ant felt the weakness of his reply as an ache in his stomach.

'So you say,' Pepper said. 'I don't see how words can do anything at all.'

'There's instructions on how to build a device that has immense power.'

'That can't be right, he's having a joke,' Pepper said.

'No. He's serious. There's one being carved into the floor at the top of the main tower. When the King returns, he's going to be very impressed and give my father a big reward.'

'Really, just for a bit of decoration work?' Pepper laughed.

'It's not just a pattern. My father says it's a very powerful device that will revolutionise the world. The King will become the most powerful monarch there ever was. And my father will have been responsible for his greater glory.'

'So it's magic, is it?' Col asked.

'I don't believe in magic,' Pepper said.

'It's not magic, it's ancient wisdom, my father says.' Ant was finding it hard to cope with his growing frustration.

'But we're never going to see it,' Pepper said. 'The King isn't going to invite us into his palace for a demonstration, is he?'

Ant took a deep breath. There was nothing else for it. 'Meet me up at the cave in the morning and I'll show you.'

***

'Show me the device when it's complete, Father. Take me to the tower again.'

Ambrose was hunched over his notebook, making scratches with a pen. A yellowing parchment, spattered with intricate drawings and strange symbols, was stretched out in front of him. For a few moments, Ant thought his words had gone unheard, but eventually, his father raised his weary-looking head. 'That would be too dangerous under the present circumstances, Ant my boy. There is someone who is intent on stealing my good name and reputation to increase his own influence over the King.'

'You mean Malachi?'

'Who else but that evil conniving man?'

'He didn't seem so bad to me, Father. A bit scary perhaps but he spoke nicely to me. I want to help more; you know I do.'

'He's very plausible and outwardly normal, but all the time he's trying to control you. Beware of his voice and his words; they coil around your mind like a rope and bind you to his will. I won't allow you to be exposed to him again. It could put both of us in deadly danger.'

'But how will I be able to learn if I can't come to the palace? Tell them I'm your apprentice and give me a proper job.'

'Your involvement has to remain a secret. We are privy to deadly secrets jealously guarded by the King and known only by me. If it was suspected that I was telling you the things I do, we would both be hanged. You must never repeat anything that I tell you outside these four walls. I've told you that often enough and I pray that you always remember it. It was a mistake to take you to the tower in the first place and one that won't be repeated.'

'In that case, I'll go myself and ask the King for work. Or better, I'll ask Malachi. I bet he'd let me help him.'

'You'll do no such thing, my boy. Any more talk like that and I'll take a whip to your hide.' Ambrose rolled up the parchment and tied it with string. 'If you've stopped all your nonsense, we need to hide this now. It has to be kept safe at all costs. I have taken from it all I need to finish the device in the tower and don't want to risk it falling into the wrong hands.'

'Nobody would dare to steal things from you, though. It would be the same as robbing the King.'

'Ah, but they would. Malachi would love to get his evil hands on my secrets.'

'Why?'

'He resents my closeness to the King and the secrets we share. If he had his way, he'd get rid of me so that he was only one that the King took counsel from.'

'But the King protects you, doesn't he?' Ant asked.

'For the moment. But the King is callous and fickle. His protection could evaporate at any moment and then Malachi would pounce.'

'Why do you devote your life to serving a king who you can't rely on to protect you?'

'Because I have no choice. He's the king, we all have to obey him.' Ambrose spread his arms.

'If he's so awful, why don't we get rid of him and get ourselves a better king?'

Ant's father's eyebrows rose, then he shook his head slowly. 'You can't say things like that, Son. Not even think them. The King is the king, that's all there is to it. We don't get a say in the matter. When he first appeared many years ago and proclaimed himself to be our ruler, there were many who opposed him, but he killed them all. Nobody could stand up against him then and now he is even stronger. The knowledge and artefacts that I bring back from my expeditions help to keep it that way. That's why I hold such a privileged position.'

Ant gazed longingly at the scroll of paper in his father's hands. 'Can I look at the parchment again, Father? Before we hide it?'

'I fear it will make little sense to a boy like you. It has taken many years of study for me to decipher even the little that I have. The device I am building for the King is but a small part of the secrets this document holds.' He unrolled it in front of Ant's wide and greedy eyes.

Ant scanned the glyphs and drawings, hungrily devouring their arcane messages. Something inside him lurched with a connection and the beginnings of understanding as if there was a part of him that knew what these strange letters meant. 'Are you going to give this to the King?'

Ambrose shook his head. 'He's not interested in ancient scriptures. Only in the physical artefacts that lie with them. I suspect, though, that this piece of paper holds secrets more powerful than any of the things he keeps hidden in the castle vaults. I'm going to keep it. Study it carefully and see if I can come to some greater understanding of what it means.'

Ant's head almost burst with excitement. 'Let me do it, Father. I can study it for you.'

Ambrose laughed. It was a cruel laugh that pierced Ant's heart and made him feel small and weak. 'You're too young for something like this. Maybe when you're older.'

'But I'm already fifteen. Old enough to be a soldier. If you won't let me do anything for you, I'll be just as useless when I do get older. You have to let me try.'

Ambrose rolled up the parchment. 'This is a very important item. Maybe the most important the world has ever seen. It has to be kept safe. Preserved at all costs. Kept from the likes of Malachi. I need you to forget all about it. I'm going to put it back in the secret place where it will be safe and you must promise me that you won't ever reveal its existence to anyone.'

Ant nodded dumbly, his heart seething with desire.

***

It was a long walk to the cave through the gate in the city's outer wall under the watchful eyes of soldiers and across the crowded hinterland of dwellings, farmland, and camps. As he cradled his father's precious document, Ant felt as if he was waving a tell-tale flag that signalled his guilt for all to see.

Ambrose had spent another night at the tower, leaving Ant free to take the ancient scrolls that described the device. It had seemed a simple thing to borrow it, keep it safe for a few hours, then return it before his father came home. As he walked, though, the significance of his transgression grew heavier with each passing minute, and he was already regretting his boastful promise to his friends.

The cave was their favourite place after the marketplace. The entrance was very narrow, too tight to allow access to an adult. Ant and Pepper could squeeze down the long, winding crack without too much difficulty, but Col's larger frame would sometimes get stuck and require assistance. Ant realised that the prospect of Col actually getting trapped permanently was getting more likely by the day, and had started to insist that Col went in first and came out last. That way, he wouldn't block his and Pepper's exit if the worst happened.

Ant pushed his way inside and opened his bundle on the dry, sandy floor. He lit a candle and unrolled the parchment his father had brought back from the North.

From his pocket, he produced a stylus that he'd attached to a length of string. This was what he'd been using for practice, inscribing the intricate pattern in the dirt outside his home until he could do it blindfolded and without the need to consult the ancient instructions.

There was a commotion at the cave entrance when his friends arrived. 'You first,' Pepper said.

'I thought I had to go last,' Col replied.

'That's on the way out, you dimwit. If you get stuck going in, I want to be on the outside, don't I?'

There was huffing, puffing, and scraping sounds before Col appeared, looking a little flushed in the flickering light. Pepper followed close behind and immediately grabbed hold of the parchment.

'Put it down,' Ant said. 'It's too precious for you to be touching.'

'Is this it?' Pepper said, unrolling the document and staring hard in the dim light.

'Leave it alone.' Ant grabbed at the scroll, but Pepper deftly snatched it out of his grasp. 'I'm not joking. That's a valuable artefact.'

'You're an artefact,' said Pepper. 'I only want to look at it. I'm not going to wear it out with my eyes, am I?'

'Let me look,' Col said. 'Bring it nearer to the candle.'

'Be careful.' Ant couldn't risk it getting ripped in a tussle.

'What's this?' Pepper poked the paper with a grubby index finger.

'Dunno,' Col answered. 'It's just whirly lines and stuff.'

'This is rubbish,' Pepper said, putting down the scroll uncomfortably close to the candle flame. 'Have you brought us all this way to look at a piece of old paper with a scruffy drawing on it?'

'No,' Ant said. 'I'm going to build the device. I've been practising. I only brought the scroll in case I forgot something. You can help me if you like.'

Col held the end of the string while Ant inscribed a big circle in carefully smoothed out sand on the floor of the cave. Ant halved the string length and drew another circle. Working slowly and carefully, with Col anchoring the end of the string, Ant divided the circumference of each circle into equal parts by drawing arcs that intersected it at two points. From each of the points, he repeated the process until there was a beautifully symmetrical pattern resembling the petals of a flower filling the inside of the circle. Then, trying not to disturb the lines he'd already drawn, Ant did the same to the inner circle. He carefully drew lines as straight as possible to join up all the intersection points on the circles. It took a long time, Col patiently holding the string and Pepper muttering impatiently as he held the flickering candle.

When it was finished, Ant sat back and viewed his handiwork. Apart from a few smudges where his feet had strayed onto a line, it seemed to be a good representation of the ancient drawing.

'Now what?' Pepper asked.

'We need some stones for the tips of the petals,' Ant said.

'I'll fetch some.' Col leapt to his feet and squeezed himself through the entrance.

'We should go and help him,' Ant said. 'What if he gets well and truly stuck coming back? Then we'll be stranded in here.'

'Naw,' Pepper replied. 'He's got in and out once, he'll be alright.'

'Help, I'm stuck.' Col's voice sounded strangled and desperate.

'You can't be,' Pepper shouted into the cave entrance. 'You fitted alright a minute ago. Try emptying the stones out of your pockets.'

'It's no use. I can't go forwards, and I can't get back. I'm trapped.'

'You are a fusspot. I'm coming out to give you a hand,' Pepper said.

'Ow,' Col was complaining.

'Hold your breath, right, I think you moved a bit,' Pepper said.

'Wouldn't it be better if he breathed out?' Ant shouted.

'Try that then. Breathe out, Col.'

Ant heard a scraping noise and a ripping of cloth.

'We're in,' Pepper said.

'Shouldn't you have pushed him outside while you had the chance? He's got to do it all over again on the way out now. He might be stuck forever.'

'What, and miss all the fun?' Col said, looking even more dishevelled than usual.

Ant carefully placed the stones on the pattern in the sand and stood back. 'There, it's finished,' he said.

'It's rubbish,' Pepper said. 'I can't see the point of it—'

'Look at that,' Col said.

The pattern had begun to glow. Yellow light, like molten gold, traced the lines in the sand then tendrils of incandescence rose upwards like burning smoke. The cave was filled with an eerie light.

Ant jumped about in excitement. 'I told you it would work.'

Col stood as if mesmerised by the shimmering light. 'Just from a few lines in the sand, who would have believed it?'

'It looks very pretty,' Pepper said, 'but does it actually do anything except light up the cave? We've got candles that do that without all the messing about drawing lines and stuff.'

'The important thing is that the design works. It's an ancient and powerful device, just like my father said it was. Imagine what the King will say when he sees the one in his tower all lit up. I bet he rewards my father really well. Maybe he'll give him a big pay rise.' Ant sat down at the edge of the circle.

'Aren't you going to find out what it does?' Pepper said.

'This is much more than I expected. Maybe we should leave well alone. Be satisfied with what we have,' Ant replied. 'What do you think, Col?'

'I think it's really nice. I love the pretty colours in the light. It doesn't feel dangerous to me. I don't see what the harm there would be in trying it out. Maybe the lights get brighter or change colour,' Col said.

'OK.' Ant took a deep breath. His heart was racing and his hands shook as he held out the parchment.

'There's something moving inside it,' Pepper said.

Ant stared hard into the swirling mist of light. Something was taking shape in there. His excitement surged. This would show them. Someone was coming through the device. Excitement was overwhelmed by fear. Maybe this was his father coming to investigate what he'd been doing using the device in the tower. Breath caught in his throat at the thought of his betrayal being discovered. Ambrose would never forgive him. Never trust him again. Life would be hell.

It was almost a relief when he realised that whatever it was that was coming through, it wasn't his father. It wasn't human. Fear of parental disapproval was exchanged for the white-hot fear for his life. Growls and snarls echoed around the cave, turning his blood to impotent water. Whatever it was, it looked and sounded hideous. A grey-green tentacle, dripping ooze and stinking of death emerged, then snaked across the sand as if searching for something. It hesitated, then changed direction towards Ant.

He'd seen and heard enough. The others were ahead of him, already pushing their way towards the outside. Ant slid through the clinging slit of stone to be confronted by Col, who was struggling to negotiate the narrowest section. Pepper had wisely gone ahead.

Behind him were scraping and snuffling noises, as if a terrible pig were pursuing them. Ant pushed desperately at Col's stricken body, but it was held fast. Something grabbed at his legs, encircled them, and began to pull him back. Its touch was disgustingly cold and wet, though he could see nothing in the absolute darkness. 'It's got me,' Ant shouted.

Col's hand grabbed the scruff of his neck and began an awful tug-of-war with whatever dire creature had come through the device. Ant felt as if he was being pulled in two. Despite Col's best efforts, he was being slowly but surely dragged back into the cave.

Ant felt Col become unstuck; then he fell headlong, releasing his hold. Ant's progress immediately became more rapid. He was being pulled towards the cave, the uneven, rocky floor digging painfully into his back. It was a relief when he neared the coruscating lights and felt the softness of the sand beneath. More tentacles began to attach themselves, squirming their way up his legs and grabbing hold of his torso as if he was being devoured by a nest of snakes.

Lying helpless on his back, he saw Col arrive and felt him pulling at the tendrils that held him. He was shouting angrily. Cursing the thing in words that a market trader would have blanched at. Ant sat up, grasping the coils that entwined his chest. They felt soft and nauseously slimy. Their smell was worse than a foul midden on a hot day. No matter how hard he tried, he couldn't dislodge them.

Pepper ran into the cave, picked up a stone, and began to strike the tentacles. Ant felt them loosen around him. The more Pepper bashed away at them, the less they clung on. Ant tore himself free, stood up, kicked the writhing mass, and felt it react. The thing was retreating under the onslaught. Col had found his own stone and was pounding away with gusto. Spurts of noisome green fluid leaked from the damaged appendages.

The source of the tentacles was still hidden within the device, a black mass lurking ominously amongst the yellow and silver strands of brightness. 'I'm free,' Ant yelled. 'Let's get out of here.'

'You two first,' Col said. 'I'll keep it at bay. It doesn't like being bashed with a stone.'

Pepper bundled Ant into the narrow passage and he began to push his way between the rocky walls. Behind, Col's yelling suddenly stopped. A terrible silence surrounded him. Pepper was no longer close behind so Ant began to reverse his progress and head back into the cave.

He emerged in time to see Col disappearing into the device despite Pepper's efforts to hang on to him. Ant darted forward to help but, with a final sickening lurch, both boys vanished into the tendrils of fire. Without hesitating, Ant dived in to join them but found himself standing amongst the cool fire, all alone. There was no monster and no sign of his friends.

His thoughts turned to his father. If the same thing happened with the device in the tower, he could be in deadly danger. A warning had to be given, even if it meant revealing his gross betrayal.

Something began to squeeze his chest. It became difficult to breathe properly. There were no nasty tentacles wrapping themselves around him, instead, he was being held in a whirlwind of soft light. The pressure increased, the lights flashed, and he found himself blinking in the harsh light of the sun.

7

The clatter of the hammers still rang in Ambrose's head even though the top of the tower was empty and still. It felt as if he were perched on top of the world up here. A waist-high stone parapet did little to quell the reaction of his stomach as he looked out over the city. Down below were the concentrated roofs of the palace that housed countless servants, courtiers, and a vast army of soldiers. The inner wall and gate kept the ordinary city dwellers at bay apart from those who worked day and night to deliver the resources greedily swallowed by the King's inner sanctum.

Far away to the north, Ambrose could detect a faint dark smudge that was the high ridge through which the North Road had to climb. Beyond that lay sweet lands which, although within the kingdom, received only scant attention from the monarch. A place he hoped to be able to keep out of the way for long enough to be forgotten.

The scattering of dwellings dispersed as he looked further away from the city. Gort was the centre and this tower the epicentre of the realm. The southern fertile plain stretched further than his eyes could see. Productive farmland fed by rivers both visible and underground. It was said that two spade depths anywhere on that land would find you water that would sustain the land even during the longest drought. Further south was the intractable desert, where water was scarce and few people ventured.

Tree-infested mountains edged the valley to the west, hemming in the rich farmland and providing wood and stone. Beyond them lay the sea. More mountains to the east, but much further away. This was the whole of the world, at least according to the King. But Ambrose knew differently. There were places he'd been that the King had no knowledge of.

He tore his gaze from the magnificent vista and back to the work completed by the stonemasons. The pattern occupied a third of the floor space with its pleasing and intricate tracery. A mixture of anxiety and relief coursed around his body. The scroll had indicated something more than a two-dimensional carving. It was supposed to be a functional device. It should have sprung to life, developed its far-seeing powers – if that's what they were. Instead, it sat lifeless and inert.

On the one hand, he'd be spared any possible accusation of witchcraft. On the other, he'd have to endure the King's displeasure. Both options had their perils. Avoiding the hangman's noose would depend on persuading the King of his continued value. A complete failure after he'd promised so much wouldn't be conducive to that aim.

The scroll was safely hidden at home, a precaution against it being stolen. He'd seen the avarice in Malachi's eyes. Under the circumstances, though, he wished he'd kept it with him. There might be some indication of how the device might be activated that he'd failed to understand.

A sudden realisation confirmed that he desperately wanted the thing to function. The King had to have his promised toy even if that might be the more risky option. Ambrose had his pride and reputation to uphold. Persuading the King that the way the device worked was nothing to do with witchcraft would be preferable to the massive loss of face involved in explaining why he'd wasted so much time and money.

Pacing around the circumference of the circle brought no fresh insight. The drawing had promised what he'd interpreted to be insights into far off places. All he'd managed was a pretty but useless decoration.

Kneeling on the perimeter, Ambrose ran his fingertips along the grooves so expertly created by the stonemasons. They felt slightly warmer to the touch than the slabs themselves, but it was an almost imperceptible difference. Crawling on his hands and knees, he made his way into the centre of the pattern and sat in the inner circle. Here, he felt sure, the warmth was more noticeable. But this phenomenon wasn't something to interest the King. It might warrant further study, though. Could it be that the device was coming to life extremely slowly and that the subtle changes were a prelude to it bursting into life?

Slow wouldn't do the trick. The King was due back in the morning and would demand something spectacular. His thoughts turned to the lake to the east of the North Road.

The North Road climbed remorselessly until it became confined by precipitous sides as the summit was approached. This was his least favourite part of the journey north. Hemmed in by the unclimbable sides that looked as if they'd been chiselled out by thousands of hands over hundreds of years, travellers were prey to anyone they might encounter. Once on that part of the road, teeth had to be gritted and the final arduous climb negotiated as quickly as possible to reduce the chance of being waylaid. The favoured tactic of the numerous bandits in the area was to follow behind at a distance while their comrades waited at the top of the pass, leaving no chance of escape. Ambrose knew he'd been lucky so far, though some of that luck might have been down to the number of well-armed soldiers accompanying him.

Getting to the summit of the North Road was always an achievement that brought great relief. It also revealed the view of a large lake to the east of the road at the foot of the gentle path downwards. Each time he'd seen the lake, Ambrose had promised himself that one day he would bring Ant with him and they would set up their home by its side. The thought created a strange tightness in his chest. His heart began to beat erratically, and he struggled to breathe amid a feeling of rising panic.

Tendrils of cloudy light obscured his vision. The tower became blurred and indistinct to the extent that he could no longer see the far wall and the sunlight adopted a milky dimness. *Heart failure,* he thought. *I'm going to die.*

As his consciousness waned, Ambrose caught a fleeting glimpse of a ghostly figure standing so close he could have reached out and touched it if his arms had been functioning. 'Ant?' Ambrose called out to the flickering image of his son before darkness overcame him.

When his scrambled consciousness was restored, he discovered that the hard stone beneath him had transformed into soft earth.

8

Malachi looked down from the tower at the awakening city and felt the chill of the early hour. Dancing sparks spiralled upwards from the cooking fires with dark blue smoke that stung his eyes and attacked his nostrils. The dust motes around him shimmered in the red light of the morning sun between him and the half dozen desultory soldiers leaning against the parapet, helmets discarded, rubbing their tired eyes into accepting the daylight.

Ambrose's device flickered with a light of its own. A ghastly light that rippled around the pattern chiselled into the floor emitting tendrils of haze that drifted upwards obscuring its centre. The sight was discomforting, but not as worrying as Ambrose's absence. Ambrose was nowhere to be found. Reports had him in the tower yesterday evening, but nobody had seen him leave. The most likely explanation was that he'd taken the prudent course of action and ran for his life at the prospect of being condemned for witchcraft and sorcery after creating this extremely worrying spectacle.

Given the choice, Malachi would have done the same, but he'd only discovered the device had activated when he'd arrived this morning. It was too late for a dignified retreat because the King was on his way and the staircase was blocked by his slowly climbing entourage.

A golden fire ran around the circles, lighting up the hexagrams and extending upwards towards the roof, bathing the whole tower in a gentle light. It was a cause of wonder that Ambrose's pattern had developed a life of its own, but there was little prospect of the King being impressed.

Despite the undoubted attractiveness of the gentle glow, Malachi knew that the King would be, at best, disappointed. At worst, incandescent with rage at this display of forbidden magic. Without Ambrose being present to accept the brunt of the King's displeasure, it would fall on him.

Having spent two years clawing his way to the side of the King and beating off any opposition with a mixture of physical and mental assaults, he was in the position he wanted to be. Needed to be. The court knew that Malachi was the right hand of the King, the King's surrogate in so many situations, and when the King was unseated, Malachi would be his successor. All he was waiting for was the means to challenge and defeat the King's power. And that was on its way.

Meanwhile, he had to maintain favour with the fickle monarch, who had forced him to stand idle while atrocities were perpetrated on the innocent, if he was to restore the old ways where people were free to worship their gods without fear of the hangman's noose. That had not been easy, and now Ambrose had left him in a very vulnerable position that might unhinge all his ambitions.

Looking at the situation positively, it might be that the King would arrive in an uncharacteristically benevolent frame of mind, decide the device was pretty enough but harmless, then take his leave. However, judging from the commotion coming from the stairwell, that possibility was fading fast.

He heard angry shouts, screams of pain, a crashing noise, then silence. More wails of anguish, more angry cries as the King hove into view, half carried, half pushed onto the top of the tower.

Courtiers hastily placed a chair underneath the royal bottom and lowered His Majesty onto it. For a moment, it seemed that all would be well, then a leg fell off, and the King was forced to cling tightly to the armrests to avoid being precipitated onto the floor. The leg was retrieved, then three men grabbed the side of the chair and raised it so that the leg could be jammed into place.

Malachi winced. In this mood, the King wouldn't be impressed by a column of dancing lights. All he'd had to do when the chair collapsed was to stand up and allow it to be fixed, but that wasn't the way the King worked. Had he been allowed to fall to the ground, there would have been several courtiers dangling from a noose before evening.

'Well?' The King settled his weight onto the rickety chair and the servants closest to him stood poised to intervene in case of further collapse.

The soldiers had stopped scratching and rubbing their eyes, replaced their helmets, and were stood almost upright to greet the King's entrance. Malachi tried to melt into their company and keep out of the King's eye.

'Where is Ambrose?' the King said.

Heads shook gently all round, as if a collective denial might absolve them all from any blame. The King's gaze alighted on Malachi and he felt compelled to step forward.

'Ambrose seems to have been detained by other matters, your majesty,' he replied.

'Then you can be the one to show me how it works, Malachi.'

'As far as I can tell, it is working, your majesty. Observe the emanations.'

'I was promised I would be able to see to the far corners of my kingdom, perhaps even peer into the future. Be aware of any and all that might pose a threat to the throne. That's what I need and that's what I expect.' The King sat back with a finality that made Malachi curse the absence of the man whose responsibility this all was. The chair wobbled but remained upright.

'Then, your majesty, I would suggest that the matter in hand is best conducted by Ambrose. We have sent word that he is to be brought here immediately. Soldiers have been sent to his home and I expect their return very soon. Ambrose is, after all, the architect of this device and his knowledge is required for it to be demonstrated. I am, after all, no archaeologist and have insufficient experience,' Malachi said. 'Perhaps your majesty would be glad of some refreshments while he waits?'

'What's with all this swirling-lights business? The thing stinks of sorcery now I come to look at it.'

'Ancient technology, if you ask me,' Malachi answered, becoming more uncomfortable with the situation by the second. There was no denying that the device was magical; he'd been saying that all along, but Ambrose had paid no heed. Anyone even remotely associated with such an obvious demonstration of magic was going to be punished. The standard, indeed minimum, penalty was hanging. Whether by accident or design, Ambrose had left him in a difficult situation, which was quickly turning perilous. A situation that could only be remedied by the man responsible turning up and facing the music, which was beginning to sound more funereal by the moment.

Malachi wondered if he'd underestimated Ambrose, who he'd always thought as being weak and inconsequential. His absence left

Malachi on a hiding to nothing. If the darn thing pleased the King, it would be Ambrose who kept the credit. If it didn't, or worse if it were considered spectacularly and fatally magical, Malachi would be caught up in the aftermath. Even if he avoided the death penalty, the years he'd spent insinuating himself into the King's trust would be wasted.

'I am asking you, Malachi, so you'd better be certain of your opinion. If this isn't magic, then I'm a fool. Do you take me for a fool?'

'Your majesty has much more knowledge and experience of these matters. I was merely repeating the exact words that Ambrose used when I asked him the self-same question. Forgive me if I am but a poor substitute for the man who you trusted to deliver this device without recourse to the forbidden arts.'

The King looked at him as if he were a piece of ordure recently scraped from a boot.

Before the King could answer, the flickering lights dimmed for an instant, then whirled about, as if blown by some unearthly wind. An apparition could be seen standing in the centre of the device. It was vaguely human in appearance, but its shape was shifting and imprecise.

'Look what I've found.' The voice from the apparition was high pitched and sounded excited.

A cacophony of voices chimed together. 'Hey, this looks juicy,' one said.

'Get out of my way,' said another.

A high-pitched squealing drowned out any further words. One of the courtiers closest to the King put his hands to his head and screamed horribly before running headlong to throw himself over the parapet.

Swirling tendrils of light enveloped the entire assembly. Malachi felt a sudden urge to inflict violence on everyone around him. It took all his willpower to resist the compulsion as he ducked desperately to avoid being decapitated by a sword-wielding soldier with a deranged look.

His attacker stumbled against Malachi's outstretched leg and fell to the ground, where he was surrounded by a group of well-dressed courtiers who began kicking him viciously. Malachi struggled with another man with wide staring eyes who grabbed him by the throat. As they grappled, the man's face darkened from red to blue to purple until it was almost black. Then his tongue flicked out, and Malachi saw that it was forked like a lizard. Concentrating hard, he felt into his assailant and discovered a dark hollow where his humanity should have been. Grabbing the grotesquely transformed heart, he squeezed with all the power of his being. The eyes widened, the hands fell from his throat and the man crumpled into a heap. As he fell, a dark cloud emanated from his open mouth and blew away over the parapet and into the city below.

Everyone was fighting, apart from the King, who was on his feet being protected by two soldiers who were hacking away with their swords at unarmed assailants. Malachi threw off a courtier who was trying to bite him with pointed teeth and stood with the King's guard.

'Get him to safety,' Malachi said. 'I'll keep them back.'

Opening his arms to feel the vibrations in the air, Malachi drew strength from the stone floor and reached into the bodies of those immediately surrounding him. With a supreme effort, he pressed hard on internal organs, squeezing out air and leaving his attackers gasping for breath. It took every bit of energy at his disposal to grip tightly for a few seconds before he was spent and collapsed to his knees.

His attackers lost interest in him and began to fight amongst themselves. Two of them threw themselves over the parapet, soldiers hacked pieces from another, while several stared at their bloody hands as if bewildered. Soldiers looked in horror at their comrades who had been chopped down and the blood that flowed across the ground.

Malachi felt the presence of evil fade, then vanish altogether. The tower became silent for a few moments before screams from the city below intensified until they reached a disturbing clamour. The King was shouting at some surviving courtiers who were struggling to manhandle his prodigious bulk towards the stairs. A few bemused soldiers were wandering about as if their brains had been addled, tripping over fallen comrades and slipping in the pools of blood released by the frenzied hacking away at each other. One was staring suspiciously at his blade, as if wondering how it became covered with blood.

Malachi took a breath, stood up, grounded himself as best he could, then turned to face the King. 'Whatever that was, your majesty, it seems to have gone.'

'Witchcraft and demonic possession!' the King screamed. 'How many times have I warned against dabbling in the black arts? And now this! Malachi, get rid of this infernal device. Then bring that dolt Ambrose to me. Now, get me out of here.’

9

As he relieved himself, Tyrant felt as if he were being watched. He'd chosen to water this particular tree, not because it looked desiccated, but because it was a respectful distance from Lone's house. Last evening's ale had stretched his bladder so that early rising had become an urgent necessity. He twisted his head and saw that he was being stared at by a horse.

It was a peculiar stare, as if the animal were fascinated by him peeing. Tyrant couldn't recall ever being stared at by a horse before. His encounters with horses tended to be brief and unsatisfactory, as he didn't see the point of them. On the positive side, it was true that they could carry things, including a rider. On the negative side, they needed looking after. Not only did they have to be fed, but they had to be protected against predators; a job they were singularly unable to perform for themselves. People wanted to steal them. Whether it was to ride or eat didn't matter, it caused trouble. Better not to have the bother of a horse. Anyway, he had no possessions for one to carry on his behalf and he much preferred the stability and comfort of his own legs to take him from place to place.

This was a peculiar animal, though. A rather pathetic version of a horse that was verging on the comic. It was mainly white with grey flecks here and there that gave it a diseased look. It was thin, horribly thin. Its ribs were there to be counted and its legs were impossibly spindly. Its backbone had a bow in it that meant the distended stomach almost dragged along the ground. Its gloomy eyes stared at him from a head with a long muzzle and flappy lips that revealed yellowing gravestone teeth. Tyrant returned the stare, expecting the beast to sidle away or at least divert its gaze. Something passed between them. Something deep and significant. Something Tyrant felt ripple through his being.

It was as if a silent conversation was being carried out that his conscious mind wasn't party to. A connection was established between what was inside him and the essence of the horse that made him feel as if he was falling down a deep well. The horse knew who he was. This realisation was both frightening and reassuring at the same time. Then it winked, and the moment was gone. He was back to normal, apart from a nervous understanding that there were more to horses than met the eye.

He looked back towards the house and saw Lone emerge. He'd intended to have a quick pee and then make tracks as far away from her as he could as quickly as he was able. Instead, she speared him with a glance, then snared him with bread smeared with meat paste.

She seemed intent on completely emptying her house onto the unfortunate animal's back, demonstrating scant regard for its continued wellbeing. As he piled the heavy saddlebags onto the horse, Tyrant expected its back to collapse under the weight. It was the scrawniest and ugliest beast he'd ever encountered. It looked so frail it was a wonder it could stand upright. Adding to its burden could only result in an imminent broken back.

'There.' Tyrant perched the last of the items on top of the horse, which was, much to his amazement, still standing. 'Thank you for your hospitality, but now I really do have to be on my way.'

'And which way would that be?'

'Oh.' Tyrant was taken aback by the question. 'I suppose I'll be heading out over those hills.' He waved his arm vaguely towards the east. 'Need to put some distance between myself and this God-forsaken place. No offence.'

'Then we have a happy coincidence. We'll be fellow travellers on the same road.'

'I'm sorry. I only ever travel alone. I like to be free to choose my own path.'

'Then I'll take whatever path you choose. Surely you can't have an objection to that? I'll just tag along and share my food with you.'

Tyrant stood dazed in the face of her implacable logic. It was true that he had, in a moment of uncharacteristic weakness, invited all this upon his own head. So he only had himself to blame, as usual. Women invariably meant trouble, which was why he avoided them as far as practically possible. A woman who wouldn't take no for an answer was a common enough phenomenon, but this particular one appeared to be so many steps ahead of him that his head was in a swirl.

The notion that Lone had hired the thugs began to trouble him. Maybe that had been some kind of audition, a test to see if he was suitable. If so, the woman was expecting trouble and that was something he most definitely should avoid.

When he considered how much paraphernalia had been heaped upon the poor horse, Tyrant couldn't help but smile. From his point of view, the small dwelling had little of value and nothing worth the bother of carrying on a long journey. Lone obviously had a different opinion because here they were, house stripped to the bone and a great pile of 'useful' items collected and made ready for transport. This was, Tyrant thought, the defining difference between the male and female species. Tyrant, representing the uncomplicated male, was entirely content to travel with a couple of knives stashed in his belt and what he could fit in his pockets. He had no need for anything else. Now he was observing first-hand the infinite capacity of the female to overcomplicate matters.

He wondered if it was witchcraft that had frozen his legs and was preventing him from fleeing. Whether or not it was a spell or his own weakness, he couldn't decide. But he clung to that explanation in a desperate attempt to absolve himself of blame for the terrible error he knew he was about to make.

10

He had to take his hat off to Lone; she really did know how to lay an effective snare. Every night now, for almost a week, she'd returned with a veritable plethora of squirrels, rats, and rabbits for him to consume. Lone herself seemed to take little interest in food.

The journey was proving slow, but uneventful. His usual navigation method of shoving himself through the thickest part of the wood and keeping in the same direction at all times, no matter what he encountered, was proving inappropriate for his changed circumstances. The pathetic horse could only amble along down the widest of tracks. If there wasn't a track, the horse just stood and waited until someone – Tyrant – managed to find it one. Tyrant believed that it would be kinder to the horse and better for her if she did her share of walking, but he kept his counsel. Lone was in constant good spirits and he wanted to keep her that way.

In any event, he was hardly in a hurry himself. Getting from nowhere in particular to somewhere else of little significance was hardly reason to rush. His stomach was as full as it had been for some considerable time and, despite the nature of the company, it was still company and it turned out that wasn't to be completely discounted.

It was after another three days of blundering around in the thickly forested hills that they had their first problem.

Tyrant awoke to the sight of half a dozen crossbows almost touching the end of his nose.

The trouble with crossbows, Tyrant knew, was that they relied on a tiny metal hook to keep them from discharging. Even if the fool holding the bow didn't pull his trigger, the device was prone to malfunction. Many an unfortunate soldier had found himself shot in the foot, or worse, when carrying a loaded bow slung over his shoulder. Hence the expression.

With a few loaded bows at the end of his nose, and the faces holding them looking as if they were only recently weaned, there was a powerful possibility of something deadly going wrong. Even if he didn't make a threatening move. Tyrant tried to appear small and unassuming; a man at ease with the world and one that welcomed the sudden appearance of military types in his campsite.

While he sat perfectly still, holding his breath and watching out for any early signs of metal fatigue, Lone greeted the soldiers as if she was also delighted to see them. 'To what do we owe the pleasure of a visit from the King's army? Are you here to protect us on our journey?' She smiled a smile so honest and true that even Tyrant felt the warmth of it.

A captain stepped forward, brandishing an unnecessary sword. He was a man who seemed barely out of his teens, but even so, would have several years' seniority over most of his troop. 'These hills are the province of the King. What business do you have here?'

'We're travelling to Endersky. We're merchants taking our wares to market.'

'Not to Gort, then? Won't you get a better price for your wares in the capital?'

'Perhaps, but we are committed to a merchant in Endersky.'

'Then you must be abnormally honest or quite a lot stupid.'

Tyrant thought he saw a flash of anger in Lone's eyes, but the look was momentary. 'Please buy some of our lace for your loved one, kind general,' she said, producing a fancy piece of cloth from her pockets that was tasselled with bright beads and much too clean to be real.

Although the crossbows were still in his face, Tyrant could feel that the soldiers' attention had shifted to their captain's conversation. Even so, there were too many crossbows held by nervous fingers for him to attempt an escape.

As she waved the scrap of material in front of the captain's face, his resistance seemed to melt and he fingered the piece gently, as if anxious not to soil it too badly.

'How much?' His voice was softer.

'Half a crown,' she said.

'Too expensive.'

'You'll not get finer work in Gort itself. Your mistress will be very appreciative in many wonderful ways should you take her this as a token.'

‘I have a wife. I’m not the kind of man to have a mistress.’

‘Not yet, perhaps, all in good time. But this would make an even better gift for your lovely wife. It would show that you’ve been thinking of her while you’re away guarding the King’s lands.’

‘I’ll give you two shillings for it. Not a penny more.’

‘Do you have daughters?’

‘Yes, two.’ The captain’s voice grew wary. ‘Why do you ask?’

‘Then I have a very special gift for your daughters.’ She pulled out two more decorative handkerchiefs and displayed them proudly. ‘All three for only one crown, sir. Think of the excitement in your household when you return. Mother and daughters regally gifted with exquisite delicate craftsmanship that will be the envy of their friends and neighbours.’

The captain dug into his pocket and fished out a coin, which he exchanged for the pieces of cloth. The cloth looked nothing special to Tyrant, but Lone obviously had a gift for selling. When he had secured his gewgaws, the soldier turned to Tyrant. ‘Who are you?’ he asked.

Tyrant struggled with an answer. He was well known in Gort, having escaped from custody on more than one occasion. Perhaps they were looking for him, in which case admitting who he was might be a big mistake.

Lone stood in front of the captain. ‘Let my husband be; he never hurt anyone in his life. I need him to protect me as I go about my lawful business.’

‘Your husband? Are you sure?’ the captain said. Tyrant thought he was being a bit sceptical for a man who had just paid a crown for a couple of pieces of rag. Maybe he did look a little dishevelled, but that surely didn’t make him incapable of attracting a wife. Maybe not a wife as attractive as Lone, but the man should at least give him the benefit of the doubt.

‘And a loyal and loving one at that. He works tirelessly for our good; there was never a better man alive.’ Lone’s fulsome praise was somehow getting into even Tyrant’s head. He found himself vowing to live up to her expectations in the future.

‘Leave him.’ The captain rubbed his eyes with both fists, as if trying to dislodge something that was obscuring his vision. The crossbowmen stood down and pointed their weapons at their own feet instead of Tyrant's face. He thought briefly about warning them of the foolishness of this, of how a smart man would immediately de-tension his bow once it was no longer needed, but decided to let them learn the hard way. His own experience had been the result of considerable suffering, so why should others get the benefit of it?

'I thought we were going to Gort?' Tyrant asked once the soldiers had left.

'We are,' Lone replied. 'Sometimes it's best to go easy on the truth in case it's upsetting. Also, if we said we were heading for the capital, it would be in the captain's report and someone might develop a curiosity regarding our real purpose.'

'Which is?'

'To find my husband, of course.'

'You told them I was your husband, and a good one at that.'

Lone's eyes pierced his soul. It was answer enough for Tyrant.

11

Ant stepped out of the device. Smooth stone had replaced the soft sand of the cave and the gloom had been dispelled by the sharp rays of the sun. He was at the top of the tower overlooking the city.

He remembered his friends and his stomach lurched. Suddenly, the view wasn't so grand, and the height was making him nauseous. Before he could decide what to do next, there was the clattering of footsteps and soldiers ran from the stairwell to confront him. 'Careful,' one of them ordered, 'he's come out of that abomination.'

Bows were pointed at him with nervous, quaking arms. 'It's alright,' Ant said, 'I'm just a boy. I won't harm you. I need to talk to my father, Ambrose. He has to be warned about this device and what manner of things might come through it.'

'Ambrose? He's your father, then?'

'Yes, that's right. He's the King's archaeologist.'

'Not any more,' the soldier said. 'We're looking for him and when we find him, the King has ordered him to be hanged. If you're his son, that order applies to you as well.'

The dire information had barely time to be taken in before rough hands grabbed hold and he was half-carried, half-pushed, down the staircase and deposited into a cell.

12

Lone remembered the grudging admiration she'd felt for the way that Tyrant had handled himself when confronted by her two thugs in Bounty. It was impressive how Tyrant managed to exude such weary resignation. He'd even tried to dissuade his attackers with an explanation of the futility of violence and the inadequacy of their weaponry before he left the two of them sprawling and their weapons in pieces.

It had, she had to admit, been a job well done, though she would have preferred him to have finished it by slitting their throats. Having said that, she could appreciate the calculated manner with which he'd acted. The risk of the mercenaries trying their luck again was tiny and had to be weighed against the chance that the townsfolk might decide to try to string him up for murder.

Of the meagre possibilities available, he was undoubtedly the best option by far to provide her with an escort to Gort. Now, however, she was finding his presence very tiresome. She was becoming so irritated by his constant whingeing that she frequently had to resist the strong urge to just feed him to Patch and be done with all the pretence and illusion.

It was important that her arrival in Gort, the cradle of what passed as civilisation in these forsaken parts, was as unremarkable as possible. The arrival of a lone woman would not fit that particular objective. Some would see her as an opportunity for molestation. Some might consider her a lunatic for venturing over the hills without a male escort. Others might even suspect witchcraft.

In her experience, men became suspicious of any woman who appeared resourceful and competent. Much better to have a husband who could take all the credit for bravely shepherding his defenceless female across the barren wilderness. She could remain effectively invisible until she got where she needed to be.

Lone took a stick from the fire with a singed dead rat impaled on it and offered it to Tyrant, who grabbed it ungraciously and greedily. 'Is your hunger approaching satiation?' she asked.

‘How many more are there?’ Tyrant replied.

‘Two squirrels and a strange-looking thing that I can’t identify for sure.’

‘Should be fine. Pity there’s no bread left. We should have brought more with us.’

‘I brought what I thought would have been plenty, but you’ve been eating too much.’

‘It’s not my appetite that’s the problem, it’s your horse that’s preventing progress. It’s a wonder we make any distance at all. I can’t believe you couldn’t find a better steed than that. You’d have been better off with a lame donkey than that abomination.’

Lone had to admit that Tyrant had a point. It was Patch. Lone suspected that he was capable of much better, but it seemed that the pathetic horse was all he was willing to offer. Her only consolation was that all of them had passed muster with the troops, and should do again when needed.

13

Tyrant's stomach was feeling very poorly. Its condition was such that he was forced to spend long periods alone in the woods, backside perched over a fallen log, listening to the terrible commotion going on behind him.

Too many squirrels, he thought, and another wave of nausea passed through his body, resulting in a very loud expulsion of wind. *Never again,* he vowed as a spasm doubled him up and he decorated the foliage in front of him with the remaining contents of his stomach that had somehow failed to find their way out the other end.

He regained a little equilibrium and began to breathe more easily. The squitters were growing less frequent and less violent, and he had the time and opportunity to consider the whole food question. It was true that Lone caught and prepared all the meat, but he couldn't recall seeing her actually eat any of it. Just a few handfuls of greens from time to time, but no meat as far as he could recall.

Then a wave of non-nauseous energy thundered through his body and left him feeling very nervous. It was the horse that suddenly began to bother him, or rather the sudden thought he'd had about it. As far as he could remember, that horse hadn't eaten a thing since they'd embarked on their journey ten days ago. If there was one thing that Tyrant knew about horses, it was their propensity to munch away constantly. No self-respecting horse would be seen without a nose bag filled with hay that was accessible at all times. Every time a horse was allowed to stand still, it would greedily devour every speck of green within reach. Not that horse, though. It would just stand there with its pathetic, hunched head and baleful eyes. He'd never seen it show the slightest inclination to graze on anything.

His bottom had quietened, but he knew from bitter experience that the volcano could erupt again at any moment and that he was wise to bide his time and make doubly sure it was safe before standing up and trying to walk.

Tyrant let go of his worries about the horse and allowed a sense of peace to come over him. This reminded him of how much he valued his own company and travelling alone. Being on his own in the woods with nobody watching him and nobody to answer to felt good. He decided to stay where he was until Lone carried on without him. They were close to Gort by now; Lone could surely manage to pilot her way across the ridge and down the escarpment. It was a big place was Gort, you could hardly miss it.

A female voice rang out through the silence. 'Tyrant, where are you?'

The voice soon became embodied and the slim figure of Lone came into view as she made her way through the trees towards where he was sitting. 'I'm shitting!' he yelled. That stopped her in her tracks.

'You've been shitting a long time,' she called back.

'I have the squitters something terrible,' he replied.

'Come back to the camp. I'll give you something for it.'

Tyrant cleaned himself as best he could with the foliage that came readily to hand, then dutifully followed her. As he walked, he thought about asking about the horse and why it never ate. The more he considered it, the less comfortable he felt about it. If he expressed his disquiet, what was she going to say? *Oh, thanks for telling me, I hadn't noticed. Maybe I should give it some food?* Whatever she said, he had the feeling that it would be convincing and that he'd accept it. She had that way with her. She also wasn't the kind of woman who welcomed questions. He decided that he'd keep quiet about the horse.

He comforted himself with the knowledge that they would be in Gort very soon and there he could slip away and make certain he didn't have to deal with this weird woman ever again.

'Here.' Lone thrust a steaming cup into his hand.

'What is it?' Tyrant asked.

'Something to make your digestive system function properly again. Drink it, then eat nothing at all for twenty-four hours.'

'Yes, but what's in it?'

'Herbs. That's all. Lovage, peppermint, sweet marjoram, and chicory. What did you expect?'

Tyrant took the cup and drank the strange but not unpleasant tasting liquid. Lone watched him with that penetrating gaze of hers – the one that made him nervous. He had the impression that she could see right through him. Once again, he began to speculate just how much of this was manipulation. Could she have put something in his food to incapacitate him? Had she been observing him all along, waiting until he had finished his business before calling to him? Was this drink really a cure or just another potion to bend him to her will?

Despite the thoughts racing around his head, he had no trouble getting off to sleep.

14

The frustration of his situation was becoming almost too much to bear. First the dreadful ignominy of being summoned into this very distasteful realm, then the manner in which he was being treated. Ordered to do things that even the most insignificant demon would find hard to swallow.

The knowledge that this was entirely his own fault for being inquisitive only made him angry. The temptation to swat his captor aside was almost irresistible.

It was the nature of the spell that caused him to hesitate. This involved ancient custom and practice. Old and powerful forces derived from deities he'd rather not upset. Absent forces that might return and make life uncomfortable. For the time being, he reluctantly decided to submit to the temporary minor inconvenience rather than flout laws that had endured for millennia. Even so, he didn't have to like it.

He felt intense irritation at her insistence on continuous manifestation. A body, for fuck's sake. What the hell, and he used the word with considerable first-hand experience, did anything need a permanent body for? No good ever came out of anything with a body. That was a certain fact.

It wasn't that this was onerous. He could generate as many bodies as he wanted with little effort. It was the nature of the body that she was compelling him to wear. First, a horse. This was a rather pedestrian and extremely docile quadruped that was the absolute antithesis of himself and everything he stood for. Nothing could be less like him than a fucking horse. If any of the denizens of the glorious underworld, which he frequently inhabited, could see him now, he might never want to go back. An infinity of derision can be wearing on even the most optimistic spirit.

He was going along with his erstwhile mistress for the time being because he was compelled. But it was only fitting that he should put up some form of protest, however minor and ultimately futile. She had insisted on the most pathetic of animals and so he provided her with the antithesis of the horse she wanted. Her mind had projected a sturdy dray horse of indomitable spirit and unrelenting work capacity. He projected something he knew was causing her constant annoyance. This, at least, provided him with some modicum of satisfaction.

Patch, for that was the shortened version of his long and glorious name, comforted himself with the knowledge that the spell would be released. Nothing, not even him and his kind, lasted forever. Although her lifespan was a fleeting moment compared to his, her death wouldn't sort out the problem. Before she died, she had to release him. The opportunity would surely come, and when it did, there would be ample opportunity to get his own back and to teach his summoner a lesson she would remember for eternity.

15

Captain Oliver was two days late already, a delay that was destined to grow longer and place him and his troop in danger of the humiliation of a search party being sent out from Gort to look for them. Bad enough to be behind schedule, but the reason they were taking so long to trek back to the barracks was itself cause for embarrassment.

One of the crossbowmen had been happily marching along when his crossbow, slung across his shoulders, had accidentally discharged. The quarrel skewered his calf, inflicting a very nasty wound that not only caused the unfortunate man great discomfort but also prevented him from taking another step.

It shouldn't have been such a big problem, but the man was some kind of distant cousin of his wife and she had specifically asked him to make sure that no harm would befall her relative. Oliver had been happy to accept this request when it seemed to him that the hills overlooking Gort contained nothing more sinister than trees and an unreasonable share of gloominess.

It was standard operating procedure for all crossbows to be ready for use at all times. There was a very good reason for this. If a marauding band of murderous assailants leapt out of hiding, a crossbow was no use at all unless it was primed and ready to fire. Once discharged, though, it became redundant, because no self-respecting attacker was going to hang around while you put your foot in the stirrup, worked the crank to tension the bowstring, fished around in your quiver for a bolt, placed it carefully along the firing groove, took aim and fired again. Crossbows were very useful if there were lots and lots of them and the enemy was kept at a safe distance by a big wall, or some other unscalable feature. Under these circumstances, the slow loading wasn't quite so disadvantageous.

Oliver's troop had been on schedule until the accident. Rulf, the poor unfortunate relative of his wife, had taken the wounding badly. He seemed to spend all of his time either screaming in pain or moaning in agony. Because of the constant noise, nobody had slept very much at all for two nights, and stretcher duty was getting more and more difficult to allocate; such was the reluctance of Rulf's fellows to spend time in his close company. The excuses became more frequent and less convincing by the hour.

'With respect, sir, Thomas and I were carrying him yesterday morning.'

'My hand is sore with holding the poles.'

'I've developed a twisted back from heaving him on and off the bier.'

'It's my ears, sir.'

Were it not for the family relationship, Oliver would have been happy to leave a couple of the protesters behind with the wounded man with orders to follow on at as good a pace as they could manage. Indeed, that was what military priority dictated. His report was becoming more and more overdue.

Not that he had anything of significance to report. In the three weeks he'd spent scouring the hills, he'd encountered only that couple. Otherwise, there had been no signs of any life, human or otherwise. When Oliver thought about that woman, an uneasy feeling began to pervade his body. It nagged at him that he should have asked more questions. In hindsight, it seemed that the rough-looking fellow she called her husband would certainly have been worth bringing back and checking out. His memory of the encounter carried the vagueness of a half-remembered dream. Anyway, they had not been heading towards Gort, at least that was something.

Oliver had decided not to include them in his report. It seemed to him that the encounter had been poorly handled and might show him in a bad light. There were too many questions to which he had no answers. He felt very nervous at the prospect of his colonel asking them.

He took out the expensive pieces of cloth he'd purchased from the woman and examined them in the sunlight. They looked disappointingly unremarkable, though he had to concede that his own expertise in the area of handicrafts was woefully inadequate. Now they looked like plain squares of cloth with a couple of glass beads fixed to each corner. When he held them up to the light, he could make out a very faint design in the weave that looked like an eye. Decorative, he supposed. But worth the outlay of a whole crown? Certainly not. Oliver resolved to present them to his wife anyway. It was either that or discard them, and he was reluctant to do that in view of their cost. He would gloss over the manner in which he'd acquired them, though. And, of course, wouldn't admit to having paid what he had for them.

By the time the soldiers reached the barracks, Rulf's wailing had subsided to a pathetic whine. His face was a sickly yellow colour and Oliver doubted he'd be coming out on patrol ever again. He comforted himself with the thought that he had at least brought his wife's cousin safely home to Gort, even if it were only to die. His wife could ask no more, surely.

'Three days late in reporting.' The colonel kept Oliver standing while he lounged back in his comfortable chair. Oliver was footsore and weary, and his need to sit down was becoming an almost overpowering urge.

'Sorry, sir. Crossbow accident delayed our return. We were slowed by the need to bring our wounded colleague home.'

'You should have left two men to assist him and got back here on time.'

'Yes, sir.'

'Your report may be vital to the safety of the King. Don't you understand the seriousness of your duties?'

'Yes, sir.' Oliver was feeling resentful as well as tired. The colonel should try wandering around those hills for three weeks some time.

'Deliver your report, then. Better late than never.'

'We encountered no possible threats to Gort or the King. The hills are clear of any potential danger, sir.'

'Good. So you encountered no one?'

'No, sir.' Oliver felt a twinge of remorse, which he quickly suppressed. He had a home to go to and a wife and daughters to be reunited with.

'Show me your patrol route on this map.' The colonel pointed to the table in front of him.

‘Here, sir. Then over here, around this and down to the edge of the forest. Then we skirted the escarpment here and patrolled these woods, here.’

‘And not a living soul encountered?’

‘It’s a wild and inhospitable area. It’s not a place where anyone would choose to be.’ A prickle of doubt intruded Oliver’s mind. Why, then, had that strange woman been there at all? In truth, there were much better routes to just about anywhere instead of across that desolation.

‘Unless they were intent on arriving unseen and unwelcome here in Gort,’ the colonel replied. ‘Which, of course, is the whole purpose of our patrols. To prevent a surprise attack on the King.’

‘Yes, sir!’ Oliver saluted stiffly in a desperate effort to be done with the debriefing. He could feel himself perilously close to confiding in the colonel about the party he had met in the forest.

‘Take your troop into the city. We have an emergency on our hands.’

‘But they are weary and in need of rest.’

‘Every available man is needed to restore order to the city. Until that’s been done, there will be no rest for anyone.’

Oliver saluted, turned on his heel and hurried away, out of the office, out of the building, and back to his men to tell them the bad news.

16

Tyrant looked at the man in the mirror that Lone was holding. Not bad, considering he'd been retching and squittering for a few days. Quite good, in fact. His hair had grown a bit wild – now it was hanging below his shoulders and he preferred it a little bit shorter for strategic reasons. No point providing something for an unscrupulous opponent to grab hold of when a few snips of someone's scissors could remove that disadvantage. His beard, which had merged nicely with the tufts of hair emerging from his nostrils and ears, was another thing. That was what gave him presence, gravitas. It marked him as a wild man who didn't give a toss. It was his special feature, his calling card, his defining look. If someone wanted to grasp his beard, they were welcome to try. Previous attempts had been dealt with severely.

'Sit still,' Lone ordered, taking up a strange folding knife and sharpening it against a leather belt that she had hung from the branch of a tree.

'Not the beard,' Tyrant said. 'You can cut my hair, but not too short. Just enough so it can't be grabbed easily.'

'The beard comes off,' Lone replied. 'You can grow another easily enough. When we get to Gort, I can't have you looking like you. I can't afford any trouble.'

With one expansive sweep of the blade, half his beard fell to the forest floor. A few more flicks of Lone's obviously well-practised wrists, and he was shorn of his pride and joy.

Lone continued to wield the knife, taking the hair on his head down to thick stubble. Then she brought him some clothes from the horse's saddlebags and placed them on the log beside him. 'Throw away your rags and put these on.' Tyrant opened his mouth to protest, but realised that the time for complaint was now long past and what was done could not be undone. Although he felt some resentment about his wishes being ignored, he was more intrigued by the way this woman seemed to ride roughshod over his every desire. *That's women for you,* Tyrant thought. *I've always found them difficult to deal with.*

The hat was almost the last straw to draw the obstinacy out of Tyrant and set his foot firmly down. It was large, flat, and very floppy. It had scarlet banding with a peacock feather poking out sideways. It was a hat to invite ridicule; a hat to start fights. A hat that no self-respecting man would ever consider wearing. 'No,' he said.

'Yes,' Lone replied, adjusting the angle at which he was wearing the hat and adding, 'there, that's perfect.'

'But I look ridiculous,' Tyrant protested.

'You looked ridiculous before. That,' she pointed to his image in her mirror, 'is normal.'

The man in the mirror looked several years younger and not at all fierce.

She handed him a sword with an ornate pommel encrusted with red gemstones. Tyrant drew it from its gilded scabbard and held it out. The feel of it was awful; it was unbalanced, too heavy, and the blade was dull and tarnished. The over-decorated handle was uncomfortable to hold, but that seemed to be the strongest part of the weapon. Maybe he'd be better using it in reverse. He sheathed it and handed it back to Lone. 'Not for me,' he said. 'I'm not really a swordsman.' He picked up his knives. 'These are my weapons of choice. I've always felt that a sword is something that invites trouble. Especially an expensive-looking one like that. It's as if you're parading it in front of people inviting them to try to get it off you.'

'Nonsense, it's a nobleman's sword and no ruffian would dare to challenge someone with a sword like this. Wear it as if it belongs. And get rid of those knives, they're crude and uncouth.'

As she walked confidently away, Tyrant found himself buckling up the sword belt. Once adjusted properly, he found it had a comforting feel as it slapped gently against his leg. He practised drawing it a few times, swished it around his head, and tried chopping a few branches. The edge of the sword was so dull that slicing through twigs was about all it could manage.

Once he was sure that he was unobserved, he lifted up his jerkin and stashed his knives securely in the waistband of his underclothes. They might be a little inaccessible under layers of clothing, but he felt comforted to know they were there. Anyway, he reasoned, an expensive-looking sword like this was surely only his to borrow temporarily. As soon as she called in the loan, he'd be back to relying on his knives.

17

If he were truthful, the tasks he had been given so far were minor and barely irritating. Apart from manifesting the stupid horse, Patch's attention was allowed to go where it wished. This allowed his spirit to wander freely, peering into human hearts and generally not liking what he saw.

In general, this was an unremarkable realm, with very little to interest any self-respecting being. There was certainly nothing out there to threaten his absolute composure. No entities of any description that might conceivably cause him any harm. The one sorcerer of any note, it seemed, was the one who had bound him. She, of course, was merely an irritation, especially as he was compelled to protect her as long as he adhered to the old laws. The one potential downside to his situation was the prospect of the one who called herself Lone becoming incapacitated before she decided to release him. If anything happened to her, he faced the prospect of being tied, albeit loosely, to this rather bland and boring place forever.

Patch was minding his own business, making gentle mischief in the market district of Gort. He had two traders at loggerheads over goods he had gently singed at the moment they changed hands. The altercation was causing him some small amusement, but this was quickly abandoned when a familiar presence wafted into his awareness.

'Cali?' he said.

'Yes, it is. Fancy meeting you here.'

'Have you been summoned and bound by some witch as well, then?' Patch asked.

'No, not at all. I just wandered in here through a portal that someone had carelessly left open.'

'An open portal?'

'Not just one of them, there's at least two.'

‘That’s interesting.’ Patch visualised the myriads of chaos-loving entities that might be gathering to pour into this unsuspecting city and cause mayhem.

‘Does your summoner know who you are?’

‘Of course not. And I would prefer it to remain that way. If you learn of anybody or anything that thinks it might recognise my presence, remind them of how petty and cruel I can be to those that displease me. Bandying my name about would be certain to do just that.’ Patch imagined the delight on Lone’s face if she ever found out the almost limitless extent of his power. It was a look that he was determined to avoid.

‘If she doesn’t know it’s you, what does she think she’s got?’

‘A demon. If you go fishing for a demon, and you catch something that announces itself as such, it’s easy to accept that without too much thought or question.’

‘How could it be that you were snared by a mere mortal?’ Cali asked.

‘The usual way. I saw something interesting, caught hold of it too casually and suddenly became aware that the rules of the game meant I was in servitude for a short while.’

‘I was under the impression it was you who made up the rules,’ Cali said.

‘True, but that’s a good reason not to break any without sufficient cause. I’ll put up with the inconvenience for a while and see where all this leads. Old magic has a habit of being wise magic. There’s likely to be some purpose involved.’

‘What exactly is it that your mistress intends for you anyway?’

‘Hell only knows. I don’t. She keeps me in the dark. From what I’ve experienced so far, I can’t imagine why she bothers dragging me along. She appears quite capable of looking after herself and doing anything else she sets her devious mind to.’

‘What about the fighter? Is he some sort of holy warrior capable of inflicting damage on the likes of us?’

‘Don’t make me laugh,’ Patch said. ‘He’s just a ruffian that she’s brought along for appearance’ sake. His sense of loyalty is about as well developed as mine. What are your intentions from here on, Cali? It might be handy for me to have you around for a while.’

‘And why would I bother to do that?’ Cali asked.

‘Well, there’s a lot of things I might help you with. Move you up the hierarchy. Get you into better circles. Maybe even provide you with some minions of your own. Now that would make life more bearable, wouldn’t it?’

‘How do I know I can trust you?’

‘You can’t. I’m notoriously unreliable.’ Patch watched as Cali’s ephemeral presence glowed softly in amusement, and then she was gone.

18

Oliver was still shaken from the orders he had just received. He could hardly find the energy to marshal his troops and move them to their post, guarding the western outer gate.

There was, it appeared, a grave threat against the King's person. This was an imminent situation and one that necessitated the highest level of security short of closing off the city altogether. Troops were to be deployed at every gate and everyone who wished to enter was to be carefully checked. What they were being checked for hadn't been made clear. 'Anything unusual' was the vague description he'd been given.

Even so, the whole situation made him feel uneasy. Oliver couldn't help but think of the woman he had met in the forest, and he shuddered at the recollection. What had possessed him to give good money for those poorly crafted handkerchiefs? Maybe it was witchcraft? Perhaps the woman was what they were looking for?

Oliver wondered if he should admit to having seen a strange woman under unusual circumstances. He'd been tempted to speak to the colonel but was stayed by the realisation that it would be difficult to explain in any rational way why he had not done anything about the encounter, especially why he'd not even reported it on his return. It was too late for regrets, he reasoned, and there was no point in throwing away a promising career and sentencing his wife and children to penury over the matter.

The western gate was busier than usual because of goods being brought to market. A long queue soon formed at the roadblock he set up as he began to question everybody carefully. The groundswell of annoyance at the inconvenience and delay was increasing by the minute and made him nervous. It soon became clear to him that what he had been ordered to perform was not practical and would result in severe disruption to city life, and most likely provoke a riot that his handful of crossbowmen were entirely unequipped to handle.

‘Go along the line and see what you can do to speed things up. Send through unchallenged anyone you judge to be unremarkable. Watch out for men who look like fighters. Oh, and witches. Any women, accompanied or not, make sure you keep them in the queue. We’re always on the lookout for witches,’ Oliver told Pepper, his sergeant.

Oliver watched as the disgruntled citizens filed slowly past, jostling and pushing, trying to overtake each other while at the same time staggering under the weight of huge baskets of fruit and vegetables. It seemed to him futile to draw each person aside and question him or her. Those he tried just stared at him in disbelief at the inanity of his questions.

‘Where have you come from?’

‘The farm.’

‘Where are you going to?’

‘The market.’

Those were about the most polite answers he received. The remainder were peppered with profanities and questions about his own sanity and powers of observation. Oliver was glad when Pepper came back to the gateway. ‘There’s a man and a woman and a queer-looking horse,’ he panted. ‘They look familiar but I can’t for the life of me think why. Do you want me to bring them forward?’

‘Yes. But first ready the bowmen and instruct them to fire at the first sign of hostility.’

Amongst a great swell of angry mutterings, the small party was ushered forward to the head of the queue. Crossbowmen flanked them on both sides, aiming at the unkempt man, the woman, and even the misshapen horse. Oliver felt a shiver of recognition as he stood face to face with the woman he had encountered in the forest.

Before he could begin his questioning, there was a loud commotion as two riders pushed their way through the throng blocking the gate. Oliver was struck by the magnificence of their steeds. The man was astride a jet-black warhorse of massive proportions. The woman was riding a pale tan horse with a beautiful blonde mane and tail. She was dressed in crisp bright linen and he was clad in gilded finery topped off by a majestic hat with a variegated peacock feather jutting from it at a jaunty angle. Both riders looked vaguely familiar, and Oliver felt sure that he had previously seen them as part of the King's retinue on state occasions. There was no denying passage to nobility such as them, so he quickly ordered his troops to let them through in order for him to concentrate on the job at hand and apprehend the weird figures who were so obviously the kind of thing he was looking for.

The woman stared at him with baleful, yellow flecked eyes. 'Where have you come from?' Oliver asked.

'Argle. Margle. Bargle. Pargle,' was the reply, or so Oliver thought.

'Where? Speak more clearly,' he ordered.

'Brumtigle. Armpittable. Glug,' she replied.

'You.' Oliver addressed the man. 'Tell me what she's saying. Where are you from? What language are you speaking? Answer or I will have you arrested.'

There was a thin, twisted smile from the man, but no verbal answer.

'Very well, you leave me no alternative but to arrest you all. You can spend some time in the King's dungeons, where you will have time and encouragement to consider your answers more carefully.'

Leaving Pepper in charge of the gate, Oliver ushered his prisoners in the direction of the castle keep. Neither of them seemed to be able to walk properly. The man kept veering off to the right and the woman could only manage a few steps at a time before collapsing in a heap and having to be dragged to her feet. The awkward horse staggered along very slowly. It was a frustrating state of affairs and Oliver was getting more and more anxious at the lack of progress when suddenly the man decided to make a run for it.

His whole disposition changed from hardly being able to stand to swift purpose. Before anyone could react, he was off, heading speedily through the morning crowds. 'Get him!' Oliver yelled. Several troopers gave chase, encumbered by their crossbows. One seemed to take Oliver at his word and loosed a bolt in the man's direction. Whether it was a lucky shot or an unfortunate one depended on your point of view. From the man's standpoint, it was doubly unfortunate. The arrow found the back of his head. On a positive note, he appeared to be killed instantly.

Oliver suffered a similar dichotomy of emotions. On the one hand, he had lost a prisoner who might have yielded useful information, or at least confirmed his intentions towards the King. On the other hand, having the prisoner escape would have been construed as a careless and incompetent act and one that would have placed the King's life in jeopardy. On the whole, Oliver was grateful for the arrow finding its mark.

On seeing the fate of her companion, the woman seemed to shake off her own lethargy and made a sprint for safety in the opposite direction. Most eyes were on the prone figure of the man and she managed to gain a few yards before several crossbows were fired in her direction. Staggering under the blows of the bolts which found their mark, she nevertheless continued her flight until the rest of the troop cottoned on to the idea and shot her down, together with several innocent bystanders who happened to get unlucky. She, too, was stone dead when they examined her.

In all the kerfuffle, the strange horse, together with its unseemly burden, seemed to have melted away into the crowd. Try as they did, they could find no trace of it despite its odd appearance, rendering it impossible for it to blend in or be mistaken for a proper horse. Oliver was disappointed, but not completely dismayed. After all, he had intercepted the very people that he had been sent to find and the King could now sleep more soundly in his bed. Two dead prisoners and a missing horse were much better than no prisoners at all.

19

The hardest part was the horses. Lone had insisted on the impressive size and appearance of the two mounts and had been adamant that there would be no compromise. Patch could do any kind of apparition he wanted, but keeping Tyrant and Lone suspended in mid-air in exact conjunction with the movement of two different sized pretend horses that weren't actually carrying their weight was a bit of a juggling trick. It needed quite a lot of his attention. Events were, however, taking a more interesting turn, so he decided to stop being awkward and get on with the job in hand in the interests of making progress.

His manifestations cut imposing figures as they rode through the crowds, though it was necessary to deflect any pedestrians out of their way to avoid the potentially image-ruining situation of the horses appearing to pass right through them in a ghostly fashion. A state of affairs that would surely raise suspicion and defeat the whole purpose of the illusion. Despite the intense concentration necessary, he was determined to make sure that everything passed off without a hitch.

His secondary job really needed a bit more attention than he had available after juggling people and illusory horses. The two unfortunates that Lone had singled out from the crowd were simple enough to control on a superficial level, but full possession was not easy, given everything else he had to do. This meant that the man and the woman remained in a somewhat catatonic state throughout. Patch was tempted to just dump the queer horse but retained it for the sake of completeness, reasoning that the whole group might be more easily recognised and therefore provide a much better means of distraction than just part of it.

Patch found himself getting more committed to the success of Lone's mission, whatever that might be. It mattered to him now, since the visitation of Cali and the information she had imparted. If he allowed his senses to stretch out to envelop the whole city, he could feel the disturbances caused by the presence of non-human entities. There were several ripples that he took to be significant demons and occult sightseers, and mischief-makers seemed to be gathering in numbers.

As Tyrant and Lone rode majestically away on their pretend horses, Patch followed them with his attention, wafting aside onlookers and keeping up appearances. This meant that he had to allow his control over the group that had been detained by the soldiers to loosen slightly. The man was the first to take advantage of his laxity and took Patch a little by surprise by breaking away from his control and making an abortive attempt to flee. When Patch saw the satisfactory outcome of the man's flight, he immediately released the woman and, lo and behold, she suffered an identical fate. Unfortunate, but very convenient. The soldiers' attention had been successfully diverted and his mistress had been safely carried to the place she desired to be. Patch relaxed. There was no longer any need to manifest the pathetic horse now. He felt that all loose ends had been nicely tied up, and all without him having to destroy any soldiers at all. He paused to consider creating some further diversions as an added safeguard but decided that he had done enough for the time being.

20

'Recall the stonemasons.' Malachi could feel the hollowness in his own voice.

'Deal with it' had been the King's parting remark and the look in his eye had carried serious menace.

The damage was done. That simple fact inflamed Malachi's anger to the point where the few men remaining in the tower were in grave danger. The flare up passed; he regained control of himself and concentrated on settling his racing heart to a steadier beat.

It was all Ambrose's doing. The long sycophantic years of insinuating himself into the King's favour had been wasted. Ambrose would surely be hanged as soon as they found him, and Malachi knew he'd be lucky if he avoided a similar sentence. Getting back into a position of influence, if not completely impossible, would take time he didn't have.

It was late afternoon before the three stonemasons could be assembled in the tower, ready to begin work. 'Get rid of it,' Malachi ordered.

The masons gripped their chisels, casting glances at the pattern with its coruscating lights, then back to Malachi. 'How?' one of them asked.

'Chisel away the line until you create a deeper hole, then fill the indentation with lime and mortar so that it is flush with the surface,' Malachi said.

'I don't see how that would help,' the mason replied. 'Why not just cement over it and be done?'

'If you think that will work, then get on with it,' Malachi said.

'I didn't say it would work,' the mason said. 'Anyway, you don't need us to mix some mortar and spread it about. We're skilled masons. That's a job for a general builder. We want nothing more to do with it, do we, lads?' The others nodded vigorously in agreement. 'There's black magic going on up here and we'll have no part of it.'

Malachi took a breath and faced the mason squarely. The man's face took on a reddish hue as he found difficulty breathing. 'You wouldn't want to displease the King, would you? It's on his command that the work needs to be done and it's you who have been chosen to carry it out.'

The stonemason shrugged, then crouched down beside the edge of the design. Bright afternoon sunlight was pouring through the windows of the tower, rendering the flickering emanations from the device almost invisible. The mason placed his chisel in position and raised his hammer to make the first mark. Before he could complete the action, he was engulfed in a burst of ghostly flame, even brighter than the sunlight. When it subsided, all that was left of the unfortunate craftsman was a pile of ashes being wafted around by the wind.

The other two stonemasons began to make their way slowly towards the exit.

21

Oliver stood stiffly to attention, sword held parallel to his chest, hastily burnished helmet squarely positioned. The epitome of a serving officer honoured to guard his king. Despite the cloying heat and the rivulet of sweat obscuring his vision, he maintained his post while the cavalcade passed.

The sweat, the dust thrown up by the passage of the King and his retinue, and the glare of the sun obscured his vision of most of the rest of his troop. Those opposite him were less formally composed than he would have liked. One recalcitrant soldier had removed his helmet and was scratching his head.

Oliver barked in disapproval until he straightened up a little and replaced his protective headwear. 'An attack could come at any time,' Oliver chided. 'Be vigilant, be ready, be equipped, be steadfast.'

His words rather petered out at the 'steadfast' bit as the cavalry passed between them, making his words redundant. For these were the cream of His Majesty's army. His personal horse guards, the elite guardians of his personal safety. Had the rattle and noise permitted, the errant soldier might well have pointed out that, in the event of trouble, it was the cavalry who would be called on to defend the King and not a motley bunch of troopers already tired from long weeks of duty.

Oliver thought himself fortunate to be spared an argument he would be unable to win. Unlike, he suspected, the elite forces, his men were prone to long-winded complaint regarding their food, their duties, their equipment, their orders, their pay, and just about anything else. It had fallen to Oliver to persuade his men to carry on with the job despite the admitted shortcomings of army life. These were not career soldiers and discipline was a fine line between threatening them with hanging and promising them something nice.

The brown and black monsters of muscle and sinew trotted past, bearing their proud riders high. One of these brutes, with or without a cavalryman astride it, could, if provoked, decimate his foot soldiers.

These horses had been bred for combat. Their nostrils flared at the prospect. Their black eyes gave Oliver the shivers.

Behind the cavalry came the coaches carrying the King and all his essential accoutrements. Five big wooden vehicles, each pulled by four carthorses even bigger than the cavalry steeds, trundling past on iron-shod wheels that ground the stony road to dust. It wasn't possible to identify which carriage held His Majesty; whatever or whoever was inside was kept well hidden behind windows slatted with wood.

Marching in the dust cloud produced by all those horses came the ceremonial pikemen. Bodies shrouded by the haze, heads adorned with ornate helmets of beaten copper, they held their poles at a slant displaying the complex ironmongery attached to the ends of the pikes. Then an almost endless stream of foot soldiers. It seemed that the garrison had been emptied of all but a few. The King was obviously expecting trouble.

Oliver's orders had been to take his men and secure the East Gate. Now that the King had safely passed out of the city, the nature of his duties seemed a little vague. 'Shall we close the gates, Captain?' Sergeant Dennis, one of the few still wearing his helmet in the oppressive heat, seemed anxious, as always, to get the job done.

Oliver thought for a moment. 'Yes,' he said. 'Of course. We are here to guard the city against the threat to its citizens. We must hold fast on their account at all costs. Tell that to the men and have them stand down from attention.'

Dennis looked towards the gaggle of men strewn around the gate. 'They seem to have already stood down, sir. Should I get them back to attention and then give your order?'

'Not necessary, Sergeant. Now get those gates closed immediately. An attack could come at any time.'

'Yes, sir.' Dennis saluted and strode off, happy to have a purpose. Oliver moved into the shade of the enormous stone buttresses, took off his own helmet, and sank gratefully to the ground.

The great wood and iron gates were heaved into position by the combined efforts of ten of his burliest men. Eventually, after much huffing and moaning, the city was cut off from the outside world and any threat that it might provide.

A crowd began to assemble by the gates. Men and women, laden with sacks, some trundling handcarts, all of them complaining loudly.

'They demand that you open the gate, sir,' Dennis reported unnecessarily.

'Tell them it's for their own safety. The city is faced with a dire emergency.'

A portly man approached Oliver. Dennis stood to block his approach, but the man shoved the soldier aside without difficulty. 'Open this gate,' the big man said, 'or it will go very badly for you.'

'I can't,' Oliver said. 'I have to defend the city.'

'The problems are all within the city. Why do you think the King has beggared off out of it. If we were under attack from the outside, he'd be hunkered down in his palace. Now, be a good lad and let us through.'

'The King must have his own reasons,' Oliver said. 'Perhaps he is taking the fight to the enemy.'

'Wherever he's gone, he won't take kindly to his bed not being made or his food prepared. We're members of the royal household and needed by your King. So let us out.'

The man had a point. The last thing he needed was some angry cavalry officer arriving to berate him over the disruption to the King's routine caused by his premature closing of the gate. 'Open the gate,' Oliver ordered.

The pushing and straining and muttering finally had the desired effect, and the gaggle of camp followers were able to resume their following. 'Shall we close it again, sir?' Dennis asked, eager for further action.

'Not yet,' Oliver said. 'I need to be sure that there aren't any more of the King's retainers galloping after him.'

'There are people entering the city, sir. Shall we apprehend them? Do you want them stopped? Arrested? Do we have your permission to shoot them if they don't take any notice of us?'

Oliver watched a group of farmworkers wander through the gate on their way home after a gruelling stint in the fields. Carts laden with produce headed to market. Children skittered around parents' legs as the tide of humanity came and went. 'By all means, ask them what their business is. But do not shoot anyone. Understand? Do I make myself clear?'

'Yes, sir.' Dennis hurried off and soon had people queuing in both directions to be interrogated. Oliver sighed. The men needed something to do. Being alert for trouble wasn't enough. Or, in most cases, too much to ask.

The nature of the emergency was unclear. For the King to flee in a cloud of dust meant that it must be real and immediate. The portly man had been correct in his assumption that the King wouldn't be exiting the city if the threat was external. Something bad was already happening in the city. Something that twenty or so foot soldiers wouldn't have a hope of influencing.

If he walked through the gate, he could be home within an hour. There, his wife and two daughters were waiting for him to protect them against whatever horrors were about to befall the city. His presence here was a waste of time. His family needed him at a time like this. It was tempting to round up his troops and take them home with him. His own little army to protect his home. It was a bad idea. When his superiors got wind of what he'd done, he'd be hanged as an example. Even if he left everyone else here, made his excuses and left, abandoning his post was another hanging offence. He was stuck. They all were. That was the way of things.

'It's Cooper, sir.' Dennis was back with his relentless, bustling energy.

'What's up now?'

'He's feeling very queer, sir.'

Oliver stood up and moved out into the glare. A group of men were gathered around a hunched figure. 'It'll be the heat. Give him permission to remove his helmet and sit in the shade until he recovers.'

'It's not the heat, sir. I really think you should speak to him yourself.'

'That's your job. If I have to speak to the men myself, there's no need for a sergeant, is there?'

'Ah, but in this peculiar case, I believe it would be for the best. The situation needs the intelligence and acumen of an officer, sir.'

The circle of men parted to allow him access to the crouching Cooper. 'What appears to be the problem?' Oliver asked.

‘I’m not feeling myself, sir,’ Cooper responded drawing a snigger from some of his less sympathetic comrades.

‘I dare say that none of us do from time to time. You’re going to have to be a little more specific.’

Cooper let out a low growl, coughed, then seemed to recover his composure. ‘It was like a dark cloud had gone across the sun. I felt very cold and frightened. Something is messing about with my insides, I can feel it. Help me, sir. Please help me.’

‘Calm down, Cooper. It’ll be a brief chill brought on by exposure and exhaustion. Hang in there and it’ll pass, you mark my words.’

Cooper looked up at him. His face betrayed no gratitude for the encouraging words. Instead, it contorted into a grotesque smile, and his lips opened to allow his tongue to protrude. It was dark blue and forked like a lizard. Cooper’s eyes widened and turned black while his pupils formed oval green slits.

Oliver took an involuntary step backwards as Cooper rose to his feet. He stood taller now, head and shoulders higher than the men surrounding him. There was a communal intake of breath as a guttural scream emerged from his mouth accompanied by a foul odour. ‘Hold him down,’ Oliver said. There was definitely something very wrong with Cooper. He might even turn out to be dangerous unless he was restrained.

The two men clutching at Cooper’s shoulders were suddenly thrown to the ground and he began tearing at their throats with tooth and claw. Gurgling sounds mixed with the screams of alarm. Blood was squirting into the air, the stricken men writhing less and less until they were still. Dead still.

Cooper was laughing, swinging his hands, which had been transformed into claws, at the nearest soldiers.

Dennis shouted in Oliver’s ear. ‘Permission to shoot Cooper, sir?’

Oliver took a breath. A soldier fell under a solid blow to his head and Cooper began gnawing at his face. ‘Shoot him,’ Oliver yelled.

Three crossbow bolts slammed into Cooper’s back without stopping his grisly feast.

‘Stab him,’ Dennis cried out, jumping forward with drawn sword and hacking at Cooper’s neck. The blow attracted Cooper’s attention and he rose to his feet, head half severed and gushing black blood. As he lunged at Dennis, two more soldiers dealt lusty blows. Five bolts smacked into Cooper's head, one of them almost disappearing into an eye socket. Dennis managed to avoid the flailing arms and finish what he'd begun, severing Cooper's head from his body, which still managed to lurch forward in search of more victims. As bodily fluids drained, the carcass ground to a halt, then slumped to the floor.

A brave soldier bent over the severed head and poked it with his sword. He drew back as the eyes and mouth opened. A black cloud emerged and covered the soldier's face before disappearing. The soldier screamed, then ran off towards the city. A couple of half-hearted bolts were sent after him, but neither met its mark.

'What was that, sir?' Dennis asked.

'Demonic possession. Someone has been dabbling in the dark arts. No wonder the King has made himself scarce. This is a job for wizards or priests, not for the military. There may be many of those dreadful things sent to destroy us. Tell the men they are dismissed. They should go home and protect their families as best they can.'

'Are you sure, sir? We're supposed to secure the East Gate.'

'We have secured it long enough for the King to escape. Our job here is finished. Gort itself may be finished. My advice is to gather up your loved ones and flee while you can.'

Oliver hitched up his sword, placed his helmet gently on the ground and set off anxiously towards home.

22

There was something exhilarating about being suspended high above the crowds with no physical means of support. Tyrant could see the image of the horse beneath him, and a magnificent pseudo-beast it was, but there was nothing substantial about it. He was suspended from the sky, it seemed, while the pretend horse lent credence to his situation. His previous musings about being the victim of witchcraft and sorcery had been emphatically confirmed. Lone had to be a witch to do this, and a powerful one at that. He made a mental note to be more careful with her in future, but had the feeling that nothing he did or thought would make any difference. He was ensnared good and proper. At least that realisation made him feel a certain relief that he had not gone completely off the rails. Wearing this damned hat was not something a right-minded Tyrant would have even contemplated. Now that they'd arrived in Gort, he hoped there was nobody he knew to observe the ridiculous thing.

He was accompanying Lone, herself astride a pretend horse, towards the inner citadel of Gort. Not somewhere he would be going as a matter of choice. Tyrant disliked large towns and Gort was the very largest. Not only was it big, it had walls. Lots of walls. Walls to stop people getting in and out. Better to stay out than risk being trapped behind the walls, but his opinion counted for nothing.

Gort had a long, sweeping outer wall that divided the open farmland to the south from the densely populated city on the inside. Further in, and nestled against the rocky crags to the north and west, was the fortified citadel. In this place, the great and the good lived together with their many servants and hangers-on. The citadel was entered through a single stone arch, which was bristling with slits through which bowmen could fire, and was fitted with a massive iron gate. The King's palace, dominated by its high tower, sat within the inner city.

With a sense of resigned foreboding, Tyrant remembered being involved in a minor altercation on a previous visit that had attracted the attention of the soldiers. During his attempt to try to calm the situation, one of the officers had received a punch in the face, which had bloodied his nose and hurt Tyrant's fist something rotten. At that point, the scuffle had developed into a full-scale fight and, when he was the only man left standing, the powers that be had taken exception to his part in the kerfuffle and decided to incarcerate him. Getting out of jail had not been easy and the unofficial manner of his release would have left some residual resentment amongst the authorities. But at least they weren't going to recognise him as long as he was wearing this hat.

They were waved through the checkpoint by soldiers wearing iron helmets with prominent nose guards. Tyrant wondered if there had been a redesign of the headwear since he had demonstrated its ineffectiveness in withstanding a well-aimed punch. Or maybe these were a different type of soldier; an elite guard perhaps. They certainly looked a bit more grizzled and capable than the youngsters he had previously encountered.

Suddenly, Lone's horse disappeared and she fell heavily onto the cobbles. Tyrant's astonishment was quickly transformed into discomfort as he was also dumped unceremoniously onto the ground. Soldiers quickly surrounded the recumbent pair.

'Magic!' someone shouted.

'Witchcraft!' someone else defined the situation more precisely.

'Get them!' a more proactive soul urged. The throng needed little encouragement and strong hands grabbed hold of Tyrant's finely crafted clothes without any regard for the damage they were doing with all their pulling and ripping. Someone even went to the trouble of swiping his hat and making off with it. Tyrant thought briefly of making some sort of protest, but decided against it. They were welcome to it.

'Lock them up, then fetch Malachi,' an officer directed.

***

Tyrant was bundled into a rather robust cell and Lone thrown in with him almost, it seemed, as an afterthought.

'Good,' she said as she got to her feet and brushed down her dishevelled clothing.

‘Good?’ Tyrant asked. ‘Surely this can’t be what you were planning. We’re stuck in here, now. This is a serious jail, believe me. It’s going to be very difficult for us to escape.’

‘We don’t need to escape. Malachi will have us released.’

‘You know him?’

‘Of course I know him. He’s my husband.’

***

As stone floors went, the one in the cell was reasonably comfortable, the slabs being smooth under his buttocks. He’d been locked up in worse places; there was even a window slit, too high to peer out of, but a welcome source of fresh air. The company had been better, though. Thieves, vagabonds, murderers, and derelicts usually kept him company while detained and they all could spin an interesting tale or while away the hours. As a man used to his own company, the alternative, being alone for long periods, didn’t bother him one bit. This was different, though. The woman pacing up and down was a disturbing cell mate. It had been bad enough her being a witch, and now she’d become that most dangerous of all females, an angry one.

‘What was all that messing about with ghostly horses and why did it go so wrong?’ Tyrant said, trying to come to terms with the situation she’d brought about. ‘Why didn’t we just walk here like normal people? Then we might not have been locked up. Have you thought of that?’

Lone’s dark eyes bored into his. A tight smile appeared on her lips. ‘That was never the plan.’

‘Good plan, not getting locked up. Maybe we should devise another for not getting hanged.’

‘This is all the fault of that recalcitrant spirit. It will be punished in due course.’

‘I don’t see how,’ Tyrant said. ‘It seems to have dropped us in it and then left. My bet is that it won’t be back.’

‘Ah, but there you would be wrong. It is bound to me, compelled to obey my instructions. Only I can release it from the ancient magic that binds us.’

‘Good,’ Tyrant said. ‘That’s a relief. Tell it to get us out of here. There’s a gallows in the courtyard outside and we could be strung up at any moment. They don't stand on ceremony around here. Keeping the hangman busy is one of their priorities.'

'We wait,' she said. 'My husband will be here shortly; I can feel his presence already.'

'Then can I be let go? After all, I got you here. You've got your husband coming to collect you and the spirit thing to do your bidding. You don't need me any longer, do you?' Tyrant couldn't understand what she'd needed him for in the first place, but refrained from opening up that line of conversation in case she felt criticised.

They lapsed into an uneasy silence. Tyrant thought about his situation and decided that he'd been in worse. At least he had the prospect of someone turning up quite soon who would release them. He presumed they'd not leave him in here to die, but presumption was a dangerous thing, even more perilous than despair.

The cell door creaked open. A hooded figure stood poised for an instant, then rough hands propelled him inside. The door slammed closed and Tyrant heard the scrape of bolts being replaced.

'What took you so long?' Lone asked.

'They were looking for me,' came the reply.

'Then they should be reprimanded for not finding you sooner,' she said.

'I was trying not to be found,' Malachi answered. 'Matters have taken a turn for the worse here. Our plan is no longer a good one. The King will not listen to my counsel anymore.'

'I hope you're not telling me that you've wasted two long years toadying your way into his trust and now, when I turn up with the means to control him, you're not in a position to go through with it? That I've spent two years of my life for nothing? I've dredged the depths of the underworld to find a demon to possess the King. Are you saying it's all been for nothing?'

'I'm not saying that, my dear, only that the timing is a little unfortunate, that's all. Yesterday, things were better. Much better. I had the full confidence of the King and ensnaring him would have been child's play. I might even have done it without the aid of a demon.'

'And today?' Lone said.

'Today, I have been the victim of a fool called Ambrose. This is a man of little intellect and smaller understanding who stumbled across some ancient ritual but lacked the knowledge to leave it alone. Instead, he inscribed a powerful magical device in the tower. One that cannot be controlled or dismantled. Powerful demons have been attracted here and are wreaking havoc in the castle and the wider city. Chaos reigns. The King is preparing to flee Gort, it's that serious.'

'The King can't hold you responsible for the actions of another,' Lone said.

Tyrant knew from experience this was a speciality of the King. Blame was something heaped on thickly and spread all around. He was beginning to realise that being in the company of these two was not going to be an advantage. On the contrary, his involvement with them involved serious trouble if the King was on the warpath.

'But he can and he does,' Malachi said. 'According to him, demons are my area of responsibility and the fact that he has been grievously insulted by one has been laid at my doorstep. No matter how hard I tried, I failed to convince him that I represented his only chance of resolving this situation. My words fell on deaf ears, I'm afraid to say. He's ordered me to be hanged at the first opportunity. That's why I was trying to keep out of the way until he cooled off and I could talk him round.'

'Hardly worth my while coming here,' Lone said. 'You were supposed to gain His Majesty's confidence while I laboured long and hard to conjure a demon to enslave him. If I'd known you'd make such a hash of things, I'd have stayed away and left you to it.'

'This demon of yours,' Malachi said, 'will it help us now? Or has it joined in with the others to wreak havoc on the citizens of Gort?'

'It is bound to serve me until I utter the words of release. This is powerful and ancient magic that can't be resisted. Unless it obeys me, it knows there's no prospect of being let go.'

'It's that weird horse, isn't it?' Tyrant said. 'I knew all along there was something very wrong with it.'

Malachi looked at him as if seeing him for the first time. 'Who is this?' he asked.

'My travelling companion,' she answered. 'It saves a lot of awkwardness if I have a man to escort me. When people see a couple, they only notice the man and deal with him. As a woman, I become invisible. Were I to travel alone, I would attract all manner of unwelcome attention.'

'Well, you're here now and have me by your side,' Malachi said.

'I hope you're not jealous, my dear.' Lone smiled. Tyrant winced. The words he was hearing sounded light and gentle, but he could feel the powerful undercurrent beneath them. Malachi, with his black hood and sharp nose exuded menace.

'Leave me out of this,' Tyrant said. 'I was just doing the lady a favour, bringing her safely back to you. Job done. I'll be on my way as soon as you get me released. You can do that, can't you?'

Tyrant's question was ignored, leaving him reluctant to bother them with all the other queries that bubbled up in his head.

'Your demon sounds as if it's been a waste of time and effort; otherwise, you wouldn't be in this predicament, would you?' Malachi's voice was like treacle running off a spoon.

'It's telling me that it is close by and waiting for my instructions. It seems that its attention was distracted by the sudden appearance of several other demons. That caused our imaginary steeds to disappear at a most inconvenient time. It has apologised and wants to make amends.'

Malachi let out a cackle of laughter that reminded Tyrant of a rock being dragged across a stone floor. 'And you trust this demon, do you?'

'As much as I trust in you, my love,' Lone answered with a look that made Tyrant want to be anywhere else but in her presence.

The cell door creaked open to reveal a nervous soldier brandishing a sword that was in every way the antithesis of the one that Tyrant had been carrying prior to his incarceration. It exuded an unmistakable no-nonsense quality that, courtesy of its honed and polished blade, threatened to slice to pieces anyone or anything that might get in its way. Tyrant liked the look of it very much. If ever he took to carrying a sword, he'd definitely want one like this.

Behind the swordsman was a bevy of bowmen, jostling to take up a position where they could shoot something other than the back of their comrade's head. It was very likely that their presence was the cause of the swordsman's discomfiture rather than being the reassurance it was meant to be.

'Out you come,' the soldier said.

'Are we free to go, then?' Lone enquired.

The soldier grimaced and one or two of the closer bowmen let out a snigger. 'Free to go to the scaffold,' he said. 'Come on now, the hangman's waiting for you.'

Malachi, black-clad and exuding menace, stepped to within an inch of the raised sword. Tyrant could see the soldier's fear displayed in the way that his quivering blade retreated slightly at Malachi's approach. In contrast to his scary presence, Malachi's voice was honey-sweet, low, and compelling. 'You have been misinformed. The King requires you cede us safe passage. Now, stand out of my way or it will be the worse for you all.'

Tyrant couldn't stop himself from believing everything Malachi was saying. Especially the last bit. An involuntary shudder wriggled its way up his spine as a succession of very bad things began to happen in his mind. From the jaw-dropped expressions on the soldiers, they were thinking along the same lines. Tyrant was glad he wasn't one of them, though he could have done with being elsewhere. Anywhere else would have done. A chilly, rain-soaked thicket in some long-forgotten forest would have fitted the bill very nicely. Instead, he was leading a more interesting life. Something he went out of his way to avoid.

There was a moment of frozen inactivity as Malachi's words rolled around the confines of the prison. The lead soldier's face was a mask of uncertainty, while most of those behind him looked terrified.

Malachi took a step forward and the soldiers backed off. Tyrant felt rooted to the spot, a spectator desperately hoping to remain just that. This was something for Malachi and Lone to sort out. His participation could only complicate matters and result in arrows being aimed in his direction instead of theirs.

'Move!' Malachi gave the word such force that Tyrant worried for the stone fabric of the building. Soldiers tripped over each other in their haste to make way. The inevitable happened and a crossbow was discharged accidentally, eliciting a scream of pain and a wail of disbelief. The bowmen melted away, dragging the stricken, bleeding, and wailing one with them, leaving the swordsman alone to defend the exit. What had looked like fierce determination on his part gave way to a struggle for breath. His face coloured pink, then red, then purple. His hands grabbed at his throat as if he were attempting to clear his airways. The sword he was brandishing clattered to the stone floor. Lone picked it up and handed it to Tyrant. 'Take it,' she ordered, and he found himself meekly accepting the weapon despite the reluctance he felt. 'Come,' she said and he found his legs moving dutifully in response.

Against his better instincts, Tyrant found himself leading the way along the stone corridor and away from the prison cell.

The corridor was barely three men wide with arrow slits on his left letting in a trickle of light and allowing the occasional glimpse of a crowd gathered outside in the courtyard. On his right was a succession of closed and bolted doors. Shouts could be heard at the far end of the corridor and soldiers hurried towards them, swords drawn.

Tyrant took stock of the chain mail, iron helmets, and grim determination heading his way. There was a choice. There was always a choice. In this situation, he could choose between fighting to the death and being apprehended. Considerable kudos would be associated with valiant but futile resistance and it would seriously enhance his reputation. There was, however, the downside of not being alive to enjoy the benefits. He lowered his sword and prepared to surrender.

The soldiers hurried past without a single sideways glance, merging into single file to negotiate the three escapees. It was as if they didn't exist. Tyrant released the breath he'd been holding and concentrated on persuading his legs to recover from the frozen state of collapse they'd adopted on sight of the troops.

'Very nicely done, my dear,' Malachi said.

'I thought that was you,' Lone answered.

It certainly wasn't me, Tyrant thought. Then he remembered the peculiar horse that had turned out to be a demon. The animal that hadn't left footprints. The weird being that had winked at him in a most alarming and disconcerting manner. He wondered about the significance of that wink. Perhaps the thing, the demon, winked at every passer-by, but he doubted it. There had been something troubling and deeply personal about that wink. It was a wink that had etched itself into his mind and left him troubled whenever he thought about it. The demon was back amongst them and offering them protection. Just how reliable that might be was open to question. The wink had made him doubt the intentions of the horse-like entity to do anything except amuse itself at his expense.

'Through here.' Malachi guided them out into the courtyard, where a sizeable crowd had gathered to enjoy the grisly spectacle of some poor unfortunates being hanged. Three forlorn figures were already swinging gently, legs twitching spasmodically as the life was strangled from them. A short queue of participants formed a reluctant line that inched forward towards the gallows, urged on by the pricking of swords. 'Mingle with the crowd,' Malachi said. 'We'll use them as cover when they leave.'

Tyrant slipped quietly into the swarm of stinking sightseers. The scaffold was raised high on a mound overlooking the city so that its macabre presence could act as a reminder of the King's power and lack of mercy. Beyond the yard that accommodated the crowd was the inner citadel wall with its watchtowers and the iron gate that provided the only way out of the palace. Malachi's idea was a good one, in that it provided the only possible means of escape. Tyrant's nervousness betrayed his conviction that, without continuous intervention from the damnable horse-thing, their chances were very slim indeed. He knew from experience that everyone that came in or out was carefully scrutinised by the guards stationed at the gate.

The miscreants chosen for today's entertainment were a mixture of children and the ancient. The King had other uses for the able bodied. Men were pressed into military service and women had a prodigious capacity for useful work. The hangings were supposed to keep everyone in line, Tyrant supposed, but he suspected that the King enjoyed exhibiting his viciousness and cruelty.

23

There were at least twenty unwashed bodies clustered in the prison cell with Ant. Some of them were old and infirm, most of them were harmless, and all of them were very frightened.

It seemed that the most common form of death in Gort at the moment was being hanged by the King's decree. Nobody was immune from the seemingly random arrests and automatic capital punishment for even the smallest perceived misdemeanour. It was impossible to judge the time in there, but he had a disturbing feeling that his was about to run out.

He was desperately thirsty and very frightened. The vision of Little Billy being strung up on a gibbet haunted his closed eyes. If he opened them, all he could see was desperation.

The door rattled open. Soldiers came in with heavy wooden staves, which they used to beat the seated, the upright, and the standing into motion. They were herded out into a corridor, Ant blinking in the stream of sunlight that came through the high windows. Soldiers were at every juncture, prodding them along. Ant stumbled, hands still tied, and was clouted hard across his back. The air in his lungs was expelled and he fell forward, face hitting the stone wall. He was pitched sideways onto the floor, where he curled up against the kicking he was receiving and began to cry.

Rough hands dragged him half upright, then flung him after the shuffling mob he was supposed to be part of. His legs felt too weak to support him. All he wanted to do was lie down and die there and then. But he wasn't permitted even that final peace. Soldiers pushed and shoved him along, so he made progress despite his collapsed state. Every time he fell down, he was hauled upright almost instantly. He rolled painfully down the steps into the courtyard and lay on his side, panting in the welcome fresh air, and looking up at the three gibbets standing side by side surrounded by a crowd of silent onlookers. Three bodies hung limply from their nooses. A young woman, face twisted in pain, stared straight at him with sightless eyes that accused him of every wrongdoing he'd ever done or imagined. Two men, necks at unnatural angles, looked the other way as if they had nothing but contempt for him.

Ant was forced into a makeshift queue, one in which nobody was interested in pushing to the front. He counted eight in front of him. He was the ninth, then. Three lots of three. He had the prospect of watching two more triple hangings before his own. Better to push forward and get it over with. The dead girl was taken down and her body cast onto a growing heap of grisly detritus.

Three more of Ant's cellmates were struggling against the ropes that were being tied around their necks. 'No!' one of them shouted. Then his cry was cut short as the noose tightened and the hangman hauled him high off his feet, which kicked furiously for a while before dangling lifelessly. The dead body was cast aside and the next trio was brought up to hang. It was as quick as that. Onto the platform, rope around neck, then that was it. No ceremony, no last requests, no speeches, no appeal, nothing but death.

Another scream was silenced. It was Ant's turn now.

He was hauled onto the rough wooden platform and displayed to the ragged crowd. The noose was placed around his neck.

24

The hangings were being conducted with ruthless efficiency, three unfortunates at a time. It seemed they were intent on emptying the prison as quickly as possible. Tyrant's throat constricted in sympathy. He was finding it hard to breathe. Every instinct screamed at him to make a run for it before he caught the hangman's eye and was dragged to the gibbet.

Blending in with the crowd was easier said than done, the assembly being comprised mainly of bent old women and geriatric men dressed in filthy rags. He was trapped between Lone and Malachi, one a striking figure in jet black and the other a vision of female loveliness. Whether they held him there by some arcane force or he was too shocked and exhausted to move away, he couldn't tell. On his own, he might have been able to count amongst the unwashed assembly, but the three of them had to be standing out like cherry trees in a wasteland of prickly gorse. Another downside to the arrangement was that he couldn't help but hear everything Malachi and Lone were saying.

'That's Ambrose's boy,' Malachi said.

'Good, maybe they've got his father as well,' Lone replied.

Tyrant winced as Malachi and Lone argued about whether to rescue the boy they were watching being led to the gallows. They were in enough trouble as it was without getting involved in some foolhardy rescue. 'We need to save him. There are things he can tell us about his father's business.' Malachi's voice was low and insistent.

'Don't be a fool,' Lone said. 'We're in enough peril as it is. Do you want to stand up there yourself and hear his dying words as you choke alongside him? Leave him. He's worthless anyway.'

Tyrant found himself in total agreement with the witch.

'I have a feeling that you're wrong,' Malachi said, 'which is unusual, I admit. Let your demon do his job of protecting us. I'm willing to gamble that the boy has been party to everything his father does and that information may be invaluable.'

‘Invaluable? What value do you put on our lives? We’re hardly out of danger ourselves and I don’t fancy joining the queue to get my neck stretched. Leave him.’

‘This could be our best chance to get our hands on the source of the King’s power and use it against him.’

‘The opportunity for that was lost when he turned against you,’ Lone replied.

‘A wise general modifies his plan of attack to suit the prevailing circumstances,’ Malachi said. ‘Our opportunity is merely postponed, my dear, and we must redouble our efforts to create another. The strategy has always been to gather power that exceeds that of the King and the boy may be the key to achieving that aim.’

25

Fear curdled in Ant's guts. His breathing had stopped as if in anticipation of his impending strangulation. He felt warm wetness cascading down his leg. The noose tightened.

The two bodies on either side swung into the air. Ant could hear their vertebrae cracking and feel the rush of air from the flailing legs. All movement ceased and the lifeless bodies were dropped to the floor with a thud.

His noose was roughly pulled off his head and he was thrown bodily onto the charnel heap, where he landed face to face with the young girl with the staring eyes.

The other bodies landed on top of him, driving the air from his lungs. Ant lay as if dead. He felt dead. Maybe he was dead. He'd been hanged, hadn't he?

Ant moved his arms to bring his head up and away from the dead girl's gaping mouth. He breathed in and the smell stung his nostrils. He rolled sideways, down the heap, and onto the ground. Slowly, he crawled towards the crowd and into their midst. Nobody seemed to be paying him any heed; there were no shouts or grabbing hands. Ant kept on crawling through the forest of legs, anticipating the inevitable arms that would take him back to the gibbet to do the job properly again.

When the arms came, they held him upright and set him on his feet. Firm hands remained pressed on his shoulders, either in support or restraint, perhaps both. Ant looked round at the hooded figure standing behind him.

'Stay still. We'll need to wait to leave with the rest of them. Be patient.'

Ant began to retch. He vomited what little was left in his stomach over the back of the man in front of him. Then he kept on heaving as if his guts needed to be expelled from his mouth.

The hangings went on and on. The sun was high in the sky and burning hot by the time the carnage was done. As if following an unspoken instruction, the whole crowd turned and walked in ragged formation towards the gate.

It was as if he was already dead and observing earthly happenings from another dimension. All he could feel was numbness. Lurking beneath lay a fearsome surge of unquenchable anger that threatened to break through and overwhelm him. He clung desperately to the numbness and observed it with a fierce detachment.

26

Tyrant watched as the three tattered figures stood trembling on the scaffold, thick rope decorating their throats. Their legs were visibly quivering, as if ready to give way and save the hangman his final heave. Two were suddenly plucked into the air, twitching and gargling.

The third, a slight boy of fifteen years or so, looked confused to find his own feet still safely on the wooden planking. When the thrashing and screaming subsided, the hangman dropped the men in a heap and threw the carcasses onto the pile he'd made in front of the crowd. Then he treated the boy in a similar fashion, as if he too were dead meat to be fed to the gathering crows. The boy landed awkwardly on the heap, paused as if in thought for a moment or two, then slid off onto the ground and began to crawl between the legs of the crowd, who were giving him no heed at all.

'Stay still. We'll need to wait to leave with the rest of them. Be patient.' Malachi spoke softly to the boy when he reached the place they were standing. 'You'll be safe with me. Rest here until we can leave.'

'Let's go,' Lone ordered. Tyrant hesitated. His head told him he'd be better off alone than in the company of a wizard, a witch, and a half-hanged boy. Lone's cat eyes caught his and held them. His resistance dissolved in an instant and he found himself tagging along.

As they neared the gate where soldiers were stopping each spectator and questioning them before allowing them through the gate, they found themselves waiting in line. Tyrant couldn't help thinking this was tantamount to surrender. Surely, they'd be recognised as fugitives and re-arrested. Maybe they'd even whisk them back up the hill and string them up. He was sure the hangmen would welcome a bit more work.

As in response to his misgivings, Lone spoke in a whisper. 'My demon will make sure that no harm comes to us.'

'I can't share your confidence. The dreadful thing is bound to protect you alone, and only then to prevent you from dying. If you're killed, the ancient magic will prevent its return to whence it came. That's its only incentive,' Malachi hissed.

'It needs to serve me well if it is to be released,' Lone said. 'I've made that abundantly clear to it. Fear not, dear husband, it is close by and will make sure that we gain the safety of the outer city.'

Tyrant could extract little comfort from Lone's words. It was hard to understand why the demon would bother with any of them. His knowledge of demons was limited to some tall tales he'd been regaled with in taverns. They were, by all accounts, wayward and unreliable. Sneaky. Mischievous at best and most commonly evil. Not the kind of ally to be pinning all your hopes on even if you were a witch.

Four sturdy men dressed in mail and wearing iron helmets with impressive nose guards stood between them and the gate. He paused, took a deep breath, and stood quietly while Malachi spoke to them. In the event of negotiations taking a bad turn, his borrowed sword would not provide them with any effective protection. He wished he'd abandoned it in the crowd while he had the chance. Now it felt stupid to have it dangling from his belt.

'Simple folk, enjoying the spectacle of a good hanging,' Malachi said and Tyrant believed him. Of course, that's exactly what they were, after all.

'Who's this?' A soldier pointed a grimy finger in Tyrant's direction.

'My manservant, of course,' Malachi said.

'Why's he got a sword?' the soldier replied.

'To protect me, of course. There are so many ruffians and vagabonds about these days, don't you agree? Look, those people over there, for instance. You should be wary of them. They look as if they're up to no good.' Malachi's voice was soft and reasonable.

'Swords aren't allowed in the citadel. Order of the King.'

'But we're leaving,' Malachi said. 'Once we're beyond the gate, everything will be as it should be. Now, stand aside, my good man.'

None of the soldiers made any move to stand aside. Instead, they gave puzzled looks at each other as if unsure what to do. Tyrant decided to help their deliberations by giving up the useless and inconvenient sword. He dragged it from his belt and offered it, hilt first to the nearest guard. 'Here,' he said, 'take it if it will make you feel better.'

The soldier accepted Tyrant's gift then examined it closely as if assessing its value. A thoroughly ungrateful gesture considering that the weapon had been donated freely and unconditionally. 'This is an officer's sword,' he shouted.

As if doused by a bucket of cold water, the soldiers' soporific state changed to urgent action. Before he could offer any sort of explanation involving his acquisition of the troublesome item, arms reached out to grab him. 'Arrest them all,' the officer yelled unnecessarily as his troops jostled to lay hands on everyone remaining within the palace grounds. Which now included only himself, Lone, Malachi, and the boy.

Although the gate was a mere ten paces away and wide open, there were too many soldiers intent on grabbing hold of him and too many crossbows being aimed his way for there to be any chance of fighting his way out successfully. An exploratory nudge felled the soldier clinging on to his right arm, but before Tyrant could capitalise on this small success, a variety of sharp objects were placed uncomfortably close to vulnerable parts of his body and he decided to refrain from any further argy-bargy for the time being.

Despite Malachi giving them his hardest stare, soldiers threw him to the ground and bundled him up in his cloak so that he resembled an angry carpet writhing around on the cobbles. More circumspection was being applied to Lone as she remained surrounded but untouched. Ant stood limply, watching when he'd have been best advised to run.

'Run for it,' Tyrant shouted. The boy made no response but remained staring back at the palace, eyes wide and mouth open. Following the boy's gaze, despite his captors making any form of movement difficult, Tyrant saw a black streak emanating from the tower. Like a dark stain on the sky, it twisted into convoluted shapes as it hung threateningly overhead. A sense of dread afflicted Tyrant to the extent that his predicament became irrelevant when compared with getting as far from the black thing as possible.

His soldier friends appeared to have adopted the same view, losing interest in anything apart from the thing that by now had thickened and assumed a tubular shape. His nostrils filled with a stomach curdling stench as it passed over the inner wall where it suddenly swooped down and covered the knot of townsfolk who were on their way home after the hangings.

Dreadful screams shattered the frozen silence. Shrieks of fear transformed into terrible wails of agony.

'Close the gate,' an officer shouted. 'Get them out of here,' he instructed. Galvanised into action, soldiers shoved the four of them through the gate and closed it behind them. Tyrant had little time to reflect on how priorities can quickly change in a time of crisis. A few moments ago, he'd have given anything to escape the citadel. Now he wished he could get back inside.

What had been a loose gathering of forty or so human beings had been swallowed by black slime that began to grow into a dark column higher than the city walls.

'Keep close to the wall,' Lone ordered. Tyrant heeded her advice and kept his back scraping against the stone as he inched his way along, keeping his eyes firmly fixed on the black thing, which inconveniently seemed to be keeping pace with them.

The blackness began to fade, revealing the awful details it had been hiding. The grotesque figure that stood before them had two legs, two arms, and a body. It resembled a headless giant formed from human bodies and stuck together with pitch. Every component was screaming. Every eye was turned towards him. A monstrous travesty of a hand reached out towards him. Each finger was a body encased in tendrils of black. Tyrant wished more than anything else that he'd not given the sword away. At least he might have had some chance to keep the thing at arm's length. He knew what it wanted. It wanted him to become part of it. It seemed intent on gathering fleshy components. It wanted to grow.

Lone started screaming as loudly as the victims. Her arms described wild circular sweeps as she confronted the awful thing. Its appendage stopped barely an arm's length from Tyrant's face. He could make out the face of an elderly woman at the tip of a makeshift finger before it disappeared under the black glue that bound everything together.

'Now!' Lone shouted, and still raving and gesticulating, ran towards the suddenly immobile conglomeration of humanity. Tyrant hesitated, saw Malachi and the boy spring forward in pursuit, then ran after them.

The soldiers behind him on the palace wall began to shoot at the monster, and arrows whistled overhead. All except one, which embedded itself painfully in the top of his shoulder. His progress halted while he came to terms with the new situation. He'd been struck with many things in various parts of his body, but this was as bad as he'd ever experienced. Without really wanting to, he stood rooted to the spot. Neither of his arms seemed to want to work anymore; they just hung uselessly from his shoulders while searing pain cascaded through his body, rendering him incapable of experiencing anything else.

He struggled to move one foot in front of the other. *As long as I can keep my legs moving,* he thought. As if in mockery of his will, they buckled underneath his weight and deposited him helpless onto the ground.

27

Lone couldn't help but feel cheated. This black demon had shot from the tower, enveloped a few dozen people, and built itself a terrible monster, all seemingly without much effort or trouble. Her demon, the one she'd sacrificed so much time and endured so much discomfort to conjure, was pathetic in comparison.

She could feel the black monster's curiosity and immense hunger as it approached. Thoughts of trying to somehow control this entity were abandoned when she detected its implacable determination to cause as much harm and suffering as possible. Properly harnessed, this demon would have been a wonderful asset and given her a tool with which to rid the land of the tyrant king. Unfortunately, she'd landed the wrong demon, and the irony was that there were plenty of better ones offering themselves now that Ambrose had opened the portal.

However much she might admire the strength of this creature, it was untameable and intent on making her its next victim. Absorbing her being into its own to make itself more powerful.

Incantations born from anger and frustration poured from her lips. Gathering energy from the earth, she projected it into the demon. She couldn't kill it, but she could weaken the glue that bound the manifestation together. She felt it lose coherence; one of its legs weakened and collapsed. People began to crawl away from the black slime that held them.

All the time, she was shouting for Patch. Ordering him to intervene. Imploring him to save her. His lack of response could mean only one thing. He was as scared of this demon as the rest of the city.

Messing up the demon's makeshift body was taking almost all her attention and energy. They needed to make good their escape before she ran out of both. Urging the others forward, she decided to try to run past the demon while it was trying to sort itself out.

Some stupid soldiers decided this would be a good time to discharge a hail of arrows at the monstrosity, and she cursed them for the extra vigilance she needed to exert to avoid being skewered. More expenditure of energy that she could have done without.

Malachi disappeared from her peripheral vision and she turned to see what had happened. He was standing over a prostrate Tyrant with the boy in close attendance. Any moment there would be a new volley of arrows that might kill them all. The demon was quickly recovering from and adjusting to her interference. When it did, she would be powerless to prevent it from absorbing the lot of them.

'Leave him,' Lone said. 'He's of no use to us.'

A voice sounded in her ear. 'Where to, mistress?'

'Get us out of here,' she said. There would be a time for questions and recriminations later.

There was a noise like the wind howling through trees. She was plucked from the ground and flown high into the air.

28

The pain was still clouding his ability to think. Tyrant could remember the crossbow bolt hitting him and also had a clear recollection of Lone's voice. *Leave him; he's of no use to us.* He tried to move, to sit up and look around him, but he was too weak to stir any of his limbs and his head just lolled about slackly on the pillow.

He was in a bed. And one with a pillow and sheets and blankets. It could be a dream, it might be some intermediate state before proper death, but Tyrant's pragmatism placed him in a relatively normal earthly bed. He vaguely recollected the agony of all that digging into him to remove the bolt. It had seemed to take hours, and there had been a lot of screaming involved. Now the pain had dulled to a constant ache, which flared to something much worse if he moved. Not being dead, he thought, was something of a bonus under the circumstances. He resolved to make the most of it.

Two young girls began spooning food into his mouth, one holding the bowl and spoon and the other using both hands to hold his head still and keep his mouth open. Tyrant wanted to be more cooperative, but willingness didn't translate to action in his present stricken state. Nor could he bring himself to speak anything more than what he hoped were grateful sounding grunts.

He had no way of measuring time other than the pain in his shoulder. The longer he lay there, the better it was. The girls were applying poultices of damp herbs on a regular basis and he surrendered to the ritual of *eat* then *rest.* Sometimes his sleep was disturbed by images of deranged people attacking him, but he usually managed to get through his dream without the need to wake up screaming. In his rare lucid moments, he would speculate about where he was and how he had arrived here. The only workable theory he could come up with was that he had been borne aloft on the wings of an angel and brought to this place of healing and succour.

A man's face hovered overhead. It was vaguely familiar. Tyrant formed some words in his head and tried to speak them. 'Waa haa hoo?' It was close to what he intended, but probably not close enough.

'I'm Oliver,' the man said. 'You were badly wounded, and we all thought you were going to die. My wife Freya, and daughters Cassie and Bee have nursed you back to life.'

'Fankoo,' Tyrant managed. His head was much clearer now, and he was searching through his memories, trying to see where this man fitted in. A horrible realisation accompanied his successful retrieval of the appropriate recollection. This was the soldier in the forest. The one who had wanted to arrest him. The one that the wily Lone had managed to extract good money from before she sent him on his way. Oh dear. Tyrant wondered how his shorn look was faring from lack of attention, and whether he had already reverted to his more usual style of having unkempt hair and a beard that was all over the place. In which case, recognition was only a matter of time. And, under the circumstances, wouldn't matter.

Oliver helped him to sit up for the first time so that he could take a proper look around. He was in a tiny bedroom in the corner of a hut. An opening allowed him a view of a cooking area where a woman was busy with pots and pans. As he breathed in, the aroma tickled his taste buds and he felt his normal ravenous state gradually returning. His arms were mobile but weak, especially his right, which buckled under any amount of weight. Still, he was relatively pain-free now, his shoulder less prone to delivering the terrible shooting pains he had become used to. He took another deep breath. 'How long?' he asked.

'You've been here two days. Like I said, we didn't expect you to live, but we had to try to help as much as we could.'

The woman came into the room holding a steaming bowl. 'It was my husband who saved you,' she said. 'He's a soldier and has a lot of experience with crossbow injuries. It was fortunate for you that you landed here.'

Tyrant gingerly took the proffered bowl in his left hand and managed to work the spoon with his damaged right. Hot food going down his throat felt so good. All he could do was to savour every mouthful and feel grateful to be alive again. When the bowl was empty, he said, 'Landed?'

Oliver smiled. 'That's one way of putting it. We were almost home when you fell out of the sky right in front of us. That took us completely by surprise, even in these days of weirdness and strange happenings.' His wife took the bowl and returned with it fully replenished. The stew was delicious. Tyrant accepted it gratefully and ate as quickly as he could manage. He had the feeling that his body needed to make up for lost time.

After the meal, Tyrant felt tired again and fell asleep. This time he dreamed of Lone and her misshapen horse. They were arguing over him; she was telling it to leave him to die. It was insisting on carrying him to safety. Neither of them seemed to prevail, and they just kept on arguing in a more heated manner the longer the dream went on. By the time he woke, all he was left with was a residual feeling of being discarded and abandoned. He was grateful to see the reassuring figure of Oliver standing over him again.

'We've met before, haven't we?' Oliver asked.

Tyrant felt too weak to care any more about being recognised by this kindly man. 'Yes. In the forest to the east. I was with the woman who sold you the handkerchiefs.'

Oliver's face twisted as if he was having difficulty remembering.

'The woman is an enchantress. It may be that she put a spell on you that stops you remembering properly,' Tyrant added.

Oliver's face changed. 'She was here,' he said. 'I thought she looked familiar. She was with the King's adviser, Malachi. I presumed she was one of his acolytes. I never connected her with the woman I encountered in the woods.'

'Then you missed an opportunity to get your money back. Pity,' Tyrant said.

A rueful smile passed over Oliver's features. 'These are strange times indeed. The world has gone mad and I fear for all our safety. I'm not sure that a few coins matter at all now.'

'Where is she now?' Tyrant asked.

'Gone. They travelled north.'

'Things are still bad, are they?'

'I fear they are getting worse. We are far enough outside the city to have been spared the worst. But I fear that will not last. There aren't enough soldiers still sane to keep our families safe, the city burns, and the King's palace is in danger of being overrun. My own troop was attacked by a demon that transformed men into ravaging beasts.'

Tyrant made his first unaided trip to the latrine, and as he went about his business, he pondered on the half-remembered details of being attended to by Oliver's family in ways that left him shaking with regret at his own weakness. He wasn't sure he could look those young girls in the eye again now that he realised they had been sorting out his waste for him during his time lying prone in their bed. As soon as he felt strong enough, he would leave. Get back to his old ways, travel alone, and look after nobody but himself. The prospect cheered him, as did his successful visit to the toilet. He was on the road to recovery and things were looking good.

Two days later, he awoke to the smell of burning.

29

Gort had been in turmoil. Ant had watched the dead stare fixedly into the distance and the dying scream in pain and disbelief. The big man, Tyrant, hit by an arrow, had sunk stricken to the ground. He remembered as in a dream that Malachi's woman had shrieked meaningless words as the four of them were borne aloft and carried by invisible hands above and beyond the carnage. They abandoned Tyrant as his blood soaked into the dirt. Even though he hardly knew the man, he was ashamed that he'd been left to die alone.

Being perched on this peculiar horse that had neither saddle nor bridle was as disconcerting as it was comfortable. He could have been floating on air. Even if he tried, he doubted he could contrive to fall off his unusual mount. Malachi and Lone had requisitioned more conventional horses, and they were all cantering away from Gort, leaving a cloud of brown dust in their wake.

Shame began to bite through his numbness and dissolve it to reveal almost uncontrollable rage. Shame that he'd caused the loss of his friends by his cowardly hesitation and failed to accompany them on their journey to oblivion. Anger at his father who had been responsible for these terrible events then left him to face the consequences. Even greater fury towards a cruel monarch who delighted in hanging children. Ant took a breath, let the resentment boil inside him, then made himself a solemn vow. He was going to kill the King. The rest of his life would be devoted to finding a way, and he didn't care what he had to do as long as he ended the rule of this tyrant.

He didn't ask where they were going, but it soon became clear that they were heading north. Nobody went north. Nobody except fools, vagabonds, fugitives and, of course, his father, who harvested the treasures of the inhospitable wastelands.

The thin ribbon of rutted dust that was the North Road began to climb. Gently at first, then becoming so steep that the mounts of Malachi and Lone struggled to keep their footing. Hooves scraped at the loose earth, sending pebbles skittering back down the slope while Ant's weird steed floated serenely and effortlessly behind. Flanks glistening with sweat, mouths snorting to catch enough breath, the horses toiled up the unforgiving slope, which stretched endlessly in the distance.

Ant's thoughts turned to his father as they made the laborious climb between ever steepening sides that trapped them within a deep groove. This was the notorious North Road, the place of ambush where escape was impossible. Ambrose had recounted this journey on numerous occasions but refused to let Ant accompany him because, he said, of the danger. Now, Ant had been abandoned to make the perilous trip in the company of a man that his father despised and mistrusted. Nobody knew the badlands of the North better than Ambrose, but when his son most needed him, he wasn't there. When the noose was around his neck, it hadn't been his father that saved him. That was wrong. Fathers were surely supposed to owe a duty of care to their offspring, weren't they? If this had been the test of Ambrose's worthiness as a father or his devotion to his son, then he had failed. Failed completely.

Then it came. The stabbing pain in his heart that was Mona. The one thing guaranteed to sweep him off-balance and throw him into a turmoil of loathing and loss. She had been his mother. Not his real mother, as his father had dismissively corrected him at every opportunity. Nevertheless, she was his only mother; the mother who remained alive to care for him and love him. His childhood had been spent in her delightful company. He had learned everything from her, becoming who he was because of her and in spite of his distant, absent father. Then, for no good reason, his father had sent Mona away. Ant couldn't think about that without welling up. His breath came in short gasps. A violent longing gripped his entire body. If only he'd had the guts to go with her. She meant the world to him, and he missed her more than he'd ever had the strength to admit.

Mona. His mother. His betrayal. Every child should have the right to stay with his mother. If only he'd been able to defy his father and gone with her. That lost opportunity was the acid that corroded his guts. That bitterness would swill around inside him forever.

Where was his father now when he most needed him? The question burned in his mind. The thought of his father possibly being dead provoked little reaction beyond cold numbness. If he were truly on his own, then so be it. Life would be simpler without that constant need to prove himself worthy. The cloud might lift from his heart and let him find himself in the fog of self-doubt.

After his mother had been torn from his life, he'd managed to avoid the mistake of attachment, knowing the dreadful suffering it caused. Until Pepper and Col had gently introduced themselves into his affection and spent every possible moment in his company. Now he'd failed them in a moment of spectacular stupidity. Hesitation had somehow prevented him from accompanying them to whatever fate lay beyond the device. Better, far better, that he also was consumed by the monster. At least they would have died together. Instead, he was left alone with an unbearable burden of remorse.

Meanwhile, speculation was tearing aside his numbness. It was as if he was waking from a nightmare. The pain and horror of his hanging lingered deep in his breast, but his mind had been freed to function again. He was on a peculiar horse heading north in the company of his father's nemesis when he should have been finding a way to save his friends. If he wasn't too late already.

'I need to go back to Gort.' Ant approached Malachi with a trembling dread. The man finished slipping the saddle from his sweat-frothed horse, then turned around to face him.

'That would be very unwise,' Malachi said.

Ant savoured the veracity of these simple words. Malachi's voice was soft and persuasive. It made Ant wonder why he had been so stupid to even think of returning. Then he remembered Pepper and Col, the device in the cave, and the nasty thing with tentacles. 'I have to find my friends,' he said.

'You saw what was happening in Gort with your own eyes. There's no point in returning; your friends' fate will already have been decided and nothing you can do will change it.'

Pepper and Col were already gone. His father had fled and was possibly even dead by now. There was nothing left in Gort for him. Apart, perhaps, from one thing. The most important of all. 'I also have to kill the King,' he said.

Malachi gave him a look that was thankfully devoid of any scorn. 'That ambition is easier to express than to carry out. The King is powerful and resilient. Don't you think that many harbour the same desire as yours? Yet the King remains the king while his adversaries suffer torture and death. A boy like you can't hope to succeed where others who were much better equipped have failed.'

'I don't care,' Ant said. 'I hate him. He's a tyrant who doesn't deserve to rule.'

'Then channel that hatred, make it work for you. Become the best that you can be. Then you might have a chance. I can help you if you want me to.'

'Help me kill the King?'

'Help you become strong enough to have a chance of success.'

Ant was excited at the prospect of Malachi's assistance. It was an offer that his father had never made, despite his desperate need to learn. He thought of the device he'd built in the cave and the parchment he'd left there. Something held his tongue from blurting out the information, though. Perhaps he was still gripped by his father's dire warnings about the wizard. 'What do I have to do?'

'Become my apprentice. Assist me in my work. Watch and learn.' Malachi's eyes bore into his, challenging him to reveal his innermost thoughts. Ant flinched as if he were under physical attack, but held his resolve not to disclose the existence of the parchment.

Lone finished tending her horse and approached them. 'So, our little hanging boy has regained his power of speech, has he? I was afraid that the noose had crushed his windpipe and throttled his voice completely.'

'Ant is going to help us find the source of the device and the ancient power that lies behind it,' Malachi said.

'Another fool to join you on your errand, then? Aren't we just running away and you're pretending that there's some point to our headlong flight?' Lone laughed, but Ant couldn't detect any humour in it. He braced himself for Malachi's response, fearing a catastrophic clash of wills and for his own safety being this close to the seat of the impending explosion.

Malachi grinned, and the tension subsided. 'We need to gather our strength and add to our knowledge. The King is no ordinary man who can be bent to our will. He's made of sterner stuff than that. Believe me, I know him too well. He's been resisting my best endeavours for years. His wisdom is not to be underestimated, and he seems to be able to anticipate every eventuality. If we're to succeed, we're going to need more than a pathetic demon in the form of a misshapen horse. The old knowledge is what keeps the King on his throne. That's what we must acquire to unseat him.'

Ant felt Lone's attention alight on him. As he met her eyes, his body reacted as if there were a physical connection between them. His nerve endings ignited and an overwhelming desire for her inflamed his heart. She was exquisite; awesomely lovely. How had he been oblivious to her beauty until now? The perfect shape of her nose, the lips that were full and inviting, hair that sparkled like dark gold. The sight of her body created a savage longing to touch and caress and explore.

Malachi had turned his back and was rummaging through his baggage. Lone shot him one final glance that might have been compassion before she withdrew her attention and sat down beside Malachi. Ant sank to the ground next to the peculiar horse. His heart was thumping as if he'd been running full pelt up the mountainside. His mind was confused by a mixture of regret, embarrassment, and desire.

'Do you feel ready?' Malachi's words spiked into Ant's heart. He was besotted with the man's wife. Was this some kind of challenge?

'What do you mean?' Ant couldn't meet Malachi's eyes, and shame boiled inside his stomach while defiance lurked dangerously inside his chest.

'Ready to begin the work,' Malachi said.

Ant took a deep breath and tried to tear his eyes from Lone, who was ten paces away, her back to him and bending over to retrieve something from the ground. She'd cast aside her cloak in the heat and was wearing a simple white shift. It clung tightly to her where a dark stain of perspiration ran from her neck to the beginning of the cleft in her backside. His eyes followed the curve of her spine down to her splayed haunches, and the terrible ache in his groin intensified. With a tremendous effort, he lifted his head and stared at the wizard, who gave no indication of having noticed anything untoward. 'Yes, the sooner I learn, the better,' Ant said. 'I want to be able to control people like you do. Bend them to my will. Cause them pain if they get in my way.'

'Understand this: there is no guarantee of success, only that the work will be long and hard. Even after many years, you might find you have none of the abilities that you desire. Everyone is different, remember that. Your talents are unique and may manifest themselves in ways that surprise us both. Your first task is to become aware.' Malachi spoke with a parental authority that gripped Ant's attention and made him want to exceed this man's expectations more than anything he'd ever desired. With the exception of his wife.

'We must continue our journey even though the hour is late and we will be travelling in the dark. It's important that we get through this narrow gorge and into more open land as soon as possible. It could be perilous were we to rest for the night in such an exposed place. This will be a good opportunity for you to practise. Observe your weariness but do not become it. Make use of all your senses and not just your sight. Become detached from your thoughts; allow them to drift across your consciousness without trying to cling on to them.'

Before Ant could begin his questions, Malachi turned away and mounted his horse. Lone shot him a tiny, thin-lipped smile as she spread her legs over her mount and urged it forward.

As they picked their way carefully up the rise, dark monoliths towering on either side, Ant listened to the echoes of Malachi's instructions and tried to obey them. A sudden movement on the periphery of his vision startled him. Heavy footsteps sounded in his ears, the hairs bristled on the back of his head, and his skin tingled with shock as he turned his head to see what was about to attack him.

There was nothing. It had been a trick of the light, something imaginary yet powerful enough to provoke his body into action. Real or not, it didn't matter. The result was the same.

The tingling residue of the fright persisted long after he knew there was no danger. It was as if his body was determined to remain on high alert, whatever his mind might decide. Ant thought about his reaction to Lone and as soon as he shifted his attention, the swelling returned to his groin and the ache began to gnaw at his stomach. She was way ahead, invisible in the darkness, yet his longing was just as great as before. What was making him feel this way? Was it her? Did she have magical powers that could invade his mind?

The scare was similar, but different in that it seemed entirely natural. His own doing. His thoughts had triggered the reaction in his body even before they had consciously registered. Was this what Malachi was trying to show him?

Ant tried to detach himself from the constant stream of ideas and speculation that drifted through his brain. Eyes closed to keep out the last glimmers of dusk, he began to catalogue the sensations he could identify. The smell of the warm wind carrying the scent of vegetation. The muted clopping of the horses ahead. Blood coursing through his veins. The thumping of his heart in his chest. There was a tree ahead at the side of the track. A large one, bent over as if shielding him from harm. He opened his eyes and saw the tree exactly as he'd imagined. A burst of excitement rippled through his abdomen. How had he known about the tree? Where had the detail come from when he'd had his eyes tightly shut? Was it the rustling of the desiccated leaves? The subtle darkening caused by its shade? Or could he really see without his eyes?

There was a lot to learn, Ant realised, and he was determined to do it quickly.

30

Tyrant was too weary to respond to the smell of smoke, but even in his depleted state, he had to take notice when his blanket caught fire. This propelled him out of his comfortable bed and into a raging inferno. The house had practically been destroyed with him still inside it.

With a tremendous effort of willpower, Tyrant resisted the urge to lie down and let the flames devour him. Moving was such a painful effort.

As the fire encroached and the heat intensified, he flung himself at the nearest wall. It gave way easily and he found himself outside, blinking in the strong sunlight, and facing an even worse situation. At first glance, he thought that everyone was dead. There were a dozen bodies, mainly soldiers, lying around. His smoke-filled vision cleared enough to discern Cassie wrestling with a crossbow. She was trying to reload the thing while a huge bastard lumbered towards her with a mace in his right hand and something even more disconcerting under his left arm.

It was Bee, his youngest ministering angel, and the hulk was holding her like he meant to crush her to death.

Tyrant wasn't a big fan of the mace. He couldn't see what was wrong with a good hammer. It was stronger, did the same job, and when you weren't hitting people with it, you could mend things.

Cassie stood upright, holding the now-loaded bow. 'Shoot him,' Tyrant said. 'And do it quick.'

She stood shaking, the crossbow wavering, and the threatening figure now less than ten paces away. 'I might hit Bee,' she said.

Tyrant hobbled over and grabbed the bow. The sudden movement set his shoulder wound singing with pain again. He pointed it at the man holding Bee and walked towards him. 'Let her go,' he said. The man let out a bellow and raised the mace above his head. Bee screamed. Tyrant released the shot. The bolt went into the man's eye socket and almost disappeared.

Tyrant's legs weren't ready for prolonged standing and collapsed beneath him. As he crumpled to the ground, the mace whistled past his head, then the man joined him in the dust. Bee's screams became even louder. Tyrant closed his eyes and tried not to listen.

Cassie was grabbing at his shirt, trying to pull him to his feet. 'Quickly,' she said, 'we have to leave. There are more crazy people on their way and no soldiers left to protect us.'

'Where are your parents?' Tyrant asked.

'They went to fetch food,' Cassie said. 'Do you think they're in danger?'

Tyrant assessed his situation. His legs wouldn't work, he felt faint, and he was wearing a cotton shift that barely reached down to below his buttocks. He wasn't capable of either fight or flight for the foreseeable future. Sitting up proved a challenge he almost failed.

The tower and city walls were far in the distance, yet he could hear the unmistakable sounds of battle. Women's screeches mingled on the wind with the guttural cries of male hatred. The awful noises were getting louder the longer he sat in the dust. *You fell out of the sky* Bee's father had said. He vaguely remembered the sensation of being borne aloft but couldn't believe that he'd flown all the way from the citadel to this village on the outskirts of the city.

Bee was clinging to her sister and sobbing. 'Get out of here.' He used what little energy remained to wave his arms at the girls.

'We have to wait for Mother and Father to return,' Cassie said.

'If you do that, the mob heading this way will kill you both for certain. If your parents are still alive, they'll find you. Better you run so that you'll be alive when they do. Leave me here. I can look after myself.'

'No, we won't,' Cassie said.

'No, you can't, you're as weak as a baby,' Bee added.

'You're our baby,' Cassie said, 'and you're coming with us.'

Both girls began tugging at his shirt and managed to drag him a few paces along the ground. Then the fabric gave way and they were left grasping the remnants while he tried to cover what was left of his dignity. 'At least find me some clothes,' he said.

Tyrant took several breaths to steady himself. The pain in his shoulder was raging, his head felt as if there were angry hornets nesting inside, and his limbs refused to perform any of their allotted functions. Getting to his feet was out of the question. When he tried, his knees buckled and he fell over onto his side where he lay gasping.

'These were on the washing line.' Cassie returned with an armful of clothing. 'Lucky for you.'

The prospect of wearing trousers again provided an incentive to which his ailing body responded. With the help of the girls, he managed to dress and even regained his feet in the process. Walking, however, was difficult on his wobbly legs and he had to endure the ignominy of being supported by the children. Despite the potential damage to his reputation this involved, being fully clothed provided a welcome boost to his morale.

Progress, however, was painfully slow. The three of them wouldn't be able to outrun a lame tortoise, let alone a murderous band of able-bodied people.

'Over there.' Bee pointed to a house that had so far escaped from being torched.

'That's no good,' Tyrant panted. 'If we hide in there, we'll be trapped and they'll find us for sure.'

'Not the house, silly,' Bee said. 'That's our cart. You can ride in it. We'll push you, won't we, Cassie?'

The cart was a flimsy contraption that buckled under his weight. The girls took up a handle each and the wheels began to turn. Tyrant felt ridiculous with his knees drawn up to his ears. If anyone saw him, his reputation would be shattered beyond repair. The knowledge that this was his only option was scant comfort.

'Go south,' he said. Weariness overcame him and, despite the cart's uncomfortable confines, he succumbed to sleep.

31

'You should have left me behind,' Tyrant told the girls. They were sitting exhausted at the side of the track, having given up trying to push the handcart up the steep incline.

'You'd be dead now if we'd left you,' Cassie said.

'I can take my chances. At least you got me out of that village.' He looked back down the road and could see no sign of habitation or of people. 'I don't know how you had the strength to push me this far.'

'It wasn't so bad,' Cassie said. 'That's why we came this way. Now there's this steep hill though and you're too heavy.'

Tyrant began to recover his bearings. This was the North Road. A long straight track that climbed through a narrow gorge for mile after mile. 'But I told you to go south. There's more towns and villages where we can get help and accommodation. There's nothing in the North but wilderness and starvation.'

'Well, we can't go back now,' Bee said. 'Anyway, it was too hard to push you south because it was too hilly. This way was best.'

'No, it isn't,' Tyrant said. 'There's only wasteland beyond these hills. It's dangerous country. South is better and safer. This road is notorious for robbery and murder. There's no place to hide. Once we're in the gorge, we'll be trapped and at the mercy of anyone who comes along.'

He managed to slide out of the cart onto the rutted road. His legs felt as if they might be getting used to the idea of performing the job they had been designed for again. He looked up the steep bank into the thick forest. 'We need to go up there and take cover amongst the trees. Find our way across the mountains that way. We can't afford to be caught on the road.'

'Why not?' Bee asked. 'If anyone comes, you can shoot them with Cassie's crossbow. And I brought these for you as well.' She held out two small knives, which he gratefully tucked into his belt.

'Even so, I'm not in any state for fighting.'

'You will be soon,' Cassie said. 'We only pulled the arrow out of your shoulder four days ago and look at you now.'

He considered the kindness he'd received from these girls. They had cared for him and healed him. He knew he owed his life to these two children and would be eternally indebted to them. This left him with a very uncomfortable feeling, one he'd been carefully avoiding for many years.

He stood up and tried to shake off his lethargy. Looking back down the road, he saw a dust cloud that heralded a substantial group of horsemen heading towards them. 'Quickly,' he said. 'Run into the woods and hide.'

'What about you?' Cassie asked.

'No time for questions. They'll be on us too quickly. If you hesitate, they will see you. Just go. I'll hide the cart, then myself.' Tyrant pushed them into the thick undergrowth.

He manhandled the cart to the edge of the track, then tried to manoeuvre it between two substantial bushes. It stuck fast in the branches and refused to budge despite all his best efforts. He was still struggling with it in full view of the road when the leading horseman stopped and addressed him.

'What are you doing?'

Tyrant winced as he anticipated the spear thrust into his back. As he turned around slowly, he became aware that these were soldiers, riding two abreast and in perfect order. There were too many of them to count; at least fifty, Tyrant reckoned, but there could be a hundred. He'd never seen so many soldiers in one place before. Not even on a battlefield.

Tyrant looked into the man's eyes and saw no trace of the madness that had afflicted the man with the mace. Then he saw the fancy epaulettes adorning the man's uniform and realised he was being addressed by a very senior officer indeed, probably a general. He took a deep breath to clear his mind for the right answer to a question that might make the difference between life and death.

'It's my cart,' he replied. 'Can you help me get it out of these bushes?'

The general smiled and waved an instruction. Two men dismounted and hefted the cart back onto the road. The general peered down from his lofty perch. 'Where are you going?' he asked.

‘Away. Anywhere. Just as long as I can escape the madness. I almost died back in Gort. People were going crazy.’

‘Have you seen anyone else on this road?’

‘No one, thankfully. I’m so glad to see that the forces of law and order have been restored.’

‘Hardly,’ the general said. ‘Gort is all but destroyed and the King has gone south.’

‘Then shouldn’t you be with the King?’

‘He has sent us on a mission to find the men who betrayed him and brought all this destruction down upon our heads.’

‘Oh,’ was all Tyrant could manage. Did they include him in this description?

Obviously not, because the general issued an order and the troops thundered off, leaving Tyrant choking in a cloud of dust raised by two hundred hooves.

When the grimy fog cleared, Cassie was there beside him. ‘What did they want?’ she asked.

‘I think they’re looking for the people I was with when I got shot.’

‘The creepy man and the strange woman and the boy?’ Bee asked.

‘You saw them?’

‘They came down from the sky like you did.’

‘I didn’t like the look of them; they looked very grumpy,’ Cassie said.

‘The boy was alright, I suppose. He’d have done for you,’ Bee said.

‘Don’t be silly, I’m marrying a man, not a boy.’ She gave Tyrant a look that made the pain in his shoulder seem the least of his worries.

‘We have to get off this road while we can,’ Tyrant said. ‘The next ones to find us might not be so friendly.’

‘If you think we’re going through those dark horrible woods, you can think again,’ Cassie said. ‘I don’t know why you’re so afraid of meeting fellow travellers. Everyone you meet isn’t out to kill you.’

‘Maybe not,’ Tyrant replied, ‘but there’s a good chance they will. Think about what’s happening in Gort. That madness may be spreading. Anyone could be affected. I can’t afford to take that chance. The forest is the only way we can keep ourselves hidden.’

'If we go up there, how's our father going to find us anyway?' Bee asked.

'You don't even know if he's looking for you.'

'Of course he'll be looking for us. Just as soon as he gets back from wherever he's been and finds us gone,' Cassie said.

'He'll find you dead and gone if you don't do what I'm saying,' Tyrant said, not fancying the steep climb one bit either. Even if he'd been at the peak of physical health, though, the North Road was a path to be avoided.

Grabbing what little food and water there remained on the handcart, he began to wade painfully through gorse and brambles. When he reached the line of trees, he looked back to see the girls picking their way carefully through the undergrowth. Both were complaining loudly.

'I'm tired,' Bee said.

'It's getting dark,' Cassie added.

'Where are we going to sleep?' Bee asked.

'Anywhere you like,' Tyrant said, ready to drop from weariness himself and glad of Bee's face-saving intervention.

'I can't see anywhere.' Cassie twirled around like a spinning top.

'We need a house or at least some shelter,' Bee said. 'It might rain.'

'Then we'll get wet,' Tyrant said. 'That's the way of the world. Now have a look around you for somewhere nice and comfortable, then lie down and go to sleep.'

'There isn't anywhere nice in this whole forest,' Bee said.

'How about that nice clump of bracken over there?' Tyrant tried to be positive and helpful despite reaching the end of his patience for this day.

'Yuck, it's damp,' she replied, 'and I bet it's full of disgusting things.'

'Then one more won't matter, will it?' Cassie laughed and Bee flew at her, shouting and punching. They fell over and began to roll around, laughing.

Tyrant left them to it and selected a mossy area under the shelter of a tree to lay his head. Apart from a few ants that stopped bothering him when they decided he was too big to carry back to their nest, there was nothing to prevent him from enjoying a well-earned rest.

As he drifted off to sleep, he comforted himself in the knowledge that his present predicament was merely a temporary one. Once they were clear of the madness, he'd find a nice family to leave them with so that he could get on with his life without their incessant chatter.

There was something pressing on him. He became vaguely aware that he was being sandwiched by two warm bodies. 'We're cold,' Cassie whispered in his ear.

'I need something soft to lie on,' Bee said.

Tyrant resisted the urge to get up and find somewhere he could lie in peace. Instead, he lay quietly, aware of the girls drifting gently into unconsciousness. Then he had to become completely still in case he woke them up and they resumed their constant complaining.

32

'Are you still here?' Patch sensed Cali's presence somewhere out there in the darkness.

'Yes,' she replied. 'I'm hanging around, as they say, seeing what's going on.'

'And what is going on?' Patch asked.

'Lots of stuff you wouldn't believe.'

'Try me.'

'There's been all sorts of things arriving through the portal. Some of them quite disgusting and very belligerent. The whole affair has become very messy indeed. That's one of the reasons I'm still here. It's too dangerous to go anywhere near a portal at the moment. I suppose I'm stuck here, much like yourself.'

'Poor you. I'm finding it extremely tedious. All I get to do is manifest a silly horse and keep well out of the way or else she-who-must-be-obeyed gets very upset.'

'Why don't you come for a wander? I could show you lots of stuff that's really interesting.'

'Like what?'

'Like lots of fighting and mayhem. Some really obscure entities. Plenty of really cool places to visit.'

'If I wander, I can't guarantee to maintain her horse. My manifesting gets a bit flaky at a distance.'

'You're lucky. I'm not able to manifest anything concrete,' Cali said. 'I can't affect the physical world at all.'

'That's not such a big disadvantage. Bodies bring with them such awkward limitations. I like to keep things as simple as possible myself. I almost feel sorry for these humans. Almost, but not quite. They really are the most parochial small-minded species you could ever encounter. They have no notion of anything other than their own internal thoughts, which are always completely at odds with reality. They really are a deluded bunch. There seems very little point to their existence.'

‘There are others who might disagree. Physical experiences are highly valued in some quarters. I’d love to have the chance to experience all of that sensation,’ Cali said.

‘There are pros and cons to every state of existence, believe me. I’ve tried just about all of them and the human one would feel much too restrictive for a free spirit like you. You’d be anchored to the earth, condemned to a slow and painful life that is beyond anything that you can influence or control. You’d be a mere passenger in a body that lurches around from one sorrow to the next. Tell me, what’s going on that might have a bearing on my own predicament? Anything?’

‘Nothing much. There’s a rather serious place ahead of you on this road if you keep heading the way you are. It’s a long way off, though, and very well hidden.’

‘Anything I should worry about?’ Patch asked.

‘It will probably be hazardous to the humans and may kill them all, but it’s not likely to bother you.’

‘That does bother me, though. If the witch gets killed, it means I’m trapped here,’ Patch said.

‘There’s an army on horseback catching up quickly,’ Cali replied. ‘They are definitely going to kill all the humans; that’s their orders. The King sent them. It appears that he’s really upset about what’s been going on and is blaming the members of your party for it.’

‘Very funny. Caught between the devil and the deep blue sea, as the saying goes. Ah well, should provide me with some entertainment at least.’

‘Are you going to communicate with your mistress? Warn her of the impending threat?’

Patch thought for a moment. ‘Naw,’ he said. ‘Let’s see how things pan out. Might be more fun that way.’

33

As the new day dawned, the steepness of the climb diminished and the three travellers reached the crest of the long hill. At this point, the gorge narrowed even further, making it difficult for two horses to pass through side by side. Ant ate his breakfast alone, preferring to try to preserve his state of calm by keeping as far away as possible from Lone's disturbing presence. The bread he'd been given tasted freshly baked and the cheese was remarkably soft and moist. Neither of these things seemed feasible after several days' travel, but he didn't feel at all surprised. Stranger things happened all the time when Malachi and Lone were around.

A couple of dozen paces from where he sat on the side of the road with his back supported by the vertiginous rock sides, Lone was rummaging through items being carried by his peculiar steed. He turned his back and tried to clear his mind of lustful notions, without complete success.

You got the hots for that woman.

The statement that popped into his head couldn't be argued with. However, it wasn't the way he would ever express his feelings for Lone. The crudeness of the thought irritated him. How could he be so crass as to be thinking in such terms?

Hello? Cat got your tongue?

There was something or someone inside his head that made him suddenly very afraid.

I'm not going to hurt you. Not yet.

'Are you the demon?' Ant asked, turning to look at his mount, which was showing no interest in him.

I suppose I am.

'So you've been carrying me all this time without talking to me?'

Not that demon; I couldn't carry anything.

'Then who are you?'

Cali.

'You sound like a girl, sorry, young lady. Are you some kind of ghost, then?'

Feminine. Not female.

'So, if you were human, you'd be a woman.'

Not necessarily. Feminine is an attribute that's not linked to gender or sex. It's very different.

'What about the horse? What manner of thing is that?'

Oh, him? All anger and resentment. I'd keep well away if I were you.

'But I have to ride on his back.'

No problem, but don't provoke him.

'How would I do that?'

You're a sensitive boy, that's why you can talk to me. Don't try it with Patch.

'Patch?'

His real name is long and complex. Knowing it is dangerous. She who trapped him is ignorant of it.

'How did she trap him and why doesn't he escape?'

She dangled shiny old magic. He took the bait. Until she speaks the words of release, he has to protect her. If she dies, he remains earthbound. When she does release him, though, she's going to be in big trouble. He likes to bear a grudge.

He wanted to warn and protect her. Prevent the nasty horse demon from harming her. The thought of losing Lone bit deeply into his chest and left him desperately fearful. 'What will he do? How can he be stopped?'

He can't. I have to leave you now. He's looking for me and I don't want him to know about us.

'Will you return?' Ant tried to hide his desperation, but she was inside his head and there was nothing he could keep from her. 'Don't leave me,' he whispered.

'Look at that.' It was Lone's voice.

Ant forced his eyes open and blinked at the harsh morning light. They had been descending a gentle incline for a few hours and he had felt the vertiginous rock walls receding to be replaced by grassy slopes. He'd listened as the birds began to sing, smelt the fragrance of vegetation, and recognised the rustle of the breeze in broad-leafed trees.

Now his eyes confirmed everything he'd been visualising. The claustrophobic imprisonment of the gorge was gone, replaced by verdant grassland and forest. Far off to the east, a lake shimmered like a sparkling jewel that needed to be possessed.

She leapt down from her horse and shook dust from her hair. Her simple dress clung to her sweat-soaked breasts, her stomach, and her thighs. 'That's where we're heading,' she said as she pointed to the lake, 'and the chance to finally scrub this grime from my body.' She smiled at Ant as if challenging him not to imagine her stripping off and plunging into the water. If it were a challenge, he failed it. Her excitement at the prospect was contagious. He found himself longing for the lake, to be cleansed and restored, but always he longed for her.

'I see you've been practising as I advised. How are you finding it?' Malachi alighted next to his wife; the perfection of his black cloak unsullied by the rigours of the journey.

'It helps that I have no need to guide my horse and can keep my eyes closed for the most part.'

'Have you experienced anything that you consider of value?'

'That I am sometimes able to perceive my surroundings without having to look at them,' Ant replied carefully.

'Very good, that's a wonderful start. Keep on with your practise and remember that it takes many years to develop true awareness and there are many who never achieve that experience. You can only do the best that you can. When we get to the lake, I will tell you more of what you might achieve and how you might use it.'

As they continued, Lone and Malachi leading the way and the peculiar horse plodding stoically behind with him perched on its back, Ant wondered how perceptive Malachi had become. Did he know about his overwhelming passion for his wife? The answer was disturbing. Of course he did. He'd have to be blind to miss it. Not only was Malachi not blind, he possessed superhuman powers of observation. If the situation were reversed, he wouldn't take kindly to anyone lusting after his wife, but Malachi seemed completely unperturbed. Perhaps he was used to men ogling her; after all, she was the most exquisitely perfect female in the whole world.

Ant felt into the situation and allowed thoughts to roll around his head without trying to grab any of them and make them right. Of all the possibilities, only one gave him a tremor of resonation when he thought about it. Ant's devotion to Lone suited Malachi's purpose. He was being manipulated by the pair of them.

This realisation did nothing to change the situation. Malachi could teach him things his father never would but she remained the icon of his sexuality. Malachi's first lesson had enabled him to realise that resisting thoughts and desires was what caused him distress. When he managed to accept the way things were, his whole being relaxed and he was able to savour the energies that rippled through his body.

They're coming! Flee while you can.

Ant's heart began to race. 'Cali? Is that you?'

A hollow silence filled his head after the intense burst of energy had almost thrown him from his mount. A debilitating fatigue immobilised his body and his mind. It became an effort to breathe. Panic swelled inside him but was unable to escape from the lethargy that held him fast. It was as if he was being forced to meekly accept whatever came his way, however terrible or dangerous.

The sight of Lone ahead, serenely undulating to the rhythm of her horse's gait, shook him out of his inaction. The peculiar horse didn't respond to his urging to speed up. Lone was twenty paces ahead and, if anything, he was losing ground. He tried to call out, but his voice refused to function as if the long journey had caked it with an immovable layer of dust.

'Lone! Malachi!' Eventually, his efforts had effect, and he managed a strangled squeak that elicited no response from those ahead. His cries rose in pitch and volume until he was screaming like an angry gull. She looked back at him, connected with his distress, and reined back her mount.

'What is it?' Lone asked as Malachi pulled his horse level with hers.

'I think someone is coming and that we should hide.'

'What makes you think that?' Malachi asked.

'It's a feeling. You know, a sort of awareness thing. The kind that I've been practising. It's very powerful.'

'There's nowhere to hide,' Malachi said. 'The horses wouldn't manage the slope up to those trees. We have to get down to the plain and those forests. Have we got time for that?'

'I don't know,' Ant said, twisting around to look back up the road. At the very top of the rise, there was the suspicion of a cloud of dust. 'Look up there, can you see that?'

'Horsemen,' Lone said. 'Many of them, by the look of it. Come on, let's get out of here.' She spurred her horse into a fast canter and headed off at speed. Malachi followed her. Ant's horse disappeared, abandoning him on the dusty track with all manner of paraphernalia scattered around.

34

'Where's Cassie?'

Bee pulled a face. 'Gone hunting. She took her bow. Said she'd bring back some poor dead animal for us to eat. Personally, I'd rather she didn't. The look of them is enough to put anyone off their breakfast.'

'We've no time for hunting or breakfasting,' Tyrant said. 'The sooner I get you to a place of safety, the better. Meanwhile, there could be all sorts of trouble heading our way.'

As time slipped by, Tyrant's impatience grew. There was nothing but squirrels out there anyway, and he'd given up eating that particular animal. The thought of them made him heave. Squirrels were wary little blighters, as well as being small and quick. That made them almost impossible to shoot. Cassie would be blundering around wasting arrows and, from what he learned of her nature in the short time they had been acquainted, was too stubborn to admit defeat and return empty-handed.

'Do you want me to go and look for her?' Bee asked as they munched their way through a late lunch of berries and nuts.

Tyrant shook his head and tried to ward off the increasing likelihood that Cassie was in trouble. Possibly dead. At best, she was hopelessly lost, an easy thing to be when following squirrels in random directions. Either way, there was little point in them staying where they were. 'We'll stick together,' he said. 'I don't want both of you lost.'

'She might come back here,' Bee said.

'If she was coming back, she'd have done it by now.'

Bee started to cry. 'You should have looked after her. It's all your fault. If she's dead, I'll never forgive you.'

They walked in a widening circle, shouting her name and getting no response until the sun disappeared and it was too dark to see what was underfoot. Tyrant sat on a fallen tree and flapped his hands at the flies that gathered around his head. 'We'll build a fire,' he said. 'Maybe it will attract her to us.' *And anyone else that might be lurking in these parts,* he thought.

As he groped around in search of dry moss and twigs, Bee stopped her sobbing and began to squeak excitedly. 'Over there,' she shouted. There's a light. It must be her.' She ran towards it, stumbled over a tree root, and fell headlong. 'Ow,' she said and began to wail again. Tyrant wondered if there was any better way to attract attention than a child's constant sobbing and decided there wasn't. If there was anybody of ill-intent out in the forest, they would surely be headed their way.

He picked up the fallen child and carried her. She responded by putting her arms around his neck and wetting his shirt with her tears. His shoulder was making a painful protest, but that was something he could ignore more easily than Bee's discomfort.

'If we don't find Cassie, you'll have to marry me,' Bee sobbed.

Tyrant was struggling to carry her weight while trying to avoid falling over roots and being snagged by brambles.

'You're both too young to be even thinking about getting married.'

'No, we're not,' Bee said. 'I'm twelve and Cassie's fourteen. Plenty old enough to be married. You could marry both of us. That would save you having to choose. What do you say to that?'

'I'm not the marrying kind,' he said. 'Now be quiet, I need to concentrate.'

The light resolved itself into a lantern hanging from the side of a ramshackle building. The smell of wood smoke was in the air. A dog began to bark as they approached.

'I don't see how being quiet can help you see better, anyway,' Bee said.

'If there's a light, then there will be people. If you don't shut up your prattling, they will hear us coming.'

'Does that really matter?' Bee asked.

'If they're unfriendly, I'd rather see them before they hear us. Then we might be able to avoid any trouble.'

'That would be nice.'

He was tired, and his shoulder was aching badly. He needed to find a safe place for them to sleep.

As he struggled through the clinging undergrowth, he wondered how he had managed to arrive at this low point in his career as a man who didn't care much about anything or anyone. Here he was, blundering around a dark forest, carrying one child in search of another. The worst aspect was that he cared. His desperation to keep the girls safe made his situation doubly dangerous.

On his own, he would have taken his chance at being a bit harder and more ruthless than anyone he encountered. He'd have made a prudently cautious yet decisive approach, then played it by ear. Now, he genuinely didn't know what to do.

Leave Bee here in relative safety and investigate the house alone? Or, send her ahead and hang back himself, ready to dive in and protect her if necessary? If there were some decent, ordinary kind people here, might it be less of a shock to them if a young girl knocked on their door and asked for shelter?

He placed all the blame for his awkward predicament on that devious woman, Lone. She was the one who had ensnared him and set him out along this path. If it hadn't been for her, he would still be comfortably alone.

'Keep close,' he whispered. 'Try not to make any noise.'

'Is it a house?' Bee asked.

'I said to be quiet. Chattering doesn't count as being quiet. Being quiet means absolute silence and that's what I need from you now.'

'Don't get your pants in a tangle,' Bee said. 'The place looks deserted to me. We should just get on with it instead of creeping around.'

'Deserted, eh?' he hissed. 'There's a lamp hanging on the outside of the building; the place is bound to be occupied.'

Tyrant took a deep breath and ploughed forward. Admittedly, his own progress wasn't entirely silent. The forest floor provided many opportunities for sound. The swishing of his feet through the foliage, the snapping of dry branches underfoot, and his generally laboured breathing were providing unmistakable signals of his approach to anyone who might be listening. Plus the incessant yapping of the dog.

The flickering light revealed a hut made of split logs, complete with windows and doors. Someone had gone to a lot of trouble to erect such a place all the way out here. Tyrant gave up speculating and made his way past the animal pens, where pigs were snoring and chickens lying dead to the world. The inquisitive dog stopped barking and wandered over to give them a good sniff.

The door was ajar. Peering cautiously inside, he was rewarded by the warm glow of a fire burning in the hearth. His stomach churned at the delicious cooking smells wafting from the pot hanging over the fire. He made up his mind quickly. 'Inside,' he said, 'before they come back.' He locked and barred the door.

'Food,' Bee said. 'Yum, let's be having some.' She went over and lifted the lid of the pot. 'Smells like meat stew; I can see carrots and turnips in it. Can we help ourselves, Tyrant? Please?'

'Be my guest,' Tyrant said. His feelings of uneasiness were growing by the moment. They were effectively trapped in here now. Whoever this place belonged to wasn't going to be best pleased to find them here. And chances were that they would return at any moment.

Bee handed him a large bowl of steaming food and he wolfed it down while straining his ears for any sounds outside. With his belly full, he began to regain his customary feelings of optimism. They were as safe as they could be in here. If the occupants of the house were unfriendly, keeping them outside was at least a decent negotiating position to start from.

Bee ate her food and settled down on the bed. Tyrant was thinking about taking a nap himself when he heard the door being tried. 'Who's there?' he called at exactly the same moment that a female voice asked him exactly the same thing.

'We're weary travellers,' he replied.

'Then you are welcome,' she said. 'But you could at least let me into my own house.'

Tyrant thought about it. Safer to leave her outside, he supposed, but hardly polite under the circumstances. She'd probably find a way in and, when she did, would cause him as much trouble as she could. Better to confront her while she was in a good mood. He opened the door and his breath was swept away by what he saw.

In that one instant of hesitation, Tyrant was lost. He hardly had time to draw breath and take in the sight of a tiny woman, barely waist high, before she was on him. His legs were somehow swept from underneath him and by the time he'd hit the floor, she was sitting on top of his chest, poking a knife into his throat.

‘What do we have here?’ Her shrill voice rang in his ears. ‘Some nasty vagabond come to steal Petra’s home and leave her out in the dark and cold?’

‘Leave him alone!’ Cassie ran into the house and began tugging at Petra’s shoulders. ‘He’s my friend, and that’s my sister.’ The pressure of the blade eased slightly.

‘We mean no harm,’ Tyrant spluttered.

‘If you hurt him, I’ll tear you to pieces,’ Bee screamed. ‘If you kill Tyrant, you’ll be sorry ’cos we’ll have to stay here with you and you’ll have to look after us for ever.’

Petra withdrew the knife from Tyrant’s throat and hopped off his chest. ‘OK, if that’s it. But don’t think you can just barge into my home and help yourselves without some form of consequence.’

Tyrant got slowly to his feet. The base of his spine felt sore and his shoulder wound had flared up once again. As much as he felt like lashing out at the woman with his foot, he resisted the urge on the grounds that he’d probably miss. The woman was the fastest mover he’d ever seen.

‘We are sorry to have inconvenienced you,’ Tyrant said.

‘Ooh, sorry are we? Inconvenienced? Is that another way of saying burglary? Breaking and entering? Invasion of privacy?’ Petra stood holding a knife, which in her tiny hands looked like a sword. Her face was scored and creased like old leather and there were sparks in her eyes.

‘What are you then? Are you a dwarf or a fairy or an elf?’ Bee asked.

‘I’m a woman,’ Petra replied.

‘You’re a midget, then,’ Bee said.

‘I don’t like that word. It’s been used as an insult too many times,’ Petra said.

‘Small person. Tiny lady. What happened to you that you’re so small? Did you just not grow up from being a child?’ Bee asked.

‘I’d rather you didn’t keep going on about my size.’

‘OK,’ the girls chorused, ‘but tell us how you got that way.’

‘My mother was normal size, but my father was small. I take after him.’

‘Where are they now?’ Bee asked.

‘They both died a long time ago. My father was killed by bandits while he was trying to defend this place. My mother died of a broken heart soon afterwards.’

‘Do you live here all alone?’ Bee asked.

‘Now I do. I used to have a husband, but that turned out to be a mistake.’

‘Tyrant’s our husband,’ Cassie said.

‘He’s going to marry both of us,’ Bee added.

‘I shouldn’t be getting into marriage too quickly, young ladies, you don’t know what you’re letting yourselves in for,’ Petra said.

‘Oh yes, we do.’ The girls let off a series of giggles that grew gradually more and more violent until they were both shaking with laughter. ‘We’ve seen his you-know-what,’ Bee managed to splutter before collapsing back into mirth.

‘It’s not as big as we expected it to be,’ Cassie squealed.

Tyrant’s first instinct was to defend his manhood from ridicule. It would have been fighting talk had it come from any other lips, but he realised that whatever he said would only add to the general merriment. With difficulty, he forced himself to remain silent and sought solace in another bowl of the stew he had been eating before Petra’s arrival.

Bee and Cassie sat eating, taking mouthfuls in turns so that one of them could continue the excited chattering.

‘It took two of us and all our strength to pull the arrow out,’ Bee said.

‘There was lots of blood,’ Cassie said.

‘It squirted all over the place,’ Bee continued.

‘We thought he’d die for sure,’ Cassie said.

‘Let me look at the wound,’ Petra said.

‘That’s not necessary, it’s much better now,’ Tyrant replied.

Petra took no notice of him. She unceremoniously pulled back his shirt and poked his shoulder with a bony finger. ‘How long ago was this?’ she asked.

‘Three days,’ Bee said.

‘Five, actually,’ Cassie said.

‘No, three, stupid.’

‘It’s you that’s a stupid baby that can’t count past three.’

'Yes, I can. Listen. One, two, three, FOUR,' Bee said and glared at her sister, 'five, six, seven, nine, twenty, and another, and another, a hundred. There.'

'That's not possible,' Petra said. 'This wound is weeks old, maybe months. It's almost completely healed.'

Tyrant winced as she stabbed his sore shoulder with her finger to emphasise her point.

'He was only just shot when we found him, and that was five days ago,' Cassie said.

'Three,' Bee said.

'Listen, you little moron. He dropped out of the sky, all dying and bleeding, right? Then we took him home and pulled out the arrow like he told us to. Next day he slept most of the time. So that's two days. The next day we gave him some broth.'

'And changed his disgusting shitty bedclothes and wiped his arse and washed his you-know-what.' Bee giggled.

'The next day he sat up and talked to us and the day after that the horrible people arrived from the city and set fire to our house.'

'And killed the soldiers. And one tried to take me away, but Tyrant killed him with your bow,' Bee said.

'So count the days, stupid. One, two, three, four, five. There you are. I'm right and you're wrong. So there.'

'Three,' Bee insisted. 'I don't count the first day. It wasn't a whole day 'cos he arrived in the afternoon.'

'What did you do to make him heal so quickly?' Petra asked.

The two girls looked at each other. 'We're 'specially good nurses,' Bee said.

'We used a magic poulstice,' Cassie said.

'No, we didn't,' Bee said. 'It was just some grass and stuff to soak up the blood.'

'I'm a good healer. Always have been.' Tyrant's intervention drew three dismissive looks, and he regretted saying anything.

'Whatever the reason, you girls have done a wonderful job. You saved this man's life, though from the look of him it wasn't worth the effort.' Petra was looking at him in a way that suggested he'd pretended to be shot in order to get attention from two children. His face burned with shame, even though he knew it wasn't true.

'Can we stay here?' Bee asked Tyrant.

'It's not up to me,' Tyrant said. 'This is Petra's house.'

'You can stay as long as you want,' Petra said, then turned to Tyrant with a very serious expression. 'The girls can share my bed. You'll have to sleep outside with the pigs.'

Tyrant nodded. He was fine with that, as long as the girls were safe. That was all that mattered. He'd had many a worse billet than a bed of straw shared with warm, docile creatures. 'Fine,' he said. 'Can I take the stewpot with me?'

Petra began to howl with laughter and the girls joined in. 'Only kidding,' she said, 'you can sleep on the floor in here. But we don't want you flashing your tiny thing around, do we, girls?'

Tyrant felt the joke was wearing a bit thin, but there was no sign of the girls tiring of it.

During the night, Tyrant was disturbed by a loud whistling noise that alarmed him until he realised that it was Petra snoring. No wonder her husband had moved on.

***

The morning brought eggs for breakfast and freshly baked bread. The girls were in a happy mood and Petra wasn't glaring at him quite so fiercely.

'Come on,' Tyrant said when the eggs were all gone. 'We need to get moving.'

'Can't we stay a bit longer?' Cassie asked.

'One more night, please,' Bee said.

'I thought you wanted to look for your father,' Tyrant said.

'You go and find him,' Bee said. 'Bring him back here.'

'We'll stay with Petra,' Cassie said.

Tyrant took a deep breath. 'Are you willing to look after the girls, Petra?'

'Gladly,' she replied.

'Then remember that the world is in turmoil, that the forces of evil have been let loose. Watch out for trouble and be wary of any visitors.'

His mounting excitement at the prospect of being on his own was countered by the realisation that he'd miss the girls and their incessant chatter. Staying in this remote place was their best chance of staying safe, though. He'd be better alone and they'd be safer here.

'We'll be perfectly fine here, won't we girls?' Petra said.

'If I do manage to find their parents, they'll have to find their way here.'

'You'd better take this map then. But guard it carefully,' Petra said.

The map was impressive, etched on pigskin using a hot iron. Petra pointed out the landmarks he had to look out for and the places he should avoid. He rolled the thing up tightly and stuck it in his belt. Whatever Petra had said about remarkable healing, his shoulder still ached terribly and he could have done with another night or two in this comfortable home.

Cassie ran over to hug him. 'When you return with Father, we'll get married.'

35

The dust cloud resolved itself into a troop of cavalry jogging towards him with the sound of jangling metal. Their horses were muscular beasts equipped with bronze breastplates to match the ones worn by their riders. Each soldier wore a helmet that reflected the red rays of the setting sun.

Ant didn't bother getting to his feet in case they thought he was trying to escape. The curved blades they were waving about looked deadly sharp and he didn't want to risk getting on the receiving end of one. The general made his imperious way through the ranks of the horsemen surrounding him. His helmet shone, and the white feathers adorning it waved gently in time with the nodding of his horse. It was as if he were attending some royal pageant in full dress uniform that bore no signs of having been worn on such a long and dusty journey. The general dismounted with a single bound and landed lightly at Ant's side, where he went down on his haunches so that their heads were level.

'What do we have here, I wonder?' the general said as he looked from Ant to Lone's scattered belongings and back again. There was a thin smile on his face that seemed to convey a modicum of good humour, but Ant couldn't be sure that it wasn't the sneer he'd expect from a high-ranking soldier.

'My horse ran away,' Ant said.

'How thoughtful of it to unload all these useful and important items before it fled so as not to inconvenience you too severely.' The smile widened as the general spoke. Ant detected a hint of amusement in his eyes that belied his haughty bearing and created a turmoil of confusion in Ant's mind.

'I can explain,' Ant began.

'Before you do, let me introduce myself and tell you a little about why I'm here. I wouldn't like you to have to go to the trouble of creating an elaborate tissue of lies that would be both unnecessary and irritating. It's important that you and I get off on the right foot. Your life depends on it. I am the head of His Majesty the King's Household Cavalry. People call me The General, but I think you already know that because you're Ant, son of Ambrose, and we have seen each other on what I fondly imagine are the corridors of power. You, young man, were hanged at the order of the King and he'd be most disappointed were he to know that you'd managed to slip the noose, so to speak.

'Your father, however, despite being under the same sentence as yourself, remains a fugitive. The King has tasked me with finding him together with another traitorous wretch called Malachi. These two, I am reliably informed, were responsible for the dreadful affliction that has caused such widespread death and destruction in His Majesty's beloved capital city. So, strictly speaking, I am not looking for you, Ant. We saw two riders leave you and head down into the valley; I presume they are the ones I'm looking for?'

'No.' Ant shook his head. 'I don't know where my father is.'

'That is indeed a disappointment if it is true. Bear with me here and tell me why I should believe that you have come all this way if it wasn't in the company of your father.'

'Because it's true.'

'Ah, the truth. It's so often hard to define, isn't it? I mean, one of us can be convinced of something, but the other somehow manages to cling on to a version of the facts that holds no basis in reality. For example, I was told by the King that you had been hanged. Now, a person in my position cannot believe that the King can be mistaken, otherwise the whole fabric of existence is threatened, not to mention my own life if I were to unwisely point that out. So, young man, hanged you were and dead you most certainly are and of no further concern to our esteemed and wise ruler. Your father, however, is another pot of stew altogether. I have express orders from the man himself to bring Ambrose back dead or alive, if you'll excuse the melodramatic phrasing. Accordingly, it would help considerably if you could reveal your version of the truth without embellishment or alteration.'

Despite his military bearing, Ant couldn't bring himself to be afraid of the general. The man spoke in a very confusing manner, but what lay behind the words felt benign, almost amused. He sat in the dust of the North Road surrounded by the most feared soldiers in the service of the

King who had wanted him hanged, yet Ant didn't feel at all threatened and was wondering why. 'I don't know where my father is, that's the truth.'

'Then who were the two horsemen who rode away from you?'

Ant hesitated, realised how bad this must appear, then blurted out as much of the truth as he felt appropriate. 'Malachi and his wife, Lone. They saved me from hanging, then brought me here.'

'Aha, so we have one of the fugitives in our sight. That, at least, might be called progress. I know Malachi well, but have to confess I've never liked him. Too shifty, I suppose. Always whispering in people's ears, suggesting what they should do. What's his wife like, then? More of the same, eh?'

Ant's head filled with words he could use to describe Lone. Beautiful, desirable, comely, shapely, wonderful, the most important person in his world, someone to be adored and protected to the last breath in his body, the woman he would die for. He took a deep breath. 'Nice,' he said. 'She's nice. What are you going to do with them if you catch them?'

'My orders are clear; I am to apprehend Malachi and bring him back to face the wrath of the King.'

'Yes, but what about his wife?'

'She's included. Can't have her wandering around loose swearing vengeance and all that palaver. Might upset the King and make him think I did a shoddy job of tidying up loose strands. Obviously, it will be better for them if they put up a fight and are killed resisting arrest. I wouldn't advise anyone who upset the King as badly as Malachi has to put themselves in the way of the dreadful torture that awaits him back in Gort. The King will have them slicing bits off him for weeks and that will be the easy part.'

'I won't let you take them,' Ant said, his head filled with visions of Lone being butchered. 'They're my friends and haven't done any harm. It's the King that needs to have bits sliced off him, see how he likes his own medicine.' He watched the general's expression slowly change from mild amusement to outright mirth.

'It's lucky for you that you're officially dead, otherwise, that kind of talk would get you into big trouble. In case it had escaped your notice, you're faced with fifty cavalrymen, less the dozen or so I left to guard the pass back there. Men like Garth here.' A huge head appeared that looked as if it had been chopped in two and put back together again with insufficient care. A scar ran the length of the man's face in its exact centre. His nose was in two separate halves and gave him a terrifying aspect that chilled Ant's blood. It was inconceivable that a man could survive such a horrific injury in the first place, but now having the story written on his face made him a fearsome adversary. Ant cringed at the thought of his outburst and wondered how he could be so foolhardy to offer resistance.

Then he thought about the demon, Patch. How his fate was bound to that of Lone. How Cali had explained that nothing could be allowed to happen to Lone until she released Patch back to his natural state. A gnawing in his guts made him nauseous with fear. Something awful was going to happen and all he could do was hope that he'd come out alive.

Ant sat in the wagon, perched on a pile of Lone's belongings that had been jettisoned when Patch disappeared. There was so much of the stuff that a second vehicle had to be requisitioned to accommodate it. In the time that it had taken for the wagons to arrive, Ant was left thinking how extraordinarily thoughtful the general was being, considering his mission was to pursue and apprehend Malachi, then take him back to meet a terrible death. The retrieval of clothing and culinary items seemed irrelevant under the circumstances, but he rationalised the situation by deciding that the general was a fastidious man who wouldn't tolerate untidiness and might have gathered the items so that they could be given to the poor and needy on his return to Gort.

The general had taken most of his troop and galloped in hot pursuit of Malachi and Lone. When they left the road and headed towards the lake, the dust cloud that betrayed their location disappeared and he lost sight of them. This left him torn between needing to know what was happening down there, and relief that he didn't need to be directly involved.

It was completely dark by the time the lumbering cart pulled up at the side of the lake. Around him were the half-seen shadows of horses grazing the lush grass and the glow of several campfires. The crackle of wood, cooking smells mingling with smoke, and murmured conversations created a peaceful atmosphere. The anticipated broken bodies and screaming wounded were mercifully absent. Had Malachi slipped away and the general given up the chase?

His musings were answered when he was taken from the cart and led to a hearty blaze, around which sat Malachi, Lone, and the general. 'Ah, there you are,' Malachi said. 'Wragsby tells me he left you behind to tidy the place up. Seems you managed to litter the road with our belongings. I hope for your sake that you've not lost anything important.' The sharp nose overhung an uncharacteristically good-humoured smile that allowed the wizard's teeth to sparkle white in the firelight. Ant's confusion grew. No signs of conflict out there and none being displayed in this cosy setting either. Even Lone looked content, her hair damp but well-groomed and her body clad in a pure white shift.

'What's going on?' Ant asked. 'I thought there was going to be a fight. I was worried.'

'That's kind of you, Ant. Your concern is deeply touching.' Lone's wide night-time eyes drew his attention and he was once again lost in the sheer attractiveness of the woman. It was a joyous thing that she'd somehow managed to avoid being dragged and manhandled and bundled into a wagon for shipment back to Gort. As for Malachi, it was as if he'd planned this friendly reunion all along.

'Remember what we were talking about, Ant?' the general said.

'You mean about the King being a tyrant and not deserving to be on the throne?'

'Yes, exactly that. Well remembered, young man.'

'But I thought you told me that even to think that was treasonous and worth being hanged for.'

'So I did, but that was a mistake. Since then, I've been thinking about what you told me. How Malachi and his delectable wife, if I may make so bold, are only trying to help. How the King has got things entirely wrong and not for the first time. If he can hang a young lad like you who never did anything to anybody, then what hope do the rest of us have of living to a ripe old age? I may be his favourite general right now, but that can change in an instant. It's not good enough. Living at the whim of some selfish despot isn't something I'm willing to tolerate any longer. Thank you, Ant. You've opened up my eyes.'

Ant watched carefully for any signs of sarcasm on the general's face, but failed to discern anything except heartfelt honesty.

'Then my friend Malachi pointed out the unique opportunity this place affords. Do you know that this beautiful lake once supported a town that rivalled Gort in size and population? That the King ordered it burnt to the ground and every one of its inhabitants was dispersed or killed in the process. I was here to witness that atrocity. It was many years ago when I was a very junior cavalryman and only capable of believing everything I was told by my superiors. Now I regret what happened and my small part in it. Malachi has convinced me that we can grow this place into a city again and defend it if necessary. The pass over the mountains is narrow and easily defended. I left men behind to monitor who comes and goes, but they could easily resist any army the King could send against us in those narrow confines. This opportunity is not to be ignored. I'm seizing it with both hands, in fact. Laketown will rise again. It will be a fitting memory to those who suffered unjustly in the past.'

As the general drew breath, Malachi leaned over to Ant and whispered, 'I don't know what you said to the man, but he's completely on our side now. Thanks to you, we can continue our journey north with Wragsby covering our back. If the King does send more soldiers after us, they'll not get over the pass.' Ant was also rewarded with a smile and a nod from Lone, which meant more than any words of appreciation from Malachi.

Wragsby raised his arms over his head in a theatrical yawn. 'It's been a long day and tomorrow we start the rebuilding of Laketown. Time for me to turn in. I bid you a very good night.'

When the general had stomped his way out of sight, Ant felt Malachi's attention descend on him like a scratchy blanket. 'He's changed his tune,' Malachi said. 'I always found him insufferably pompous and so close to the King's backside he was in danger of disappearing forever. What did you say to him?'

Ant thought about his encounter with the general and his tirade against such an unjust King. 'I spoke from the heart, that's all. Told him what I thought of his King and his appalling cruelty. Maybe I opened his eyes a little.'

'Whatever you said, it was beautifully done,' Malachi said. 'Thanks to you, the rampaging bunch intent on murdering us on behalf of the King are suddenly our allies. Now, we are free to continue our quest to find the powerful wisdom of the past that has kept the King on his throne all these years. You have a gift, Ant, and I'm going to help you develop it to the fullest extent possible.'

'Don't delude yourself. He's nothing special.' Lone shot Ant a sideways glance that set the blood pounding in his ears. She rose gracefully to her feet, smoothing down her tight dress over her thighs. 'If he's lost any of my things through his carelessness, he'll not be developing anything because he'll have no future. I can't wander the North dressed in this flimsy piece of cloth and nothing underneath. It's not decent and I'll catch my death of cold.'

'It's all in the carts. Everything. I made sure they retrieved it all.' Ant could hardly draw breath to answer. His eyes followed her hungrily as she left the circle of firelight, then his efforts to remain calm began to bear fruit. His head stopped banging and his limbs regained their ability to function.

'Take no notice of her,' Malachi said. 'She's peeved that her demon ran off at the first sign of trouble and left you to take care of everything.'

'Demon?' Ant decided to appear ignorant. The alternative would have been to risk revealing that Cali had spoken to him.

'The strange beast you've been riding for days. Surely you noticed that it was no ordinary horse?'

'I did wonder,' Ant said.

'That was the manifestation of a demon that my wife spent two long years finding and entrapping. We had both hoped that it would become a powerful ally, but it seems to have very limited powers. Very disappointing. What happened to it when the soldiers arrived?'

'He just disappeared. Poof. Just like that. I don't think Patch wanted the general to see him.'

'Patch?'

'That's what I call him. He's my horse, after all. He has to have a name so I can tell him where to go and stuff like that.'

‘That’s interesting because that’s what Lone calls the useless thing.’

‘Maybe I heard her talking about it and presumed it was the name of my horse.’

‘Well, I’d keep things like that to yourself while she’s around. You need to be wary of her, but I don’t think I need to remind you of that. She’s a remarkable woman in many ways, but patience is something she lacks. Try not to antagonise her.’

‘I like her,’ Ant admitted without meaning to. His cheeks flared with the heat of embarrassment.

‘You mean that you’re attracted to her. That’s to be expected; most men are affected in that way. She exerts power and domination because of it. Men become obsessed with the desire to possess her and she uses that for her own ends. Poor things have no chance of resisting her.’

‘She’s your wife; doesn’t it upset you when other men look at her in that way?’

‘She may be my wife, but she’s not the kind of wife to be making a home and cooking my food. Our relationship is that of equals. She has complete autonomy and nothing binds us apart from common purpose. In a way, that aspect of her is the most dangerous of all. Our society insists on women being subservient to men. They do all the menial tasks and have little say in their own lives. Women like Lone are a danger to that archaic and mistaken way of life, so they are branded as witches as a way of eliminating their threat.’

‘Isn’t she a witch, then?’ Ant asked.

‘Oh yes, she is a very powerful exponent of the black arts. She has other powers than her femininity, though that may be her greatest one. Try to understand the feelings you have for her, Ant. They are natural ones and all the more compelling for that. She will amplify them, stoke that raging fire in your belly so that you become her willing slave. Do you know of a creature called a mantis?’

‘No.’

‘It is an insect, a sort of grasshopper, I believe. The female is much more powerful than the male. After mating, she bites off the male’s head.’

‘And will Lone do that?’ Ant found himself adopting the position of the male mantis and decapitation seemed a reasonable price to pay for the consummation of his desires.

'Figuratively speaking, yes. But long before anyone gets close enough to even attempt mating.' Malachi laughed. 'She's not well disposed to that kind of activity. I can tell you that from experience. Let's say that she likes to keep herself to herself.'

Ant stayed by the fire and fell into a restless sleep where questing tentacles chased him into darkness where something dreadful lurked.

***

He was grateful when the morning light began shimmering on the surface of the lake and he could sit on the shore and be comforted by it. When he thought about Col and Pepper, he was seized by anger and frustration. If only he'd been quicker to dive into the device. If only he hadn't been such a fool as to create it in the first place. Could they still be alive? Had they been devoured by that monster?

The scroll in the cave was surely the thing that Malachi was looking for. So why hadn't he revealed it? They had passed almost by the entrance to the cave when the long journey north had begun, and it would have been a simple matter to present it to Malachi. He owed the wizard at least that, didn't he?

The gentle lapping of the water eased his troubled state. He'd done his best. He was doing the best he could. The past couldn't be changed, and the future didn't exist. There was only the shingle beneath him, the breeze in his face, and the beauty all around him. Peace settled on him like petals falling from an apple tree in blossom. Here, by this beautiful lake, everything seemed to be exactly as it should be, if only for this particular moment in time.

Like it here?

'Cali? What's going on? They think that I persuaded the general to disobey the King.'

Let them. Good for you, might keep you safe.

'But it wasn't me, at least I don't think it was.'

It wasn't you, silly.

'Then it must have been Patch.'

It could have been me.

'Was it you?'

No. Just teasing.

‘I didn’t realise that demons could be so…’ Ant struggled to find the right word.

Subtle?

‘I imagined demons would be more inclined to violence, you know, fiery destruction and that sort of thing.’

Confusion more powerful.

‘I miss my friends.’

What friends?

‘They were taken by a thing with tentacles and dragged into the device I’d made. I think they’re dead and I wish I could have saved them.’

Show them to me.

‘How do I do that?’

Think of them.

‘Col’s the big one; he was kind and uncomplicated. Pepper was always busy. I really miss them both.’

Found them.

‘How is that possible?’

I’m not tethered. I can go anywhere.

‘Tethered?’

No body. Nothing to drag me back. Not like you.

‘Where are they? Are they alright? What happened to the monster?’

Only a grabber. Didn’t hurt them.

‘That’s great. Tell me where they are and I’ll get on my way.’

North. Long way north.

‘I don’t care how far it is. Tell them I’m coming.’

Can’t. Only you hear me.

‘But you can guide me, can’t you?’

Yes. Need help when you get there.

‘What sort of help?’

Bad things there. Very dangerous. Hurry. Friends in big trouble.

36

Up here, sitting on a rocky outcrop, Lone could watch as the other members of the party rested by the stream. 'It's time we went our own way,' she said to Malachi, who was sitting, hood uncharacteristically thrown back, obviously enjoying the warm sunlight.

'Nonsense. We have to stay with Ant. He may be the key to the whole situation. I believe he knows much more about Ambrose's activities and the origin of the portal. We might be able to uncover other powerful artefacts with his assistance.'

'That's a long shot, even for you,' Lone replied.

'Spoken by a woman who devoted two years of her life to finding a way to summon a demon. Now that's what I call a really long shot.'

'There was a clear purpose to everything I did. If it hadn't been for Ambrose's stupid meddling, we'd be the controlling influence behind the throne now. Our power would have been unlimited.'

'Well, it didn't happen and the King may no longer have a kingdom for us to rule.'

The two sat quietly for a while, Lone wondering whether Malachi knew more than he was saying. After all, he had spent the last two years as a member of court and must have been party to many secrets, including those revealed by Ambrose to the King.

'Another thing,' Malachi said. 'Release the demon. Let him go back to whence he came. We have no use for him now and demons can be unpredictable things. We're likely to find him more trouble than he's worth.'

'No, Patch stays bound to me. He has to look after me; if I die, he faces the prospect of being stuck here forever. He's already saved both our hides by flying us over the city walls when we faced being torn apart by the mob.'

'So he's done his job. Served his purpose. Now's the time to let the devil go and be glad that we're rid of him. Demons are tricky beings at the best of times. If you aggravate them, they have long memories and infinite determination. Make your peace with him, thank him kindly and part on the best terms possible, I implore you. Give this world one less problem to deal with.'

'Infinity is a long time, Malachi. Patch is here to serve me for what must be an instant in his terms. Whether I let him go now or in a hundred years' time, it will make no difference to the level of resentment he harbours. Or to the opportunity he may have to vent his frustration upon me. There's nothing to be gained by an early release, and in these perilous times, the aid of a demon might make the difference between life and death on many more occasions.'

'If you're set in your resolve, I can understand why,' Malachi said. 'It took you long years of toil and frustration to snare this imp. But bear in mind what I have said and watch for signs of wilfulness and deceit. Be on your guard at all times, my dear.'

'Look down there if you want evidence of wilfulness.' Lone pointed down the hill. 'Look at that abomination of a horse. It's Patch's way of showing me his displeasure at being here. I know that he's capable of manifesting perfect horses, or anything else for that matter, but he amuses himself by creating something that must scream out witchcraft and sorcery to anyone who sees it.'

'My point entirely. Is our situation more dangerous with Patch than without him? I can't help feeling that ridding ourselves of him would simplify matters.'

'I hear what you say but, on balance, I want to keep him for the time being. More importantly, you need to decide when to stop babysitting the weak and defenceless and leave him to fend for himself while we get on with the task at hand.'

37

Oliver was devastated to find his home destroyed and his daughters missing. There were bodies strewn all over the village, houses smouldering, knots of inhabitants huddled together in hiding from the terrible carnage. There was no sign of his girls, and the few survivors of the rampaging mob had no words of comfort to deliver. Only tales of brutality.

He clung to the desperate hope that they'd made their escape before the mob arrived and left with Tyrant. He wondered about Tyrant. The big man had been in a bad way when they'd left Bee and Cassie alone with him. Surely he couldn't have recovered enough in that short time to have taken flight with them? And what if he had? They had no means of judging the character of the man. He'd been dropped from the sky with what seemed to be a fatal wound, and they'd tried to help him as much as they could.

He looked at Freya, her face etched with effort and worry. Leaving the girls with Tyrant had effectively been her decision. She'd refused to let him return to Gort without her and was now regretting that decision as much as he was.

'There's no use staying here,' Oliver said. 'They must have left before the trouble. The sooner we get going, the sooner we'll find them.'

'They'll have gone south,' Freya said. 'There's nothing in the North. They're smart girls and will know that.'

The churning in his guts stopped momentarily before a sharp pain took its place. 'I'm not so sure,' Oliver said. 'North is the easier way if they only meant to escape the village.'

'Then you go north and I'll go south,' Freya said, face bright red and eyes swollen.

'We should stick together,' Oliver said. 'I'll come south with you.'

'I'm worried that the North Road is narrow and dangerous. If they did go that way, we need to find them before anyone else does,' Freya said. 'We should check there first before we go south.'

Oliver looked at his wife, who had developed a more determined look in her eyes as she climbed back on her horse and galloped off.

By the time the horses slowed to a tired walk, they had reached the long climb up the narrow pass without having seen anyone. The evening was drawing in and the light was getting duller by the minute when they came across the abandoned handcart.

Oliver alighted from his horse and examined it. 'It looks like ours,' he said, 'but I can't be sure.'

Freya joined him, running her hand over the smooth wooden handles. 'It's ours, alright,' she said. 'I've pulled it far enough to know it when I feel it. This means that they are on this road and they can't be far ahead.'

'The horses are too tired to continue and so are we,' Oliver said.

'Nonsense,' Freya replied, taking her horse by the bridle and plodding off up the dusty road. Oliver walked wearily after her.

The horsemen were almost on them before he realised they were there. Three men had broken into a gallop and were heading towards them. Oliver unslung his crossbow. There was hardly time to string it and load it before the men were within range.

The leading horseman had a military bearing. He was wearing a leather jerkin and bright green trousers, unlike any uniform that Oliver had ever seen. The other men had more conventional garb of grey shirts and black pants. Each of them wore an impressive-looking sword, and one of the men was carrying a lance as well.

'What's your business on our road?'

'My wife and I are travelling north on the King's business,' Oliver replied.

'The King appears to have reached a very low ebb when it comes to representatives in these parts.' The man with the leather jerkin leaned down from his horse as if to appraise Oliver in more detail. 'You do look like a soldier, but more like a deserter than an active one. You know the penalty for desertion in the face of the enemy, don't you?'

'I am far from that, though I doubt the same thing could be said about yourselves. King's Own Light Cavalry, wasn't it? And now turned to common thieves preying on loyal subjects with legitimate business on behalf of His Majesty?'

'We were disbanded.' The man smiled. 'Maybe it's not entirely official, but now we're only loosely attached to the palace; a situation that we seem to have in common.'

'I am Captain Oliver of the First Regiment of Foot. My men were scattered while fighting the demons that possess Gort. Now I am seeking members of my family who became separated during the fighting. I ask in the King's name that you escort us safely over the pass and help us find our children.'

The leader paused for a moment; Oliver gripped his crossbow more tightly in anticipation of how he might respond. To his relief, the officer broke out into a smile. 'My name is Marshall. I'm glad to meet you, Oliver. In these difficult times, it's hard to know whom to trust. We, like yourself, suffered terribly in Gort. The way that ordinary men and women threw themselves uncaring at our swords and lances made me sick to the stomach. If you are who you say you are, we'll do what we can to help.'

His face quickly broke into a parody of a smile, then he looked down at a bloody spike that had suddenly appeared from his chest. Without any further words, he toppled from his saddle and lay face down in the dust, a long spear protruding from his back.

The soldier whose lance had done the damage echoed the dead man's smile with a horrible grin of his own. Then, still apparently amused, he drew his sword and slashed at his colleague, who managed to pull away from the blow, turn his horse around and speed off up the track. The deranged soldier turned his attention to Oliver, who was standing next to Marshall's body.

Faced with a sword thrust that threatened to decapitate him, Oliver raised his bow and discharged it at the man's face. The blade swished towards his neck, the trajectory of the blow changed, the sword dropped from the soldier's hand, and he fell off his horse and landed on top of his dead leader.

Freya stood by the cart and gave a short scream of anguish. Oliver looked back at his assailant and saw him getting to his feet despite the feathered shaft sticking out of his left temple. Oliver drew his sword and began hacking at the dead man's neck. Still, he lurched forwards, seemingly oblivious to injury or pain. As empty hands dripping with blood reached blindly towards him, Oliver kept striking out with his blade in an effort to halt the attack. One hand grabbed hold of his sword and wrenched it from his grasp, the other fastened around his neck. Foul breath soiled his nostrils as the life was squeezed from him. All he could think of was Freya and that she'd be next. The girls were not much farther up the road and the half-dead parody of a human being would be upon them in a few hours.

The grip on his neck loosened as his attacker sank to his knees. Oliver saw Freya stabbing away with a spear as he retrieved his sword and took a mighty swipe that almost severed the man's head completely. Even that dreadful wound was insufficient to douse the arcane life that had possessed this poor soldier's body. Yet the injuries were becoming too serious for the body to function as an offensive weapon. Slowly, his attacker succumbed to the inevitable as each limb became uncontrollable, the advance stopped, and he collapsed in a bloody heap.

The eyes glowed brightly, a dark cloud issued from the gory face, and Oliver found himself engulfed. He could feel the evil thing trying to take hold of him. Trying to pass from the cadaver to his body. This was even worse than death. If it succeeded, he'd be used for murder and Freya would be his first victim.

Freya screamed, 'Get away'. Standing between him and the black cloud, she took the star-shaped amulet from around her neck and held it in front of her face. 'By the power of Persephone, I command you to be gone.' The words were spoken with a weak and wavering voice, and the trembling in her hands was amplified by the leather thong so that the tiny fragment of moonstone danced about in the air, catching the rays of the setting sun.

The demonic fog coalesced into a dark column as tall as a man that hung threateningly barely an arm's length away. Reflected sunlight, transformed into a coherent white beam by the amulet, pierced the blackness and punched a hole which burned wider and wider until there was nothing left. Freya sank to her knees.

Oliver glanced around nervously, but saw no sign that might herald the demon's return. He helped his wife to her feet and held her frail, shaking body in his arms. 'It's fortunate that nobody else is around,' he whispered. 'Any mention of the goddess is forbidden by the King. We could have been in a lot of trouble.'

Freya stopped crying and unclasped her arms from around his waist. 'That's because he's afraid of her power,' she said, her face regaining a flush of colour. 'When she returns, everything will be different. His tyranny will cease and women will be respected as equals.'

'That's treason, my love. You shouldn't even be thinking it. Our whole family would be in danger if it came to his attention that you were harbouring dissent.'

'Danger? What do you call this? Our children are missing, the whole of Gort has gone mad, evil is stalking the highways, and you threaten me with the King? If he's so powerful, why did he allow this to happen?' Freya's eyes were ablaze.

'I don't have an answer. All I know for sure is that the King had the temple destroyed and your god did nothing to prevent it.'

'We had grown lazy and complacent. Our worship wasn't sufficient to attract her attention. But things are changing; I can feel it in my bones. There are many of her worshippers remaining and, despite our unworthiness, she will heed our pleas. Didn't you see? It was her intervention that banished the evil spirit that threatened to devour us.'

Oliver felt a frisson of fear shake his body. Persephone had the reputation for being a harsh and cruel deity and a despiser of men. Freya was the epitome of kindness and he trusted her judgement in most things. Perhaps religion was something best left to her.

Forcing his thoughts back to practicalities, he realised that they now had two extra horses. These were huge cavalry mounts, much bigger than their steeds, and enormously powerful in comparison. 'We need to get going before anyone else catches up with us,' he said. The big horses were, thankfully, perfectly docile and stood patiently while he helped Freya clamber into the saddle of one and he mounted another. Taking the bridle of the third, he urged his mount forward and was happy to see that the loose horses were content to follow.

They rode through the night. The mountains closed in on both sides until they were riding in a steep gorge barely wide enough for two horses abreast. Their new mounts seemed indefatigable and negotiated the climb without complaint or falter.

***

The first rays of dawn were illuminating the highest point of the ravine on their left when they found their passage blocked by soldiers.

A huge man stepped forward to confront them, his face disfigured by a scar running from his crown to his chin. For all his fearsome appearance, his manner seemed friendly.

'We're fleeing the madness in Gort,' Oliver said. 'Looking for our young daughters who have been separated from us.'

'Those are our horses,' the man said. 'Where did you get them?'

'The men who rode them are dead, killed by a terrible demon,' Oliver said.

'Sounds like you did well to escape all that bloodshed,' the big man said. 'We're guarding the pass against any troublemakers heading north. You're welcome to continue, though I should warn you that returning might not be so easy.'

'Have you seen our girls?' Freya asked. 'They might be in the company of a big rough man who calls himself Tyrant.'

'You're the first to come this way since we took up position. If they came this way, I'm sure you'll find them with everyone else at the lake.'

Once past the guards, Freya began to cry again. 'I shouldn't have left them with Tyrant,' she said. 'We should have all kept together. Now I'm scared that we'll never see them again.'

38

There were many groups of people camped out at the lakeside, but none of the Gort madness seemed to have afflicted them. Oliver had found a nice spot for him and Freya, away from the other inhabitants, but still with a good view of the road.

It was another gloriously sunny day, so Oliver sat by the lake and fished. His favourite pastime had been a bone of contention in the past, with Freya accusing him of spending far too much time away from the family. Now there was little else to do but fish and wait.

The fish in the lake were small and plentiful, with the useful characteristic of being very keen on being caught. At times, it felt like they were vying with each other to take Oliver's hook. The fish were tasty and a very welcome addition to the flour and water flatbread that had sustained them thus far. So far, there were no complaints from Freya about his fishing, only a constant lament about his decision-making.

Oliver threw his catch onto a large flat stone and began to prepare the fish for cooking. Freya came over from tending the horse to help, her face stained with tears.

'What are we going to do?' she asked.

'All we can do is wait,' Oliver said. 'If we leave here and they come, what will happen then?'

'They should have been here before us. Something terrible must have happened.'

Oliver bit his tongue, not for the first time. This had been Freya's constant theme for days now. He knew now that he should have kept his family together. It was a regret that gnawed away at him during every waking hour and haunted his sleep as well.

Something had delayed them, that was certain. The possibilities were endless, ranging from being attacked and killed to getting lost. He had to believe they were alive and well, but in that case, why were they not here?

'I think we should wait for a couple more days at least. Give them a chance to find their way here by whatever route they can.'

'You said that yesterday,' Freya said. 'And the day before. I don't think you really care. As long as you've got your fishing to do, you're happy. But I miss my daughters; they're the only important things in my life even if they don't matter to you. Stay here and catch fish if you like, but tomorrow I'm going to look for Cassie and Bee.'

'But you don't know where to look. They could be anywhere.'

'If I don't do something, I think I'm going to go mad with worry. I'm going to go back over the pass to the place where we found the cart and start looking there.'

'That's crazy,' Oliver said, regretting his choice of words as soon as he had spoken. 'What I mean is, they won't be there. That's the last place to look.'

'They must have gone up through the forest. We can at least look for signs.'

'But what if they arrive at the lake and find us gone? What will they do?'

'We leave a message with the cavalrymen,' Freya said.

'They might not get it.'

Freya looked all around her. 'That's a risk I'm willing to take,' she said. 'Anyway, we can also leave word with the other families on the lake. You can stay here if you like, but I'm going in search of my daughters.'

Oliver realised that she was talking sense. He should have thought of leaving word. That might have changed his mind about leaving several days ago. Though her idea of retracing their steps seemed to him to be a mistake. He had a better idea.

'OK, we'll take the horses and try the path to the west over the mountains. If they are coming that way, we have a better chance of intercepting them.'

'What if we don't meet them?'

'Then, I suppose, we turn round and come back here. I don't know, Freya, it just strikes me that if they are heading this way, that must be the route they've taken. Apart from the North Road, it's the only way to the lake from Gort.'

Freya continued gutting fish in silence for a while. ‘We’ll leave tomorrow, meanwhile, you’d better get fishing. These paltry few will hardly make a decent dinner for tonight,’ she said.

39

Tyrant sat on the steep mountainside, eating the last of the food that Petra had provided. It should have lasted him longer, but the unfortunate combination of excessive hunger and lack of progress had conspired to make it run out completely. If he didn't take good care on these treacherous slopes, this might well be his last meal.

As he munched the flatbread, Tyrant looked at the map. He recalled her pointing out the best route, detailing the landmarks he should look out for and explaining all the places he might go wrong. There was something about not taking the track to the east of the three peaks, but that was all his mind could recall. He'd never been one for maps.

Try as he might, he could make no sense of the lines and squiggles on the skin. Truth was, he couldn't even figure out which way up the darn thing should be held. There was writing on the map, but for all the use it was to him, it might as well be finger marks, of which many had accumulated during his frequent attempts to orientate himself.

He was high in the mountains and completely lost. This was a new experience, as his usual method was to set off and see where the path took him. All this *maps* nonsense was unnecessary when you didn't care where you were going and it didn't matter when you got there.

He could feel the frustration building inside him. He was letting the girls down. He was failing in his promise to find their father, an obligation that weighed heavily on shoulders that were unused to any form of commitment.

Tyrant pored over the map. He turned it around and stared at it again. Now the mountains were in the right place, it seemed to him. What was the point of a thing that changed its information depending on which way up you held it?

He was tempted to retrace his steps back to the house. His memory was pretty good and he felt he could rely on recognising where he'd come from. What stopped him was the burning shame of failure. It was a major concern that the wellbeing of two young girls had begun to matter so much to him.

The unwelcome responsibility precluded the usual solution to this kind of problem. Normally, he'd forget about anything he was supposed to be doing and just relax into the things that actually were happening for him. After all, he was well fed, at least for the moment, the weather was fine if a little chilly, and the scenery around him was breathtaking. A man without a mission couldn't ask for anything more.

Tyrant rolled up the map and tied it carefully to his belt. It might not be of much use to him, but it was essential that he gave it to their father so that he could retrieve his children. Finding Petra's house without it would be nigh on impossible. He surveyed the landscape, looked down into the valley, and across at the hills beyond. The road he sought could lie beyond the hills he was traversing or those others far away. There was no means of knowing which. Walking down into the valley didn't seem to make any sense. He decided to stick to the path he was on, even though he could see it winding ahead of him for miles, with no signs of taking him to the other side.

Face set with determination, he strode off at a fast march. The job, however inconvenient, was one he had to complete. It meant encountering the army and asking about their father, a prospect he didn't relish at all. It was the only way he knew of finding Captain Oliver and letting him know his daughters were safe and giving him the map. Then Tyrant could make his own way in the world once again. The anticipation of that freedom brought a new spring to his step, and he decided that everything would probably turn out for the best. After all, there was a first time for everything.

It was getting dark by the time he got over the mountains and looked down at the small town. He now knew for sure that he was on the wrong side of the wrong mountain range and further from his intended destination than when he had set off.

40

Endersky was a dump. It was reputed to be an utterly drab and dismal place, but it was much worse than that. Tyrant wandered down what had to be the main street, on account of the fact that it was the only discernible street for him to wander down, and thought about how reputations could be misleading. It made Gort, even in its present state of possession by bloodthirsty mobs, seem like paradise.

The only reason anyone would live here, Tyrant reasoned, was because they had run out of places they could live. The town, if a muddy patch surrounded by dilapidated structures unfit for farm animals could be described that way, smelt of a combination of human sewage, animal faeces, and more human sewage. The nearer he got to the centre, the worse the stink became.

Nestled at the bottom of the almost inaccessible hills, Endersky was the last outpost before you reached the Northern Wilderness. Nobody ever went into the Northern Wilderness; there was no point. Better to stay in Endersky than venture into the wilderness.

So, Tyrant thought, Endersky must be full of people on the point of turning around and going back to where they had come from. That must be why the place was so dismal. Nobody had any intention of staying any longer than absolutely necessary.

Tyrant happily and enthusiastically added his own name to that list.

As he trudged through the mud, he ran a tentative finger through his hair. It was getting thicker and matted together by dirt. He felt his chin. There was a satisfying length of beard now extending from the base of one ear to the other. He sighed with pleasure. His appearance was close to being restored to its lack of former glory. He was alone in a strange place, no money, no food, no accommodation, and certainly no friends. It had started to rain, a cold heavy rain that quickly soaked through his clothes. He was back to his old life, the one he knew and understood. It felt good.

There was one inhabited hovel in the middle of the town. It smelt like a latrine, but when he poked his head through the makeshift door, instead of being greeted by the sight of people squatting, he saw what must have been the entire population of Endersky sitting on benches and logs while they drank and shouted at each other. It was perfect. Tyrant knew he would fit in well here.

The absence of any coin in his pocket was not a new sensation, nor was it a surprise. He'd spent a long time in a nightshirt without pockets and the girls had gathered his current attire from a washing line.

He sat down at the edge of the nearest bench to the door. Two men were clutching tankards and arguing. 'Hello,' Tyrant said. The men paused in their conversation to give him dirty looks.

'What do you want, stranger?' The man with a hooked nose and warts stuck his face closer to Tyrant than was comfortable.

'Directions,' Tyrant answered.

'Fuck off… er…' – the man waved his arm in the air then pointed at the door – 'that way. There's your directions.' He laughed and his friend joined in.

Tyrant smiled and took hold of the man's throat with his left hand, which was the least uncomfortable hand to use for this sort of activity. 'Can you feel something in your groin?' he asked.

The man nodded, Tyrant's grip preventing any other means of communication.

'Well, that's not what you hope it might be. It's actually my knife and I'm going to slice off your gonads one by one for the insolence and unfriendliness you just showed me. I'm a sensitive man and can't stand rejection. It sends me all funny. I start doing things that other people might regret.'

The man's eyes were beginning to bulge, so Tyrant loosened his grip slightly. 'I'm sorry,' the man said, with difficulty.

'That's alright, then.' Tyrant let the man go, even going to the trouble of smoothing down his ruffled clothing. As the man gulped and looked at his companion for guidance, Tyrant continued. 'Buy me a drink and we'll forget all about it. I'll put it down to a misunderstanding and we can all start again with a clean slate.'

The two men looked at each other as if weighing up their options. After a minor amount of head shaking and nodding, they both seemed to agree and the unmolested one fetched three frothing mugs of local brew.

Tyrant drank the first in one gulp, then guarded the other two pots within the confines of his elbows. After emitting a loud sigh, his benefactor went away and brought back two more drinks, which he placed out of Tyrant's reach.

'Now that we're all friends, let me introduce myself,' Tyrant said. 'I'm Tyrant. I'm in a particularly good mood today, otherwise things might have been different and we could have fallen out badly. Now, to whom do I owe a debt of gratitude for this…' Tyrant paused, searching for the correct word to describe the awful liquid he'd been provided with.

'I'm Alvin,' the drinks bearer said.

'I'm Hal,' the other said, rubbing his throat with his hand.

'And do you gentlemen know these parts well?' Tyrant asked.

'As well as most, I suppose,' Hal said.

Tyrant took the map from his belt and, after sweeping as much of the spilled beer from the table as he could, laid it out in front of the men. In order to further aid their perusal, he reached over to the neighbouring table, borrowed a candle stub which flickered out a paltry amount of light, and placed it squarely in the centre of the pigskin. 'There,' Tyrant said, 'that's my map. Can you point out where we are?'

The men huddled together and ran their grubby fingers along some of the lines. 'That could be the northern road,' Hal said.

'This might be the Barren Hills over here.' Alvin made a smudge mark with his thumb.

'Who made this map?' Hal asked.

'A friend of mine. I'm supposed to find a road and a lake but I might have taken a wrong turn somewhere.'

'This lake?' Hal pointed.

Tyrant looked closely at the marking on the map. It could be a lake, he supposed. He'd assumed that it was a symbol, or letters, or even a word written in joined-up writing. But it could be a little picture of a lake. He wondered if some of the other squiggles were the same sort of thing. Like that line of pointed hats could, he supposed, be mountains.

'Is it near a road?'

'Yes. The North Road.'

'Then that's where I have to be. How long will it take me from here?'

'Hard to say. We're way over here, not even on this map. First, you have to go over the mountains behind us, then across the valley to the next ridge. That's this one on the edge of the map here. Then you have to be careful not to choose the wrong path. But the map is quite clear, it even has little arrows to guide you.'

Tyrant squinted hard, saw the little arrows that he'd never paid any attention to. 'What's that?' He pointed to another arrow with a letter standing on top of it that was in the far corner of the map.

'That's the north pointer. It tells you which way up to hold the map.'

Tyrant felt that the map made a bit more sense now and that he might have a better chance of navigating himself to where Oliver might be patrolling. He drank the third beer and wiped his mouth with his sleeve. He was feeling a lot more confident. This tavern was even beginning to feel like a good place to be. He laid his head on the table and closed his eyes for a moment, just to give them a well-earned rest while he gathered his thoughts.

When he opened them again, light was coming through the windows, the tavern was deserted, and the map was gone.

41

Tyrant finished turning over every table in the tavern without finding his precious map, then went outside to have a few handfuls of rainwater for breakfast. He looked around the town, which looked even more dismal than it had in the dark. He walked over to an old man who was trying to fix a hole in the side of his house by nailing some rotten timber across the gap.

'Have you seen two men? They were called…' Tyrant tried to remember their names, 'Al and Melvin.'

'No.'

'They have my map. It's a valuable map made of pigskin. There's a reward for anyone who returns it.'

'And what's on this map? Treasure?'

'No. It shows me the way I have to go, that's all.'

'You can eat pigskin,' the man said.

'Not this sort, it's been made into a map.'

'I'll bet if you crisp it up in front of the fire it'll taste delicious.' The old guy stuck his tongue out and began to lick his lips.

'Have you seen my map or not? Or the two men who stole it?'

'These men, Al and Melvin, you say they've stolen your pigskin map?'

'Yes,' Tyrant said.

'Are you sure they've not eaten it? Or did you eat it yourself and forget about it? I'm always searching for things that I've eaten but can't remember doing it.'

'It's not been eaten, it's been stolen,' Tyrant said, wishing that he'd not bothered to start this conversation.

'Why would they do that if it's worthless?'

'Well, we had a bit of a disagreement. Got off to a bad start. They may have taken it to punish me for taking their beer.'

'You stole their beer?'

‘Not exactly. They gave me the beer and I drank it. Then I fell asleep. When I awoke, the map was gone.’

‘Hold the other end of this timber while I fix it.’

Tyrant stood dutifully while the nails were hammered in.

‘There.’ The man stood back in obvious satisfaction at his handiwork. The whole section of wall, including the recent repair, fell forward and landed at his feet.

Tyrant decided that nothing could be gained from further discussion and walked up the muddy street, eyeing each passing face intently.

By mid-afternoon, he felt he had examined every face in Endersky at least ten times without any success. The only conclusion he could reach from this exhaustive exercise was that the two thieves had left town with his map.

A dreadful possibility began to occur to him. Maybe they were using the map to find their way back to the girls. In which case, he’d better get going.

He might not be great at reading a map, but he was very good at remembering where he had been and the route he had taken. This talent was normally used to avoid returning to places, but it could equally be applied to getting back to Petra’s house. Once there, he could explain that he’d lost the map, without being too specific about how, and perhaps get a new one.

Tyrant’s instincts were true and he made no mistakes in retracing his arduous path through the mountains. By the time he reached Petra’s house, he was very tired and had a mighty hunger.

This didn’t stop him from approaching the place cautiously and it was well that he did so. As he peered through the trees, he could see smoke rising from the chimney and smell cooking on the wind. But there was a dead chicken lying in front of the door and all the other animals seemed to have gone.

Something was badly wrong.

42

Tyrant thought through the situation. His first instinct was always to take the direct route. In this case, that would involve kicking in the door and taking it from there. *Sounds reasonable*, he thought. *It's worked before, no reason why it shouldn't work again.*

Then he visualised the possibility that the girls were in there and still alive. Whoever was in there with them would only have to put a blade to one of their throats and he'd be left with a hard choice. Back off or watch Cassie or Bee die. That was a scenario he didn't really like.

He had no idea who was in the house or even how many of them there were. If the girls were gone, or dead, he would be best served to walk away, head back to Gort, and try to forget about Oliver and his family. That was a real temptation. His weakened state meant that if there were more than two of them, he'd probably be killed. Two might be doable, but even one big hard bastard could be beyond him the way his shoulder felt at the moment.

He could wait. Lie low, watch, and see what happened. See who emerged from the house; get a better idea of what he had to contend with. Patience might be the best option.

It was starting to get dark. Tyrant faced the prospect of another cold and hungry night outside. Nothing new there, but the occupants of Petra's house were probably in for the night, with food cooking on a warm fire and beds nicely prepared. His stomach curled up with the thought of the food and the patient option began to seem less desirable. Maybe his normal robust approach would work best.

By waiting, Tyrant could be abandoning the girls to a night of unspeakable horror. Bursting in now might prevent them from harm. And the prospect of getting something hot and nourishing was also a big incentive.

He took a few deep breaths and loosened the knives in his belt. Before he could make a run for the door, it opened. Out strode Melvin or Alvin or maybe it was Al or Hal. Whatever the bastard's name, it was one of the men who had stolen his map from the tavern. It was all he could do to restrain himself from bursting out of hiding and taking the man apart. Tyrant's breathing was fast and shallow; he could feel his heart pumping. He waited, gave himself time to think. *Was it just the two of them? Or had they brought some others with them?*

Tyrant watched as Hal stood in the doorway and pissed all over the poor dead chicken. It was a very uncouth way to act, particularly as Tyrant had had his eye on that chicken for emergency rations in the event there was nothing else. Once he'd finished relieving himself, the thieving bastard went inside and slammed the door.

Tyrant made up his mind. He had to get them out of the house and an idea had just presented itself. He crept towards the door, picked up the sodden chicken, and threw it onto the roof. He hauled himself up after it, tiptoed gingerly across the ramshackle shingles, took the wet fowl and shoved it down the belching chimney. A chorus of shouts came from down below, then the door burst open, emitting some of the smoke that the chicken had redirected into the building. Two men emerged, coughing and spluttering.

Tyrant jumped off the roof onto Hal's back, making sure he landed with his knees just below the man's neck. There was a satisfying crunch as he hit. Tyrant rolled sideways onto his bad shoulder and felt some considerable pain of his own. Alvin, standing close to his now prone friend, reacted slowly, seemingly more concerned with the sting of smoke in his eyes. Without pausing in his roll, Tyrant swept Alvin's legs from under him. Then he rolled onto his knees and stuck a knife into the base of the man's skull for good measure.

When he got painfully to his feet, a quick appraisal told him that neither man was going to be bothering him again. That was more than he could say about his poor shoulder, which was sending sharp reminders of its condition down through his body. He went to the door of the house and peered inside. The smoke inside was too dense for him to see if there were any more occupants. He clambered stiffly, knees creaking, onto the roof and fished the charred chicken from the chimney. Then he waited for the smoke to clear before he cautiously entered the house.

He found Cassie first, tied to Petra's bed. He used his knife to free her and carried her outside. As she lay gasping on the ground, uncomfortably close to the dead thieves, Tyrant returned to find the smoke had cleared enough for him to see Bee, curled up in a corner of the room like a frightened dog. He grabbed her and took her outside to join her sister. 'Where's Petra?' he asked.

'Inside,' Cassie spluttered.

Tyrant went back into the house, but there was no sign of Petra anywhere. He even tried looking under the bed. Nothing. He was about to give up and go back out when Cassie came in to stand beside him. 'They put her in there.' She pointed to a substantial square of timber lying flush with the floor.

Tyrant pulled it aside and, in the depression beneath, found a tiny figure trussed up like a parcel. She had a piece of rag in her mouth secured by a leather strap. Tyrant lifted her out gently and placed her on the bed. Even when he had removed all her bindings, she remained still. Bee joined her sister, and they both tried to revive their friend. Nothing seemed to be able to rouse her and Tyrant feared that she might be dead.

He turned his attention to the girls. Apart from watery eyes and some soot stains on their faces, they both appeared to be unharmed. Tyrant breathed a sigh of relief. 'How about some of that stew?' he asked.

Cassie remained seated on the bed, intent on Petra's condition, and ignored his request.

'You don't deserve anything after what you did,' Bee said.

'I just saved you from those men,' Tyrant said, feeling very surprised at the girls' lack of appreciation.

Bee made no reply, but his hunger got the better of him, so he fished a great dollop of stew from the pot and put it on a plate. Cassie made a loud sigh as he did so.

As he took a spoonful and put it to his mouth, there was something about Bee's face that made him hesitate. 'What?' he asked.

The two girls remained silent. Tyrant sniffed at the food. It smelt delicious but there was a faint whiff of something that he couldn't place. 'You've poisoned it,' he said.

No answer.

'Come on, tell me. Yes or no. Is there poison in the stew?'

Bee was nodding, but Cassie shook her head. 'Go on, try it,' she said.

Tyrant put down the plate, then went over to the kitchen cupboard and started rummaging around for an alternative source of nutrition. Just as he triumphantly retrieved a hunk of bread with hardly any green spots in it, something heavy landed on his back. He was knocked forwards, hitting his head painfully on the edge of the door. Another twist of his head and he found himself lying face up with a knife prodding at his Adam's apple.

'I should slice you to pieces after what you did to me and those girls.' Petra was sitting on his chest, looking like she'd made a sudden and complete recovery.

'I already had this from Bee and Cassie. I just saved you. What have I done wrong?'

'Those were horrible men,' Cassie said. 'They killed all the animals and wrecked the place.'

'They said that Cassie would have to warm their beds,' Bee said.

'They'd have done terrible things to those young girls, and it's all on your conscience.' Petra kept the knife pressed hard against his neck.

'Those men were nothing to do with me,' Tyrant said.

'So why did you give them your map?' Petra asked.

'I didn't,' Tyrant said. 'They stole it. As soon as I found it was missing, I came straight back here.'

'I don't believe you,' Petra said.

'Then go outside and have a look at the men you think are my friends and accomplices.'

'He's right,' Bee said. 'He did kill the men as soon as they went outside to avoid the smoke.'

The knife point retreated slightly.

'Don't eat the stew,' Cassie said. 'We put belladonna in it. There's enough in one plateful to kill a horse.'

'Thanks for the warning,' Tyrant said. 'It seems a bit late.'

'Oh, we wouldn't have let you eat much. Just enough to give you the stomach ache you deserve for sending those men here,' Bee said.

Petra leapt off his chest and put down the knife. 'I suppose we have to believe you, considering you did kill the men. But you must have been very careless to let that map get stolen.'

'I was lost,' Tyrant said. 'I was asking for directions. They must have taken the map while I was sleeping.'

'Drunk, more like,' Petra said.

Tyrant kept quiet, even though the accusation stung. He took the piece of bread from the floor where it had fallen and began to eat.

'We've got some more stew without the poison if you'd prefer it?' Cassie took a pot from behind a chair and placed it on the fire.

Tyrant smiled. His belly ached for the food and he could hardly wait for it to warm up. Now the two youngsters were all smiles again and even Petra seemed glad to see him.

He was just congratulating himself on a job well done when two soldiers appeared in the open doorway and trained their crossbows at his head.

43

Tyrant shovelled stew down his throat as if it were his first meal in a long time and might turn out to be his last. A big, dishevelled man pushed between the crossbowmen and came into the house. His eyes were wide and staring. It wasn't his deranged expression that worried Tyrant though. It was the battleaxe in his right hand. And the way that blood was dribbling off its edge.

'Get out,' the big man said.

Petra rose to debate the order, but Tyrant placed a gentle hand on her shoulder. 'We'd better go,' he said. 'Take what you can easily carry and let's get out of here while we still can.'

Petra gave him a fierce look, then turned to the girls, who were huddled together on the bed. 'You heard what the man said, let's go.'

The big man came a few steps nearer and stared at Petra. 'What's this?' he said. 'An imp, maybe?'

Tyrant sensed her reaction and stood between her and the obnoxious visitor. 'I'll thank you not to speak disparagingly of my wife,' he said.

'I'll speak disparately, er, desperately, anyway, I'll talk about anyone I care to and you'll do nothing about it if you don't want my axe in your head.'

Tyrant picked up the item nearest to him and also nearest to his heart, the smaller of the two stew pots.

'Wait, we need that food,' the man said.

'There's a bigger pot over there which is brimming with stew. This one has only scrapings left.' Tyrant held out the pot for inspection, but the man pushed him aside, picked up the other pot and looked inside it before placing it on the fire.

Tyrant ushered the girls outside. They were clutching blankets and a few items of clothing and looking shocked. The bodies of Hal and Alvin lay where they had fallen. One on his back staring sightlessly at the sky, the other face down in the mud. Next to them lay a new companion with the back of his head stoved in and fresh blood still running from the wound.

Several men were climbing the hill through the trees. There were sounds of angry exchanges and the occasional thud as blows were exchanged.

'It's the Gort madness,' Tyrant said. 'It seems to have spread all the way out here. Let's go.'

'I can't leave my house,' Petra said.

'Yes, you can,' Tyrant replied. 'You can either lose your life or lose your house. You choose. Now let's go before any of these mad bastards takes a shine to Cassie and Bee. You can always come back here when it's all over and people have returned to their normal, slightly less homicidal, ways.'

'Which way?' Petra asked.

'We'll have to go over the mountains, but this time I'll have you to show me the way.'

'Are we going to find Father?' Bee asked.

'Yes,' Tyrant said. Petra shot him a look that was something between gratitude and malice then led the girls off into the relative safety of the forest. As he followed, he couldn't resist shouting back towards the house. 'Enjoy the stew, you mad bastards.'

44

Ant awoke with the sun burning through his eyelids. He'd been lying close to the water's edge and been alerted by Lone running past him and into the water. As his eyes became accustomed to the harsh light, he was rewarded with a glimpse of her naked back down to where the curve of her buttocks met the lake before she slipped gracefully beneath the surface.

'Good morning,' Malachi said. 'You chose a good place to rest.'

'We have to go,' Ant replied.

'Go where?'

'North. There's no time to lose.'

'What's the hurry?' Malachi smiled. 'Those ancient things we seek have lain undisturbed for such a long time that a few days will make no difference. Lone likes it here and has decided we should rest for a while. I need to keep our friendly general close for a while to make sure he continues to do the right thing. You, too, need to exert what influence you can while he's in an amenable state of mind. His defection could be our most significant achievement, far outweighing the pursuit of artefacts of uncertain value. Relax, Ant. There are families living all around the lake. You should take the opportunity to meet some new people while you're here. I'm sure there will be girls of your age desperate to find themselves a nice boy like you.'

Lone's head broke surface far out into the lake, then her body arched sinuously and she was gone again. The glint of sunlight on her torso burned an image into his mind that remained even when he closed his eyes. 'I know of a scroll that has secrets beyond anything you might ever have hoped for,' Ant said, knowing that he was treading on dangerous ground. At least this was the truth and whatever Malachi's powers, it couldn't be contradicted. 'My father also knows of it.' Also true. 'It's a race against time.' True again.

'Do you know what this document contains?' Malachi's beak protruded inquisitively from the recesses of his hood.

'Instructions about the device that my father installed in the tower. How to make one and what its powers are. Plus, much more information that my father says is even more powerful. If you want to succeed in your quest, then you have to have it.'

'What is it that's so important?' Lone stood up in the water, rivulets ran down her body, dribbled off her fingers, and trickled down her legs.

Ant gasped for air and tried to avert his gaze, but it stubbornly remained fixed on the wet triangle between her legs and the dribbles of lake water that were running down her thighs.

'It's a scroll,' Malachi replied on his behalf.

'How do you know about it?' Lone was making no attempt to cover herself.

'My father.' Ant tried to steer as close to the truth as possible. Being caught in his deception would be disastrous for him and his friends and Lone seemed to be able to stare straight into his soul. The thudding in his head and chest wasn't making things easy while the straining in his groin was becoming an even stronger distraction. 'He told me about it. He's seen it and wanted to make sure that nobody else, not even the King and especially not you, Malachi, should ever know about its existence.'

'So why wait to tell us now?' Lone asked.

'Because you both want to stop here and rest when every hour lost might mean that someone else will get to it before us.'

'So, Ant, you know where this treasure is, do you?' Lone squatted down so that her eyes were level with his.

Ant greedily drank in the sight of her legs splayed apart. There was a constriction in his throat, burning sensations rippling through his head, and a painful throbbing in his guts. It was only with a great effort that he was able to form the word 'yes'. As soon as he spoke, his tension eased, and he began to breathe again. Lone took her dress from Malachi's outstretched hand, flicked it over her head, and stood up. 'Let's go,' she said.

The peculiar horse had been waiting for them, ready laden with the paraphernalia it had dropped on the road. Ant was positioned on its imaginary back and they resumed their journey north.

That was tasty.

'Cali? I was worried you'd abandoned me when I need you to guide me to my friends.'

She really gets to you. Delicious.

'What do you mean?'

She's playing with you.

'Why do you say that?'

Naked and dripping wet. The oldest trick in the book.

'She was swimming.'

She likes making you aroused. It stirs a fire inside her.

'She's very attractive. I can't help feeling the way I do.'

She's controlling you with desire. Yum.

'You sound like you're eating.'

Enjoying your energy. That's why I like to be with you. All that passion, even if it is directed towards her.

'Is that what demons do? Feed off human emotions?'

Some like to do it. Some need to do it. Some aren't bothered.

'Which sort are you?'

I like to do it. That's what first drew me to you.

'Will you help me find my friends?'

You'll find them.

'But I don't know where to go.'

'Do we stay on this road or take that track into the hills?' Malachi called out, half turned in his saddle.

'Cali? What do I say?'

'Do you know the way or not?' Lone shouted.

'Keep going on this road,' Ant replied, trying not to let the anxiety in his voice betray his uncertainty. Cali might at least have said something helpful about the route instead of all that stuff about passion and energy. Still, he was learning things about her in particular and demons in general that he was sure would come in useful in the future. As for the effect that Lone was having, wasn't it normal for a boy of his age? Maybe even healthy?

Cali did have a point, though. It's a big lake, so why pick that place to swim? She must have walked past him while he was asleep. Maybe Cali was right and Lone derived pleasure and excitement from the reaction she was getting. Just thinking about the possibility was making him hot and bothered again, so he closed his eyes and tried to detach himself from the cascade of thoughts and images about Lone.

The North Road deteriorated from a band of bare earth to a barely discernible rut. Ahead, looming on the skyline, was the black shadow of the wastelands. He didn't need Cali to tell him that was where they had to go. His father had said little about the place and nothing positive. There was something in the air or the rocks that precluded life, he'd said. Nothing could live there; few people ventured into the wastelands, and even fewer returned.

Lone was sitting cross-legged with her eyes closed and her palms flat on the earth beside her legs. The moonlight reflected from her thighs, accentuating the dark, forbidden shadow between. Even though she was twenty paces distant, he could still feel the warmth and breathe in the heady scent of her.

'What happened with the general?' Malachi asked.

His attention snapped painfully away from Lone. 'I don't know,' he replied automatically.

'Think about it. What was his demeanour when he caught up with you? Was it always his intention to mutiny against the King or did you say something to persuade him?'

'I said lots of things, I suppose. The truth about what I was doing and where I was going. That's all.' *The man had been intent on hunting them all down then he changed completely. It must have been the demon, Patch. Maybe he could make anyone do anything and Malachi was unaware of his powers.*

'Whatever you said had a remarkable effect, Ant. I'm very proud of you. You're learning very rapidly.'

It wasn't me. I was helpless. This knowledge wasn't enough to disabuse Malachi. Praise was something he'd been starved of, and Malachi's honest admiration felt good. So good that he wanted to keep what he had and earn more.

'Now that your awareness of external stimulations has improved, I'd like you to begin the enormously difficult task of observing your internal processes,' Malachi continued. 'For example, when you feel strong emotions, see if you can manage some separation from them. Become a witness rather than a helpless participant. Watch yourself as you react. This is very hard to do and some spend a lifetime attempting it without much success. I think you're special, Ant. You have a rare talent.'

Ant followed his eyes over to Lone and his heart jolted with desire and shame. 'I'm not sure I understand what it is you want me to do.'

'Look at my wife and tell me what you feel.'

Blood pounded his ears, washing his mind with shame. Fear filled his heart before desperate disappointment overwhelmed him. The raging desire he carried for Malachi's wife was wrong. Forbidden. Shameful. Unnatural. It was betrayal of the highest order. 'I don't know,' he spluttered.

'Relax.' Malachi's voice was calm. 'She has that effect on everyone.'

'You know what I'm feeling?'

'You can't help but make them very plain. The helplessness you are experiencing is an opportunity to learn. Though I doubt you'll ever be able to cope with her, at least you have a clear example of how you can so easily lose yourself in emotions. When you think of her, you become your passion and cease to be Ant. You're off balance. Easily influenced. You have no centre, no attachment to the ground. It's as if you're dangling from a rope and swaying in the direction of any breeze that comes along.'

'How do you know all this?'

'Because I have exactly the same experience as you. Our only difference is that I recognise what's happening to me.'

Ant's breathing began to settle back to a more even rhythm. 'So you can prevent yourself being carried away?'

'Sometimes, but not always. Lone is a powerful woman, possibly the most dangerous person you will ever encounter. I've not met any man who could resist her influence. We are like soft clay in her hands; she can squeeze us into any shape she chooses. Or choke the life from us. Don't be hard on yourself, Ant. You can't help your feelings for her. All you can do is to practise recognising them for what they are. Become the observer of the raging torrent without being dragged into its turbulent depths. You can't stop the strong current, but you don't have to enter the water. Watch it sweep by if you can; resist the temptation to immerse yourself and become swept away. That is the most valuable lesson you can ever learn.'

'I'm not sure how to do that,' Ant said.

'You'll learn, if my judgement is sound. Use Lone as an extreme example to help identify other occasions where you give yourself away.'

'Give myself away?'

'Act against your true nature. Think about something that you regret doing. That wasn't in character, if you like. An action provoked by someone else that now seems strange and irrational. That's what I mean about giving yourself away. We all do it constantly to a greater or lesser extent. It may not seem important most of the time, but it is. Learn to recognise this in yourself and you are possessed of a formidable weapon. Not only can you become resistant to manipulation but, by seeing your effect on others, you can bend them to your will.' Malachi stood up. 'Incorporate this into your practice. Bring your mindfulness to bear on yourself. Watch. Observe. Know that you can experience emotions without becoming them.'

Ant became aware of Lone's eyes boring into his soul. Panic boiled his blood. She knew. Everything.

Malachi walked over to her as if answering a silent call.

45

Tyrant's hair was whipping across his face, the cold wind piercing the thin blankets it was trying to tear from his grasp. Cassie was sat on one leg, Bee on the other. Petra was sandwiched between the girls to conserve what little warmth they could. He did his best to keep as much of the flapping cover around them.

The awful gales had made progress impossibly dangerous, and they had been forced to spend the night perched precariously at the very top of a ridge. Tyrant sat in the lee of the rim, taking what shelter he could from a large boulder that jutted from the ground. His broad back was taking the worst of the battering, providing some comfort for the girls. Sleep was impossible. He was in constant fear of them all being blown away down the mountainside.

As the morning sun began to bring the respite of a cold light to the night's constant stress, the wind began to ease. Tyrant became aware of Petra's voice. 'We need to get a move on. My old bones won't survive another night up here.'

'Ready when you are,' Tyrant replied. Then added, 'I'm really sorry about your house, Petra.'

'So you should be. You were responsible for those men destroying my home. Whether or not you meant it to happen doesn't matter. If it hadn't been for your carelessness, we would still be warm and snug.'

'Maybe,' Tyrant said. 'But I doubt we'd have been left to enjoy it for more than a short while. The madness soon arrived from Gort, as I feared it might. It was a good thing that I came back when I did. I can't believe that you let Hal and Alvin get the better of you. I'd have thought they'd be no match for your speed and guile.'

There was an awkward silence before Petra spoke. 'They took me by surprise. I was asleep and they wrapped me up in my blanket, and tied me up like an old carpet. There was nothing I could do.'

'Carelessness. If you ask me, that's what you owe your troubles to. Not me.'

'I'm not asking you. I'm blaming you.'

'Then you should stop.' Tyrant felt an unusual desire to have this tiny woman stop blaming him for what happened and was surprised by his own reluctance to let it go.

'Never. I'll always remember what you brought down on us. How my beautiful home was wrecked because of you.'

'But I came back to save you. I killed those men and freed you. Doesn't that count for something?'

'It counts for very little. Those men would have been dead in an hour, in any case,' Petra said.

'You can't be sure of that,' Tyrant said.

'Yes, I can. They were hungry, the stew was poisoned. They were sure to eat it and then they'd be dead.'

'Who poisoned the stew if you were tied up?' Tyrant asked.

'Cassie. She's a remarkable girl. She knows such a lot about plants and herbs. How to poison with them as well as heal. She gathered them and made the food.'

'Yes, I did.' Cassie sounded very proud of herself.

'I helped,' Bee said. 'And I'd have chopped up the bodies and fed them to the pigs once they were dead.'

The girls clambered to their feet. Tyrant felt the warmth evaporate and realised that he would have been hard pressed to survive a night up here without them.

'So, I saved you that trouble at least.' Tyrant laughed.

'No trouble,' said Bee. 'I'd have enjoyed it. Those men were horrible. They kept leering at poor Cassie. I don't know what they would have done to her.'

'I do,' Cassie said. 'That's why I put the belladonna in the stew. Men are such filthy animals. I'm never going to get married.'

'I thought you were set on marrying me,' Tyrant said.

'In your dreams,' Cassie replied.

The descent from the mountains was arduous. Tyrant found the effort of walking down the slope almost as bad as climbing up it. There was pain in both his heels and his knees were beginning to hurt. The girls were full of energy and excitement, scampering enthusiastically, showing little signs of fatigue. Tyrant wished he felt as lively as they looked.

The makeshift path bordered an immense scree slope, and the loose rocks shifted dangerously whenever a foot strayed onto them. 'Be careful,' Tyrant called out to Cassie and Bee.

'Wimp.' Petra uttered her first word since she'd finished castigating him. 'Watch me,' she said, then jumped into the loose stones and began to move her feet as if she were kneading dough. The whole hillside seemed to start moving. Slowly at first, then gathering speed at an alarming rate, Petra was carried, standing triumphantly, down to the bottom of the slope far below them.

Seeing what Petra had done and the way she'd completed the long descent in a few short minutes, Cassie and Bee stood together a little unsteadily on the scree and began to paddle their feet. First Bee began to slide, carried down on the crest of a wave of loose stones. Then Cassie followed, waving her arms frantically in an attempt to keep herself upright.

Tyrant watched as three specks waved to him from the foot of the mountain. He now had two choices. An hour or more of a painful walk followed by inevitable derision from Petra and the girls, or risk his life on the scree slope. He stepped tentatively onto the loose stones, finding it difficult to remain standing as the ground shifted alarmingly under his feet. One foot tried to head off on its own and he found himself almost split in two before he managed to retrieve it. Keeping his feet together so that they were touching each other, Tyrant waited for the same effect that he'd seen with the girls. Nothing happened. It seemed that he'd somehow managed equilibrium and he and the stones were finely balanced and stable. He heard shouts from far below and, although they were too faint to decipher, he felt safe in assuming that they were not complimentary. What the three women had achieved with ease, he was having obvious difficulties with.

Cautiously, he began to paddle his feet in unison. He felt himself sinking into the stones and his feet were soon buried up to his ankles. Suddenly, the pile of rocks he was partially buried in decided to turn itself into an avalanche. He was swept down, more and more stones accompanying him, getting faster and faster. Soon he was travelling faster than running speed. The figures below were getting closer and he could hear their shouts of encouragement.

Tyrant began to enjoy the sensation. It was a wonderful way to descend a mountain. He felt proud of himself at mastering a new technique. Then overconfidence struck and he found himself falling forward onto the sharp rocks. The avalanche continued unaffected by his body position and he was delivered cut, battered, and half-sensible at Cassie's feet. A shower of stones bounced off his head as he lay panting. As he looked up into her face, he saw her concern turn to mirth as she realised he was unscathed. Disconcertingly, he felt that a few bruises were a small price to pay for the recompense of her amusement. He'd climb back up there and do it all over again just for the look in her eyes.

They crossed the line of rutted mud that delineated the North Road and made their way across a meadow with twenty or so fine-looking horses, grazing unfettered by saddles or bridles. A group of men were working at the side of a large lake, felling trees and clearing ground. They looked like soldiers to Tyrant, but they wore no uniforms, just a variety of makeshift clothes fashioned from blankets and sheets. Their appearance wasn't their most unusual feature though. Tyrant could hear them singing. All of them. In unison. The same fragment of song over and over again.

A man walked over to them. He was even bigger than Tyrant and had a wicked scar down the centre line of his face. Whatever had caused it had split his nose so that it now consisted of two separate nostrils joined by a flap of skin. Despite his rough exterior, Tyrant felt no sense of threat from the man. 'Are you looking for somewhere safe to live?' he asked.

'We're looking for someone,' Tyrant replied. 'The father of these two young girls. He's an army man, name of Captain Oliver. Do you know him?'

'No, but there are many of us here who once served. Soldiers arrive here daily, some to escape the madness and others sent by the King to prevent us rebuilding the township here.'

'If the King forbids it, he'll send soldiers to stop you,' Tyrant said. 'That sounds like another kind of madness to me.'

'This place is safe, don't you worry. Any discussions take place high up there.' He pointed to the mountain pass from which the thin brown smear of the North Road emerged. 'We've blockaded the road and nothing can come north that we don't want to. Including the King's army. You'd be surprised what a few determined and well-trained men can do in that narrow gorge. An army, no matter how large, can only engage a few at a time.'

Tyrant knew the road well. The man spoke the truth. If they had fortified the narrowest point, then even the biggest force would find it difficult to make progress. Still, these men were obviously deserters and the King couldn't afford to let them go unpunished or else his whole army could dissolve into chaos. There had been a rich and prosperous town on this lake before, but the King had ordered it destroyed, presumably because he viewed it as a potential threat to his sovereignty.

'There are families down by the lake; you are welcome to join them,' the man said and resumed his construction activities.

They walked over to some makeshift buildings that housed mainly women and children, who ran out excitedly to greet them. Tyrant's whole body relaxed for the first time in ages. The girls would be safe here. He could go on his way in the knowledge that he'd done what he could.

As they wolfed down the welcome offerings and prepared to settle down for the night under a makeshift shelter, Cassie voiced her concern. 'Father won't be able to come here according to that ugly man, will he?'

'He might already be in these parts,' Tyrant said.

'But even if he was, he'd be fighting them, wouldn't he?' She looked worried and Bee's face had also clouded over.

'They're having a war,' Bee said.

'Not necessarily,' Tyrant replied, but couldn't think of an alternative.

'And we're on the wrong side, aren't we?' Cassie said.

Tyrant felt shivers run down his spine. *I'm definitely getting soft,* he thought, *and it may prove the death of me.*

46

Freya's face was surrounded by stars. Oliver felt the cool earth beneath him and remembered where he was. He sat up. His head began to swim and he felt dizzy. 'Let me get my breath then we'll be on our way.'

'It's not even dawn.' Oliver struggled to wake up.

'We can use the starlight until the sun comes up. I can't wait any longer. When I think of what might be happening to my poor girls while you're snoring in bed, it makes me so angry that we didn't do something before now.'

'We had to give them chance to arrive here,' Oliver said.

'There's been plenty of time for that. They're in trouble, I know it. Trapped on the mountains most likely. Waiting to be rescued before they die of cold and hunger. While we sit around doing nothing.'

'At least wait until first light,' Oliver said, pulling his blanket over his chest. The stony look on Freya's face was enough of an answer to make him climb to his feet, fold up his bedding, and secure it to the bulbous pack that Freya had set down in front of him.

They trudged together in silence until they came to a roaring fire next to a makeshift shelter.

A man was squatting next to the fire, intent on whatever it was he was eating. When he turned towards them, Oliver recognised Tyrant and his heart surged with joy. Freya let go of his hand and shouted, 'Cassie! Bee!'

Oliver had never seen a sight so wonderful as the two beatific children who emerged, wrapped in blankets. Their faces were lit up with smiles as they hugged their mother.

Oliver threw down the pack and joined in the group hugging, tears streaming down his face.

'Tyrant lost the map,' Bee was saying.

'So these men came. It was all his fault,' Cassie said.

'They were going to make Cassie warm their beds,' Bee said.

'They were horrible, so I put belladonna in the stew. That wasn't a bad thing to do, was it, Mum?' Cassie said.

'No, no. As long as you're safe now,' Freya said.

Oliver looked over at Tyrant, who was holding his peace and smiling from time to time. Oliver knew that he'd get plenty of opportunity to hear Tyrant's version of what had happened, but right now it was time to bask in the warm energy of his joyous family.

He fell asleep listening to the girls' account of their adventures and the morning light found him lying by the fire next to a recumbent Tyrant, who was snoring softly like a giant cat.

A tiny woman appeared at his side. 'I'm Petra,' she said. 'Your girls were staying at my house.'

Oliver looked at her smooth skin like polished leather and bright brown eyes. 'Pleased to meet you,' he said. 'And thank you for helping my daughters.' She shook his hand briefly then walked off towards the lake. Oliver heard a faint splash and presumed she'd gone for a swim.

When Tyrant woke up, he rubbed his eyes and smiled. 'I may have made one or two bad decisions along the way, but at least we're all safe and sound.'

'Thanks for keeping them safe,' Oliver said.

'Petra had a lot to do with that. If you listen to the girls, she did much more than I did. I only want you to know that I did my best, even though it didn't always work out the way I'd hoped.'

'Oh, I heard all about the men who came to the house. What did happen to them?' Oliver said.

'When I realised the map had been stolen, I got back to the house as fast as I was able and dealt with them. They gave me very little trouble. It was the next lot to arrive that was the real problem. That's why Petra is with us; she had to abandon her house. The Gort madness is spreading, it seems.'

47

The path up the rocky escarpment became steep, and the horses began to scrabble for purchase on the loose stones. Patch continued as serenely as ever, seemingly unaffected by the change from soft brown dirt to sharp black rock underfoot.

As they climbed higher onto the escarpment, the vista slowly changed from verdant green to cold black. Ahead lay an unremitting carpet of black rocks, sharp and undulating. The darkness seemed to crowd in on Ant as they progressed. Ahead lay nothing, it seemed, but desolation.

A cold wind began to blow in his face, cutting into his throat and chest, making him wince and shiver. It was only the thought of Col and Pepper and the deadly peril he'd put them in that stopped him from turning his back on this desolation.

They spent the night in the sparse shelter of a rocky outcrop. It was impossible to get comfortable on the hard, uneven ground. The fire they made soon spluttered and died from lack of fuel, leaving him huddled, shivering, in his blanket. Although Lone's sleeping figure was barely a hand's breadth away, the presence of her inaccessible warmth only made his night more lonely and uncomfortable.

The morning light did little to dispel the gloom. The sun was shrouded by a white haze, and it seemed as though the black landscape absorbed any light that did manage to penetrate the clouds. Ant felt tired and miserable. The prospect of another day spent on that abomination of a horse was a depressing one.

Progress was slow. The horses had to pick their way carefully across the jagged rocks. Lone and Malachi spent more and more time out of the saddle. Even while being led, the poor horses were finding it hard to stay upright and sharp rocks had produced bloody lacerations on their legs. The wilderness was a vast sea of blank rocks stretching ahead further than his eyes could see. A black vista of crenulated lava, broken only by an occasional shrubby tree. There were no birds at all. It was as if they had abandoned this place long ago, given it up to the blackness of the rocks and the cold, biting wind.

Malachi decided that the biggest threat would be the lack of fuel if the nights became colder, and without a fire, they would find it hard to survive. So they gathered fuel where they could, zig-zagging their way north from one stunted tree to the next sparse bush. The wood they gathered was attached behind Ant's steed, which dragged it without any noticeable effort.

Ambrose had told him that an advanced civilisation had once inhabited this region, but that seemed impossible now that he had seen it for himself. He wondered about Col and Pepper and what they were making of this horrible place. Cali had remained silent for days now and he was wondering if the wilderness had driven her away as it threatened to do to all of them. It was only Malachi's grim determination that kept them going.

It was towards the end of his third miserable day in the wilderness when he saw movement in the rocks ahead and realised that they didn't have this dreadful place all to themselves.

His voice echoed in the eerie silence. 'Over there, behind those rocks,' he called.

A dark face appeared briefly above the rocks in front of him. He dismounted and the three of them advanced cautiously on the place where the movement had been. As they approached the outcrop, Ant's anxiety rose to screaming point.

Malachi strode forward. 'Nobody. Nothing,' he said.

'Whoever it was couldn't just have vanished,' Ant said.

'Well, they did, because there's nobody here now,' Lone said.

Ant cast around the area, looking for signs of life. There was nothing to indicate that anyone had been here, and he was beginning to wonder if he'd been mistaken. Maybe the light had been playing tricks on them.

'Over here!' Malachi's sudden shout made him jump. Ant scrambled over the uneven rock and jarred his shins painfully as he misjudged the height of a particularly vicious outcrop.

'It's a cave,' Ant said, pushing his way inside the narrow entrance. As the sides squeezed and pinched, he felt as if he was back in their cave in Gort. The passage was narrow but, with a squeeze and a squirm, he negotiated the narrowest section and into a dark passageway.

'I'm in,' Ant shouted back at Malachi and Lone.

'It's too small for me to fit,' Malachi said. 'Come back out. We'll find another way.'

'Do you want me to see what's in here?' Ant said.

'No,' Malachi said. 'I don't think that would be wise. Come out until we know it's safe. We have no idea what might be down there.'

'I say we let him have a look. He's in there now and this might be the place that we've been searching for,' Lone said. 'We can't just ignore it.'

Malachi shouted back at him. 'Take a quick look around and then come straight out.'

A sharp bump on his forehead from the low ceiling brought Ant back to the here and now. Steadying himself with a deep breath, he closed his eyes and felt into his surroundings.

Ahead of him was an impression of openness and no feeling of danger. He pressed on, comfortable in the darkness. The passage narrowed again and he became stuck, unable to move either forward or back. The muscle memory of their cave calmed him. He relaxed in the familiar feeling for a moment, then calmly explored the subtle changes in posture that might extricate him. Bending his knees, he exhaled completely and inched his way through. The cave opened out, allowing him to straighten up and walk normally.

His hands detected a passage off to the right which seemed to be heading upwards and might lead to the surface and an entrance large enough to admit Malachi and Lone.

Their absence, for the first time since his hanging, felt liberating. The prospect of being reunited with them wasn't attractive. At least not yet. The intense scrutiny he'd felt could only be truly appreciated now that it was lifted. Alone, in the blessed darkness, it was as if he'd become his own man again and not dancing to the witch's tune. The flare of intense longing was still kindled by any thought of her, but Malachi's words had loosened their grip on his heart. There was even perverse pleasure to be gained from recognising the over-blown desire for her that, in her absence, no longer consumed him.

There was a faint greenish glow that might have been light from the surface, but felt unnatural. He remembered the terrible tales of sickness, death, and suffering his father had attributed to the glowing caverns and decided it was prudent to avoid the upward path even if it meant continuing alone. He was convinced that this was the place to find Col and Pepper. Reaching out with his mind, he tried to contact Cali to guide him, but she wasn't willing to be found.

The going became easy. The floor was smooth, sloping gently downwards, and the passage remained wide enough for him to walk normally. He made good progress, eyes firmly closed, relying on his enhanced senses to keep him away from the walls.

A rush of air brushed his cheeks, bringing with it a clean, fresh scent as he emerged from the darkness into a great cavern, the size of which took his breath away.

48

Tyrant woke up feeling tired and sore. The scree slope had left his arms scraped and bruised and his backside painful. The expression on Cassie's face wasn't helping either. It was as if he was abandoning them to some terrible fate. Selling them down the river. Instead, he was just leaving them in a safe place with their parents so that he could carry on his life as it had been before he'd encountered Lone. Surely she could understand that there was nothing more he could do. The girls would just have to live here by the lake until things quietened down.

'But we need you here with us,' Cassie said.

'You'll be just fine without me. You've got your father to take care of you now.'

'But we need you as well. This place is just as dangerous as Petra's house and look what happened to us there,' Bee said.

'You said that when you left them at my house and look what happened,' Petra said. 'You sent horrible men to molest us. If you hadn't been so stupid, things might have been very different and we'd all still be there now.'

'We can't change what is,' Tyrant said. 'Be thankful for this place and the chance to live quietly. I have to be on my way.'

'Not so fast,' Petra said. 'I'm coming with you.'

Tyrant's heart, buoyed by the prospect of being his own man again, plummeted back down to earth.

'You can't come with me. I travel alone. That's what I do. I don't do company. I need to keep myself to myself; that's always been my way,' Tyrant said as he walked through the field of horses, Petra struggling to keep up with his big strides.

'Did you expect me to stay with them?' Petra said.

'Yes, why not?'

'Because I don't fit in. I'd be a hanger-on, just getting in the way.'

'So you're inflicting yourself on me rather than them?' Tyrant said.

'It's the least you owe me after I lost my home because of you,' Petra said.

'You lost your home because of the crazy bastards that invaded the forest. Nothing to do with me.'

'Those men you sent wrapped me up so I couldn't breathe and shoved me into a hole in the ground. I thought I would never get free. Imagine how that would feel, being condemned to suffocate slowly in a shallow grave. Now don't try to tell me that wasn't your fault. It was you who lost the map. Or did you give it freely to the first drunken slobs you met who fancied a bit of fun with two little girls?'

Tyrant stopped and looked down at her. 'You know that none of that is true,' he said. 'What you're forgetting is that I came back and saved you. It was me that pulled you out of the hole and untied you.'

'Only after you almost asphyxiated us all with your dumb trick with the chimney.'

'I'm not arguing with you any more,' Tyrant said. 'Like all women I've ever encountered, there's no reasoning with you. You can't keep up with me. I'd be forever waiting for you to catch up. You'd slow me down and, worse still, invite trouble. I'd be forever getting into fights with people who called you inappropriate names and, to cap it all, I don't like you. All you do is berate me for doing my best, and you drive me crazy with your incessant chatter. It won't work, Petra. You'll have to go your own way and I'll go mine.'

'We could take one of these horses,' Petra said. 'I'll sit quietly at the front of your saddle and the horse won't even know I'm there.'

'Yes, but I will.'

Petra walked over to the builders.

'Can I borrow one of those horses?' she asked the nearest worker.

'The horses belong to nobody, my friend. If you have need of one, please feel free to take it. There are saddles and bridles stored over there.'

Without any further response to Petra's constant badgering, he picked a nice docile animal, saddled up, and then, very reluctantly, pulled Petra onto the horse to sit in front of him.

'I'm heading back to Gort,' he said. 'Does that fit in with your plans?'

'Sounds good to me,' Petra said.

Tyrant gently coaxed the horse forward with the uneasy feeling that this new arrangement was going to bring him a lot of trouble.

As he travelled smoothly along the road towards Gort, Tyrant pondered on the advantages and disadvantages of having a horse.

The big advantages were obviously speed and ease of travel. Although his backside was getting sore from sitting in the saddle, it was small discomfort compared to the aches he would get in his feet and legs if he was walking. He would arrive wherever he wanted to go much more quickly and in better shape physically. These were the advantages. He couldn't think of any others.

The disadvantages were many. Sitting up there on a horse, he felt exposed. It was advertising the fact that he was somebody worth robbing, at least of his horse, if nothing else. Walking was much lower profile. Without a horse, he could duck into hedgerows and hide from passers-by and avoid confrontation.

There was also the problem of what to do with the beast when he arrived somewhere. Tying it up outside a tavern was a waste of time, because someone would inevitably untie it and make off with it. That prospect made Tyrant anxious and irritable. He was used to having nothing except the clothes he stood up in, his knives and, in the best of times, a few coins in his pocket. He'd been perfectly content with that state of affairs for as long as he could remember. Now, he had this horse to take care of. Beside the need to keep it secure, there were also other obligations to go with it. Food and water. Grooming, or so he believed, was another essential activity to maintain the wellbeing of a horse, though he had little concept of what it might actually entail.

Getting where he was going a lot quicker than he would on foot was not really an advantage when one considered the fact that he didn't need to get anywhere at all. It was the journey of life, not the arrival of death, which should be embraced, as some old drunk had once shouted in his face. It must have touched him somewhere because he still remembered the phrase, unlike just about every other pub conversation he'd had.

Petra was another problem. She was unpredictable and feisty. A combination that was bound to lead to trouble in even the most placid of company. Gort had been anything but placid the last time he'd visited.

He'd had to be magically flown out of harm's way with a crossbow bolt in his shoulder. At least, that was his recollection. He couldn't be certain of the details.

The sooner he got rid of the horse and, especially, Petra, the easier he'd breathe.

'We'll be in Gort sometime tomorrow,' Tyrant said.

'And then what do you propose?' Petra answered.

Tyrant thought for a moment or two. 'Maybe we should steer clear of it. There are some nice towns further south. Let's give Gort a miss and keep on going.'

They halted for the night by some rocky cliffs that provided a little shelter from the elements. They were very close to Gort now and could have entered the city within the hour if he'd wanted to. Better to arrive in the light, he'd decided. There was more chance of avoiding trouble that way.

Tyrant explored the crevices in the hillside, looking for a nice dry cave to camp in. He'd just settled on a shallow scar in the rock that would afford them reasonable comfort when Petra's shrill voice broke the silence. 'Over here,' she shouted.

Tyrant reluctantly abandoned his comfortable position and went over to where she was standing. 'I've found a cave,' she said.

Tyrant managed to get a few steps inside the cave entrance before becoming wedged between the walls of rock. 'It's too narrow. I can't get through.' He extricated himself with difficulty and stood facing Petra. 'Forget it, I've found a good place over there.'

'I can get inside,' Petra said. 'It's not too narrow for me.'

'Then off you go. Be my guest, have your own place to sleep. I'm all in favour of that.'

Petra disappeared inside the cave. 'I can see some light,' she said.

'Then come back out. Now!' Tyrant said.

He waited, but there was no response. After an hour or so of waiting and shouting, he gave up and retired to the place he'd chosen to sleep.

***

Tyrant woke with the sun casting sharp shadows over his face. He'd enjoyed the best sleep he'd had in a long time and he put that down to the fact that he'd been left mercifully alone. Petra finding her own place to sleep had been a godsend.

He roused himself into action, drank a little water, and picked some berries off the bushes that grew all around him. He walked over to the cave entrance and shouted through it. 'Wake up! Time to get moving. We'll get a good breakfast in Gort. Hurry up, I'm starving.'

Tyrant heard no reply and shouted louder. It was as if she had walked into the cave and out on the other side of the hill. He had a bad feeling about leaving her and decided to wait for a while in case she emerged. The bushes were almost completely devoid of berries by the time he decided to carry on without her. It was obvious she wasn't coming out of the cave. Either she'd found another exit or she'd slipped away in the night. It didn't really matter which was correct, Tyrant felt completely justified in leaving. His problem was that he couldn't get rid of the vision he had of Petra's displeasure when she emerged and found she'd been abandoned. She already disliked him because of the incident with the map. Leaving her now might just tip her over the edge, and then he'd end up having his throat cut by an angry dwarf.

Tyrant rode slowly into Gort. The place looked even worse than he remembered it. There was hardly a building that hadn't been damaged in some way. Most of them seemed to have been torched to the ground. What had been a vast area of comfortable habitation was now a wasteland. There were a few sorry-looking people picking through the ruins, searching for scraps of value. He felt depressed at the sight of what the once-thriving city had become.

The west gate was open and unattended. He rode through with trepidation, vaguely remembering how some arcane force had somehow whisked him airborne and carried him over the wall with a bolt stuck in his shoulder. He winced at the thought and his wound responded with a slight twinge.

As he rode towards the inner city walls and the King's palace, Tyrant could feel his horse getting more nervous. It began to pull on the bridle as if it was trying to get him to turn around. Up to that point, it had been as good and docile an animal as any Tyrant had ever encountered.

Some thin trails of smoke rose from within the walls of the inner citadel, and as he rode closer, he could see soldiers clustered around the main gate into the city proper. He wondered if these were the same troops that had shot him as he passed through with Malachi and Lone.

On the positive side, people seemed to be going about their business in a normal fashion again, and it appeared that the madness had been a temporary affliction.

'Where do you think you're going?' A burly soldier confronted him as he approached the massive portcullis.

'I'm heading into the city,' Tyrant said. 'Is that a problem?'

The soldier was looking closely at Tyrant's horse. 'It is for some thieving vagabond riding a stolen cavalry horse with the King's mark branded on its flank. I'm placing you under arrest. You'll be getting a fair trial in the morning before you're hanged as a thief and murderer.' He waved to the cluster of men who had trained their bows on Tyrant. 'Take him away.'

Tyrant's newly learned respect for the hurting power of crossbows kept him from attempting escape. At least they weren't proposing to hang him right away. He had until morning to find a way out.

'I didn't steal the horse. It was given to me by the cavalry officer who used to ride it,' Tyrant said.

'After you killed him, no doubt. Doesn't matter, anyway. Being in possession of the King's property is enough to get you hanged. At least there's a full jail up there in the castle, so you'll have lots of company.'

Men bundled him off the horse, extracted his knives from his undergarments in a most insensitive manner, dragged him through the gate and up to the castle. He was thrown into the very same cell he had occupied with Lone. On the good side, he was at least free of that odious woman, but on the negative side, her husband was unlikely to be on hand to get him out.

His dozen or so cellmates were a smelly crew, the debris of the unwashed and the unfortunate. A man with wide, staring eyes lurched up to Tyrant and grasped his collar. 'What do we have here?' he asked. Tyrant smashed his forehead onto the bridge of the man's nose while simultaneously bringing his knee up into his groin. The man's question remained unanswered, and he didn't look to be in any state to repeat it.

Tyrant surveyed the faces of his fellow inmates. Most of them were pretending not to have noticed the violence, keeping their eyes fixed on interesting patches of damp on the walls or blobs of excrement on the floor. Nobody made a move.

'OK, listen up!' Tyrant shouted. Several men carried on their low conversations, keeping their backs to him. Tyrant went over to the nearest and hit him hard in the back of his neck, just where it connected to his skull. The man fell down as if his legs had been severed and Tyrant's injured shoulder made only a slight protest. Looking around for someone else to test his fitness, he saw that the remaining men were giving him their full attention.

'The next time that door opens,' Tyrant said, 'it has to stay open. Then we fight our way out. It's either that or be taken one by one to be hanged. Your choice. Fight or die meekly on the gallows. Any questions?'

The man he had hit in the neck rose to his feet. Tyrant's fists bunched automatically as he looked the man straight in the eye. 'Do you mind repeating that?' the man said.

'Door opens. Soldiers will be standing in the door. Rush them. Push and fight your way out. Then run. Are you clear?'

'Won't some of us get stabbed or shot?'

'All of us may get stabbed or shot. Some of us might escape. It's our only alternative to the gallows. Remember, we all have to do it together if it's going to have a chance of working.'

The man rubbed the back of his head with his hand. 'Have you done this kind of thing before?'

'Lots of times.' Tyrant allowed himself a brief laugh that was meant to sound more like a snort of derision.

'And did it work?' A voice from the back of the room.

'Oh, yes,' Tyrant said. 'Every time.'

Tyrant sat down behind the door so that he could grab it when it was opened. It was a long wait, but eventually he heard the sliding of bolts and creaking of hinges.

Tyrant grabbed the edge of the door and heaved it fully open. He was now protected by it as the mayhem began. He remained where he was as the screams of the inmates and the shouts of the soldiers filled the room.

The sounds of fighting seemed to be getting a little further away; less than half of his fellow escapees remained in the cell and they were pushing hard to get out. The soldiers were forced back further as the surge of bodies finally emptied the cell. The last man to leave was the man Tyrant had felled. He gave him a rueful grin as he pushed his way into the melee.

Tyrant waited. The battle was obviously raging hard, and he hoped the soldiers weren't having it their own way. Maybe there were too few of them, perhaps they were unprepared. Perhaps they'd turned up with a few crossbowmen to back up the prison guards on the assumption that bows would provide sufficient deterrent. Once all the bolts had been discharged, the soldiers would be fighting on equal terms and without the incentive of a hangman's noose to spur them on.

Tyrant ventured from behind his door and looked out of the cell. Everything was going on to his right. The passage was full of brawling men, and the floor was littered with fallen bodies. He slipped out into the corridor and turned left. At the end of the corridor, he found a wooden door, which led to a spiral stone staircase. Another door at the foot of the stairs opened out into a continuation of the passageway he was in. When he cautiously peered around it, he saw several soldiers heading his way. He decided it would be more prudent to climb the stairs and keep out of the way in the hope that the soldiers would go off to join the fighting. After all, that was what they were paid for.

The staircase was narrow and designed to be defended easily. *One man with a sword could hold off an army.* The only problem was that he didn't have a sword, or anything else for that matter. Using a bare arm for the job was not a great idea. Even a man with a crossbow would be able to overcome a bare arm. Most of the time.

It was a long and arduous climb. As he puffed his way upwards, Tyrant wondered if he might have made the wrong decision. Footsteps and voices echoed from below. He was being followed, though the noises didn't sound like pursuit.

As he reached the top, panting and sweating, Tyrant found himself in a high tower and thankfully alone. He emerged into a quadrangle bounded by a low parapet and overtopped by an arching roof. In the centre was a circular area in which a complex pattern had been chiselled out of the stone. Above the pattern, there was a weaving display of ghostly light, wisps of illumination that drifted about, forming a cylinder of eeriness that stretched up to the roof.

Tyrant stepped to the side, giving the lights a wide berth. This had to be the device that Malachi and Lone had been discussing. The terrible portal that had summoned evil into the world. His body shivered at the thought, although he blamed this on the cool breeze that wafted through the open sides of the tower.

Leaning over the parapet, he commanded a view of the whole city. Faint sounds of conflict reached his ears, and he could see a few men engaged in hand-to-hand combat with an awful lot of soldiers. Tyrant's opinion of his cellmates rose considerably. He hadn't expected them to get far; they'd done amazingly well. In truth, he hadn't held out much hope that the motley crew would have had the balls to get out of the cell, never mind fight their way from the building.

They were all doomed, of course. Even if they managed to get across the courtyard, they would still have the soldiers at the gate to deal with. The ones who shot crossbows at people from the safety of the turrets on either side of the huge portcullis. Tyrant rubbed his shoulder wound in memory of what it felt like to try to get past those particular archers.

The mildly scented air carried a hint of smoke and the teeming human presence below. The feeling of power that came from being able to watch people without them being aware of his presence was a powerful one. No wonder kings went to great expense and trouble to build high things from which to look down on their subjects. It was a spectacular reminder of superiority and Tyrant was catching a whiff of it.

It felt good up here. Moments alone were to be savoured, especially when there were footsteps on the stairs getting closer.

49

Tyrant was squatting on the opposite side of the tower to the stairwell. His head was below the level of the parapet and in the sharp shadow of the setting sun. The two soldiers who nervously emerged seemed preoccupied by the coruscating lights and stared into them as if mesmerised.

These two soldiers, carrying regulation crossbows held protectively in front of their chests, were the only ones to appear. Tyrant hoped any colleagues had eschewed the long climb, and that this was a mere formality of a search. The alternative was that they knew where he was and had planned accordingly. Two men, with crossbows. Tyrant found he had a newly won respect for the much-maligned weapon after one had almost ended his life. He'd been shot many times before, but these were nicks and scratches in comparison. The pain and anguish of being skewered by that bolt was something he was hoping to avoid in the future. Now the first test of his resolution was here.

Slowly, as if it might suddenly jump out and bite them, the men circumnavigated the device and their attention fell on Tyrant. He kept perfectly still, hoping to give them no excuse for shooting him where he sat, though that would have been his own preferred course of action had he been in their shoes. He'd at least had time to devise a plan that should make them hold fire at least for the present.

'You!' the lead soldier shouted, far more loudly than necessary considering he was within ten paces of the person he was addressing. 'Stand up and explain yourself.'

Tyrant stayed on the floor where he was. 'Thank goodness you've come,' he said.

The soldiers exchanged glances. 'What are you doing here?'

Tyrant put his head in his hands and began to sob. He noticed with satisfaction that the soldiers had lowered their crossbows and were looking at him as if he were an errant child instead of what he really was; a hardened criminal who would cut their throats given half a chance. 'It was that thing.' He pointed to the lights. 'It brought me here. One moment I was peacefully having supper in the safety of my own home, then there was a flash of light and here I am. Where am I, anyway?'

'You are in the King's palace,' the guard said.

'Thank goodness! And thank you for rescuing me. What are your names?'

'I'm Quinn and he's Barda,' Quinn said. 'But that's of no consequence. Who are you?'

'But it is of great importance! My name is Tyrone and I'm a cousin to our King. A distant cousin but one that, thank heavens, is looked on kindly enough by His Majesty. When I tell him how I was saved and who did it, I'm certain he will be handing out a suitable reward. I'll wager you'll both have a bag of cash and a promotion out of this!'

'Tyrone?' Quinn said. 'I've never heard of a nobleman called Tyrone.'

'Then we must belong to different social circles,' Tyrant said. 'Not really that surprising, don't you think?'

'We're going to have to take you down some stairs to show you to our officer,' Barda said. 'He'll know what to do with you.'

'That will be perfectly in order,' Tyrant said. 'But first, let me catch my breath. I'm feeling very weak at the moment, perhaps the effect of being magically transposed. It also appears to me that the climbing of those aforementioned stairs has taken its toll on you two fine gentlemen and you might benefit from a brief rest yourselves. Sit a few moments, then we'll go and see your officer.'

Quinn dutifully sank to the floor and sat directly in front of Tyrant, his back to the flickering lights being projected by the device. With a little more reluctance, his partner followed suit, crossbow on his knees, but now pointed to the side rather than directly at Tyrant. Quinn had placed his weapon on the floor and was busy rubbing his legs and sighing with relief.

Tyrant flexed his knees, rising a little, then settling back on his haunches. The soldiers were a couple of steps out of reach. If he were to succeed, he'd need to get to them both before either could shoot him. The way they were arranged, Barda had to be the first one to go, being the more ready of the two. Tyrant had to find a way of getting across the three paces between them before they became alerted to his intentions. All the bullshit about being the King's cousin seemed to have found its mark, but now he had to put the matter to bed, so to speak. There could be reinforcements arriving at any moment, and he doubted that they would be as gullible as these two.

Tyrant allowed the seconds to pass slowly. He rose completely to his feet, then sank back down to a squat. The soldiers remained unconcerned. Barda wasn't even looking at him, instead, tracing imaginary lines on the floor with his finger. There was a sense of calm about the whole situation that was even beginning to affect Tyrant. Thoughts of what might happen if he convinced the rest of the guard that he was the King's cousin began to drift dangerously through his mind. He was beginning to delude himself, which was fine during the attempt to trick the guards, but very dangerous if he allowed it to take the edge off what was going to have to be decisive and bloody action.

'No!' Tyrant shouted at the top of his voice, rising to his feet and pointing at the device behind the soldiers' backs. Both of them turned around and Tyrant ran over to Barda and grabbed him around the arms, trying to strip the crossbow from his grasp. The guard reacted surprisingly quickly, ducking out of the embrace and swinging his weapon to strike Tyrant on the side of his head. Tyrant was used to being hit on his head and it wasn't one of those debilitating blows that left his senses befuddled and his head ringing. It was more of a sharp tap and it brought the crossbow within Tyrant's reach. He managed to find the trigger and discharge the bolt into the ceiling. Grabbing hold of Barda with both hands, he heaved him sideways, hitting Quinn, who was bringing his crossbow to bear.

This seemed to enrage Quinn, who threw his colleague to one side and leapt at Tyrant. Surprised by this whirlwind of spite and anger, Tyrant stumbled against the parapet and had to grab the edge to prevent himself from falling off the tower. Quinn was stronger than he looked and the frenzied attack sent him reeling under the onslaught. No matter how hard he tried to avoid them, he kept on being battered by Quinn's fists.

Long fistfights weren't Tyrant's forte. He was used to much less gentlemanly disorder. Keeping his back to the parapet and his hands protecting his face as best he could, Tyrant waited for Quinn to run out of steam. He didn't. Instead, he drew back slightly and swung a haymaker that thudded into Tyrant's head and befuddled his brains. He felt his legs weaken and realised that a few more of those could have him in real trouble.

Sure enough, before he could clear his star-encrusted vision, another identical right hook was heading his way. In desperation, Tyrant bent over, his head descended to waist level and the blow swung viciously into thin air. That unbalanced Quinn to the extent that he fell over the stooping Tyrant, and it was an automatic gesture that helped him over the wall. By the time Tyrant managed to peer over the parapet, Quinn had already hit the ground and would not be swinging any more punches at anyone.

Tyrant sat down heavily. His head was still ringing and he felt the soreness beginning to seep into his consciousness. Although he was glad that Quinn had gone, as it meant that he was no longer being battered, he wished it could have ended a little more tidily. The bloody mess Quinn would have made on landing, not to mention the loud squelching sound, would be attracting attention by now and they'd be pounding up the stairs very soon. When they got to the top, this time they'd surely shoot first and ask questions later. Barda made this a certainty when he scrambled to his feet and shot down the stair like a rat down a pipe.

Tyrant reviewed his options. There were only two ways out of the tower. Down the stairs and into the arms of a bunch of soldiers hell-bent on avenging their fallen-from-a-great-height comrade. Or there was the same way that Quinn had gone, over the wall. It was a long way down. Tyrant leaned over to check whether there might be some footholds that would allow him to climb down rather than plummet to a soggy death. The tower was inconveniently constructed with a large overhang directly below where he stood. Even a very capable spider would have trouble negotiating that.

The stairs or the cobbles? It was a tough call. Cobbles would provide a quick death and there would be the interesting experience of flying to take his mind off things immediately prior to being dead. The soldiers on the stairs might not be so accommodating. Depending on Quinn's popularity, they might inflict a long and grievous punishment on his killer.

Something to fight with would be nice. His knives had been confiscated when he'd been arrested, and he didn't fancy his chances of fighting his way down the stairs with his bare hands. If he could get himself a weapon, making a stand on the spiral stone staircase was going to be the prime choice.

To do that, he would need a sword, preferably, or a very good knife. A right-handed man with a good blade could shield himself behind the central column and present little or no target for an advancing foe to hit. Quinn's abandoned crossbow was good for one shot and then he'd be too busy defending himself to reload. Still, it was all he had.

The whirling lights above the device caught his eye. Cautiously, he approached the trails of fire, but could feel no warmth from them. There was a shape lying on the stone floor within the pattern. It looked like a sword, or at least a long knife, but he couldn't be sure if it was real as the image shifted and changed thanks to the tendrils of brightness.

Cautiously, he put his face as near to the thing as he dared and stared at the sword. It looked real enough. He wondered if it were Quinn's, and had fallen in there during their altercation.

Tyrant was reluctant to risk putting his hand into the device, even though it felt cool and unthreatening. There was some strange magic going on, and he was mightily suspicious of it. Tentatively, he placed the little finger on his left hand into the shimmer of yellow light. It seemed to him the digit he would least miss were it to be sliced from him or consumed in the blaze. Nothing happened. There was no change in the feeling or appearance of his finger when he withdrew it. Now, he had to seriously consider going in to retrieve that sword. It might be his only chance of defending the stairs, even if it was a slim one. He'd likely or not be dead in an hour or so. Whether from the effects of the device or the attention of soldiers mattered little in the great scheme of things.

Sounds were coming from the stairs. The army was arriving, and he had little time to act. Tyrant took a deep breath and walked into the lights. They swirled around him in a manner that suggested they were reacting to his presence, but nothing untoward seemed to be happening to him. There was no discomfort, no change in temperature, only the disorientating effect of the shifting patterns of light. He bent down and picked up the sword. It weighed heavy in his hand. The blade was sharp and bright and the handle had been forged as part of the sword then polished and wrapped to provide a wonderfully comfortable grip. It was as if the weapon had been custom forged for his exclusive use. His exultation at discovering such a weapon was quickly extinguished by the sight of soldiers running into the room. The staircase defence was now no longer an option.

50

Tyrant watched as the soldiers filed through the doorway and fanned out into the room. Most of them were carrying crossbows, but there were spearmen and swordsmen as well, a dozen at least, and far too many to fight.

The good thing was that none of them seemed to have noticed him standing amid the flickering lights in the centre of the device. It was as if they were reluctant to look his way. In fairness, they seemed eager to view the crumpled remains of their colleague from the vantage point of the tower and there was much leaning, jostling, and sucking breath in through teeth.

'Captain Cornwell, sir, we've found the body.' A crossbowman approached a tall, dark-haired swordsman with prominent sideburns.

'It's rather hard to miss it. But thank you for pointing it out. The question I'd like answered is where is the person responsible for the death of our colleague? Come back when you can tell me that.'

'He must still be here, sir,' the man said.

'Must he? Then why can't we see him and why haven't you shot him? You do know how to work that bow, don't you?'

'Oh yes, sir, I'm well practised.'

'Well practised or not, I'd thank you for not pointing it in my direction, or anyone else's for that matter. Those things, especially in the wrong hands, tend to go off unexpectedly. We lose more men in accidents than we do in battle. Try to remember that.' Captain Cornwell sounded tired and exasperated. Tyrant hoped he was the type to quickly give up and leave before he took the relatively easy option of looking directly at the device. It was as if they all held it in such dread that they believed they could be harmed just by looking at it. If that were the case, Tyrant felt he might just get away after all.

'Make yourself useful; get Sergeant Lee over here,' Cornwell said.

Tyrant wished the captain would move away from the device. He was standing a mere ten feet away and Tyrant could have leaned out of the whirling lights and prodded him with his newly found sword. If he'd been in lesser company – with fewer lethal bows around, for example – it might have been a reasonable option.

A small sandy-haired soldier grasping a short spear as if it meant the world to him bustled up to the captain and gave him an elaborate salute. 'Sergeant Lee reporting, sir. You wanted to see me, sir. Here I am.'

'I can see that you're here, Lee. Tell me what you've found and what you make of this situation.'

'Yes, sir. Certainly, sir. There's a dead man. It's Quinn, sir. He's fallen from the tower. His head is splattered all over the cobbles. It's a right mess. He's dead, sir.'

'Thank you, but I can see that from here. Where is the man who killed him?'

'I don't know, sir. Maybe he jumped?' Lee said.

'Could a man survive such a fall?'

'I don't know, sir. I could ask one of the men or even try it myself, sir.'

The lack of response from the captain might have been interpreted as an invitation to his subordinate to jump from the tower, but Lee appeared to require more than subtle silence to goad him into action. Tyrant considered it to be a pity; another soldier falling to his death might provide sufficient distraction for him to slip away unnoticed and unskewered.

Without something cataclysmic, though, his prospects were poor. Anyone with half a pair of eyes had to be able to see him if they could be bothered to look. Making a break for the stairwell was out of the question. Reaching the stairs unscathed would require a remarkable lack of accuracy from a dozen bowmen that even this motley crew were unlikely to manage. The law of averages meant that he'd be killed before he confronted the guards that had been posted at the top of the stairs. In the unlikely event that they were asleep, and they were showing no signs of tiredness at the moment, he would be only be able to run down the stairwell and into a secure area teeming with troops. Then there would be a dash across the courtyard under the watchful gaze of the patrols on the walls before reaching the heavily guarded gate where he'd been shot previously. Getting out of the tower unscathed was impossible, but relatively easy when compared with his chances of escaping the castle.

Tyrant saw the sergeant's face screw up into a wrinkly mess. 'I think it must have been a demon, sir.'

'Really?'

'Yes, sir. A demon came out from the device and threw him off the tower,' Lee said.

'Where is that demon now?' Cornwell asked. 'Shouldn't we be worried about our own welfare?'

'Yes, sir. We should, sir.' Lee's eyes wavered a little then fixed on Tyrant, who tried not to stare back at him but found the impulse impossible to resist. There was a connection, a moment of recognition. Lee's face became wide-eyed and open-mouthed. 'The demon, sir. In the device. I can see it and it can see me.'

'Where?' Cornwell asked.

'Right in front of us, sir. If you look directly at it, you can't see it at all. You have to look slightly to one side and half close your eyes. Sir.'

'Oh, yes. There it is. Looks like a big man holding a sword to me.'

'It can't be a man, sir. Remember what happened to poor Mark the stonemason? In fact, there he is, or at least there's the scorch mark that he left when the device incinerated him.'

'Nevertheless, get some of your best men to cover it with their crossbows and shoot it if it moves,' Cornwell said.

'But, sir, is that wise? If we shoot it, that might make it angry and it might make us all explode into flames or turn to stone.'

'And if it's a man with a sword, he just might chop off your head with it.'

'Yes, sir. I'll get some men.' Lee gathered half a dozen men and arranged them around the circumference of the device, then reported back to Cornwell. 'Men in position, sir. I've told them to shoot if it moves.'

'I can see that, Lee. Do you think it's wise to have them standing in a circle? If they all shoot at once, they stand a very good chance of either hitting each other or, heaven forbid, one of us.'

'Point taken, sir. Sorry, sir.' Lee reassembled his men.

Tyrant stood very still. He could feel the bristling menace of the bolts aimed at him. They only had to fire and he would be dead for sure.

Thoughts of all the places he would rather be than here in the tower drifted through his mind. There were a lot of them. Just about everywhere that he wasn't in immediate danger of being turned into a human pincushion. Petra's image popped into his head. There was a lurch of guilt when he thought about her emerging from the cave to find him gone. He should have stayed and waited for her. Anything, even Petra's company, was better than this. A memory of the arrow piercing his shoulder triggered a sharp pain in his chest. The arrows were about to stab him again, and this time there would be no recovery. No Bee and Cassie to tend his wounds. No Petra to admonish him for being stupid enough to end up like this. The pain in his chest increased. The strings of incandescence that separated him from the soldiers became more solid. They coiled tightly around his body, restricting his breath. His arms were pinioned, his legs immobilised. It was impossible to move. His view of the tower was becoming blurred, and he could no longer hear what was being said.

51

As he entered a great cavern lit by a soft glow from the walls, Ant followed a stone-flagged path that led to the entrance of a great building, which stretched high and wide before him. Even the King's palace in Gort was nowhere near as magnificent. Ant wondered what his King would make of such an obvious challenge to his supremacy.

As he climbed past small, beautifully manicured plants that were somehow growing deep in the earth, far away from any sunlight, Ant marvelled at this wondrous place. It was a long climb, and his legs were aching before he passed through another archway and into a courtyard. The sound of chanting grew as he approached.

There was a square raised bed of plants ahead of him, and sitting on the wall was a boy dressed in dark red robes, swinging his legs in time to the distant voices. He looked up as Ant approached and invited him to sit on the wall. Ant, glad of the respite after the arduous climb, hopped up beside him and rested his legs.

The boy was about Ant's age and had long dark hair fastened at the back in a horse's tail.

'It's a wonderful day,' the boy said.

'That really depends on what's going to happen to me next,' Ant replied.

'No, it doesn't. All that exists is the here and now. You're sitting on a wall; you're sweating from your journey. That's the reality. Is it wonderful or not?'

'This place is wonderful. Amazing,' Ant said.

'There you are. Be with that wonder. It's all there is.'

Ant felt something settle inside him. Feeling the stone against his backside and allowing the ambience of this peaceful place to seep through his body brought him a sense of peace after days of turmoil and fear. He breathed more deeply. The silence between the boys was long, but not uncomfortable. Ant kept thinking of things to ask, information that he wanted to gather, but something inside him resisted the urge and let things be as they were. Ant found a glorious feeling of contentment creeping over him.

Occasional thoughts about Lone and Malachi, Col and Pepper drifted through his mind like clouds in a summer sky. He managed to let them go without grabbing at them and becoming enmeshed in their inevitable complications and anxieties.

Ant began to realise that it was, indeed, a wonderful day in every respect.

After what seemed like a few minutes, but could easily have been much longer, the boy slid off the wall. 'Come with me,' he said. 'I'll find us some refreshments so that we can sit comfortably and have a chat.'

He led Ant to a large square room festooned with banners and flags, with a raised wooden dais in the centre. The boy took Ant up onto the raised platform and they sat on cushions clad in the same deep red cloth as his robes. Two men came into the room from a side entrance. They were dressed in bright orange robes and carried a bowl of fruit and a pitcher of water, which they put at the boys' feet. They bowed as they left.

Ant took a welcome swig of water, then quickly ate an apple. It was sweet and luscious. The boy sat opposite him, sipping appreciatively at a cup of water.

'What is this place?' Ant asked.

'This is a monastery,' he replied. 'It is the home of many hundreds of monks and acolytes. It's very old.'

'What do you do here?'

'We live and pray.'

'Is that all?'

The boy's expression remained serene. 'Some would regard this as sufficient and ask what else is there to life?'

Ant looked at the fruit remaining in the bowl and felt a shiver of doubt. There were no trees in these sunless caverns. How did hundreds of people feed themselves down here? 'Where does all the food come from?'

'It is a gift from nature. We also have gifts bestowed upon us in gratitude for helping to alleviate some of the suffering in the world.'

'If that's the case, how do your patients get here?'

‘We’re not doctors; our work is spiritual. Life is full of sorrow and we offer the means to reduce the suffering.’

‘How?’

‘Through prayers and teaching.’

There was a mystery here, but the boy’s enigmatic replies weren’t providing any useful answers. ‘I’m looking for my friends,’ Ant said. ‘Have you seen them?’

The boy smiled. ‘Tell me more about them.’

‘They’re called Col and Pepper. Col is a big lad and very quiet. He hardly says anything, whereas Pepper never stops talking, mostly about becoming a soldier. They were dragged into a magical device by a demon, but when I followed, they were gone. Or, at least, I was transported to a different place. We have a horrible king who likes to hang people, and I was sentenced to death. If it hadn’t been for a passing magician, I’d be dead.’

Ant paused, waiting for some comment from the boy who sat attentively opposite. None was forthcoming. It gave him a chance to think of what to say next, a luxury he never had when talking to Pepper. Most of the time, he doubted his friend was even listening, preferring to compose his next interjection and take over the discussion. Talking to this boy was very different.

‘You see, my father discovered this magical device, and I learned how to build it. I was showing my friends how it worked when this thing got hold of us. I could make one for you if you want. Then you could leave this cavern and travel to the real world.’

A deep, booming sound echoed through the cavern. The boy smiled and rose slowly to his feet. ‘Come with me.’

Ant followed him down a wide corridor decorated with brightly coloured banners until they reached a vast space with an arched roof supported by ornate pillars and an intricate latticework of stone and metal. Men sat on the floor in perfect rows and columns. Some wore bright orange robes, but most were clad in dark red.

The boy led Ant through the silent ranks and showed him to an empty mat in the centre of the front row. ‘If you would like to sit here, we would be happy for you to join in our morning devotions.’

Ant had no idea what he meant, but felt very nervous about sitting directly in front of the big chair.

The boy climbed onto the plinth and sat cross-legged on the massive wooden chair. Ant felt his heart miss several beats. Who had he been talking to all this time? Surely this boy couldn't just take the prime position without being someone very special?

They all sat in silence for a very long time. Ant's backside became sore, and he had to reluctantly shuffle about to get comfortable while everyone else remained perfectly still. The silence was palpable. Ant could feel the power of it. All those people and all that stillness combined to carry his thoughts away and let him rest in the tranquillity of the moment.

After the silence, the monks began to chant in low tuneful voices. The strange words evoked deeply peaceful feelings, and he found himself able to relax, listen, and enjoy.

When the monks lapsed into silence again, the boy stood up. 'Let me show you the rest of the monastery; I'm sure you'll find it most interesting.'

The darker recesses of the monastery were illuminated by the red glow of burning coals, which cast shadows that picked out the indentations on the walls. This place looked as if it had been hewn from the solid rock, one chisel stroke at a time. Ant struggled to imagine the enormous task that had been. It must have taken hundreds of years.

At the end of one dim corridor, a new, brighter light appeared. When he recognised the familiar coruscating lights of the device he'd created, Ant felt foolish at first and then relieved.

'That's one of those things I was telling you about,' Ant said. 'I created one by drawing a pattern in the sand.'

'The pattern, as you call it, is very simple,' the boy said. 'Almost everyone is capable of drawing it with a little practice. Very few have the ability to activate the energies and open a portal. If you are capable of that, you are very special indeed.'

'How does the device work?' Ant asked.

'You just step into it and out on the other side,' the boy answered.

'But how do you know where you'll be ending up?'

'Ah, that is an art that has to be mastered over several journeys. Some never get the hang of it; it's quite subtle. The key to directing the vedhana, as we call it, is intention.'

'Does there have to be another vedhana at the other end? Or can I go anywhere.'

'Normally, yes, there has to be one at the point of arrival. But it's not unknown for a traveller to find himself in an unexpected destination, one that hasn't been previously visited. Like all of life, there's a mystical element to the whole process. It's a matter of acceptance and of surrender to the forces that guide us.'

'So there's something controlling the vedhana?' Ant asked.

'Yes.'

'So what is that? And how do I know if what it decides is best for me?'

'In essence, it's you that decides everything. Again, as always, it's a matter of being aware of the real you rather than the one that is projected into the world as a defensive screen. Trust that all will be well.'

Ant stood at the edge of the vedhana and looked into the swirling pattern of lights. This was his chance; all he had to do was take a couple more steps and he would be gone and the boy wasn't doing anything to stop him. He thought of Pepper and Col. He remembered their special cave. Then he jumped forward and felt the flickering pattern surround him and solidify. His breath was forced out of his body, then everything went black.

***

He awoke to find soft sand beneath him.

Ant recognised the cave at once. It was *their* cave, and his device was still glowing as strongly as ever. The familiar smell of the damp sand and the faint aroma of spent candles hung around the place. His excitement that the device had brought him back to Gort was tempered by his need to find his friends. And Lone was still trapped up there in the harsh wilderness.

He pushed his way through the narrow entrance. Outside there were signs of people having camped close by, but the embers of a fire were completely cold and there was no sign of anyone now. Ant took a deep breath and looked over to the familiar walls of Gort. He wondered if the madness had subsided and thought about what the boy had said about the device being purely a means of transport.

Ant went back into the cool sanctuary of the cave and sat by the vedhana. He allowed himself to become still, as if he were in the Great Hall with the boy and the other monks. Calmness descended on him and his thoughts began to clarify. He realised that he hadn't escaped. On the contrary, he had been allowed to leave. The more he sat and thought about it, the more obvious the next step became.

Ant rose from his sitting position and took the few steps back into the centre of the vedhana. He took a deep breath and visualised the monastery.

When he stepped out of the wavering lights, the room was empty. The boy had not waited for his return.

The Great Hall was packed with monks sitting silently in devotion. Ant crept quietly in, and picked his way through the serried ranks until he reached the place he had previously occupied, which, much to his relief, had been left empty. He settled down and then looked at the occupant of the big chair for the first time. It wasn't the boy. It was Col.

Ant saw Pepper sitting two rows away from him with his eyes closed. He allowed a feeling of happiness to wash over him, let it sink deep into his body and fill his mind with ease. It felt like the most joy he'd ever experienced.

When the hall emptied of silent monks, Pepper met Ant in front of the big chair, where Col sat in stately serenity. The two boys embraced awkwardly. 'You took your time getting here.' Pepper smiled.

'I've journeyed long and hard to find you two. It's wonderful that you're still alive and we're all together again.'

'All you had to do was to follow us into the vedhana,' Pepper said.

'I did, believe me, I did. But I ended up in the tower and,' Ant tried to swallow but his mouth had become too dry, 'things got complicated.'

'Doesn't matter,' Pepper said, 'me and Col got along fine without you.'

'Now I know how to work the vedhana, we can all go home together,' Ant said.

'Col thinks he is home already so he's not going anywhere. Me, I don't really mind the monk's life. At least I get to see interesting places. It's a bit like being in the army without all the marching.'

'You get to leave this place?'

'Sure, anytime I like. Mostly we go to gather food. There's a big city, even bigger than Gort, where it's very hot all the time. The markets there have everything anyone could ever want.'

Thoughts of Malachi and Lone stabbed his chest. They would get here soon with the demon to guide them. When they did, they would discover what they needed to overthrow the King and rule the world. These gentle monks would be unable to resist even if they wanted to.

52

There was a brief moment of blackness, then the light became dizzyingly bright. Tyrant was out in the open, the sun was hot on his back and there were, most significantly, no soldiers aiming weapons at him.

The device from which he'd emerged was a much cruder affair than the one in the tower. Fashioned from pieces of rope held down with small rocks, it looked temporary and ramshackle in comparison with the elaborately carved version he'd been standing in.

Sitting gratefully on the sandy ground, the realisation that he'd managed to escape certain death by some kind of miracle overcame him. Leaping to his feet, he waved his arms in the air and danced a little dance.

When he grew tired of dancing, he plunged his hands into the dry sand and raised his head towards the hot sun. This was somewhere south, he thought, and a long way from Gort. That notion made his smile even broader and provoked another bout of dancing.

When his nostrils caught the faint scent of wood smoke, his demeanour changed instantly. The someone who had fashioned the device might be close at hand. He gripped his newly found sword tightly and looked all around him with a heavy dose of suspicion. There was a thin tendril of smoke coming from the other side of the rise. Tyrant crawled quietly up the sandy slope and then peered cautiously at the scene below him.

There was a small fire in the valley, crackling and smoking as if it had recently been ignited. It had been placed next to a rough shelter fashioned from leafy branches, which had been arranged in a pyramid shape. There were no occupants that he could see. That worried him. Someone was probably watching him. He hoped they hadn't seen his little dance of joy. That would be bad for his reputation.

Before he could decide how best to deal with the situation, there was a blow to the back of his head and he felt a knife at his throat.

'It's lucky for you that I have a kind and forgiving nature.' The voice in Tyrant's ear was a familiar one and his state of electric alarm subsided immediately. He rolled over and sat up to face Petra, whose leathery face was wrinkled by a wide grin. In her right hand, she was holding a wicked-looking machete, which seemed like a broadsword in her small hands.

'You,' Tyrant said, catching his breath, which seemed to have deserted him.

'Me, indeed. How did you get into that cave?' Petra asked.

'I couldn't. You just disappeared in there and there was nothing I could do except wait outside for you.'

'How long did you wait?' Petra asked as they walked down the hill towards the tiny encampment.

Tyrant thought about his answer carefully. If he told her the truth she might fly into a rage and accuse him of reckless abandonment. If he lengthened the time period, it might seem lame and unmanly for him to have been parked outside an empty cave. 'A day or two,' he said.

'Are you sure you don't want more time to think? Maybe it was an hour or two? Or a minute? Do you want to try again?'

'I camped the night, then when you still weren't answering my calls, I left for Gort,' Tyrant said.

'So how did you get here if you didn't get inside the cave?'

They sat down by the fire, where a pot of water was boiling merrily away. Petra took a small handful of brown powder from a white bag and threw it into a decorative porcelain pot. Then she poured the hot water into the pot.

'I went into Gort and ended up in the King's tower. There's a device like the one over there, but carved into the stone rather than made of string.' Tyrant accepted the cup of tea and sipped it suspiciously. It was surprisingly fragrant and tasted quite nice. Anyway, Petra had given him it to drink, so there wasn't much option but to make the best of it.

He told Petra the whole story as he drank. How the cavalry horse had betrayed him, his arrest, and incarceration. The way he had, single-handedly, broken out of the cell, taken on the entire guard, forced his way to the staircase and defended it vigorously for hour after hour. Then he related how he had been gradually overcome by the weight of numbers and tiredness, retreated to the top of the tower and escaped by means of the device.

Petra sat and listened politely throughout. Tyrant detected an air of slight disbelief in her posture and wondered if he might have embroidered the story a little too much.

'There was a similar device in the cave, all flashing lights and suchlike,' Petra said. 'I walked into it and was transported here. That's why you couldn't get any answer to your calls.'

'But who put the device here?' Tyrant asked. 'And do you know where we are?'

'There was a man already here; he's the one who built the camp and brought the teapot and cooking things. He was a nice man, bald head with long red robes. He said he was a monk, having some time alone to reflect.'

'Where is he now?' Tyrant asked.

'He left using the vedhana, which is what he called the device. He said to wait for his return. He was going to find somewhere appropriate for me to travel to.'

'Appropriate?'

'It seems that this is a very remote part of the Great Southern Desert. Nobody ever comes here; it's too far from anywhere. There's no water to be had for hundreds of miles all around. That's why he needs to take me out through the vedhana. There's no other way.'

'But it looks OK around here; there's lots of greenery. There must be water here,' Tyrant said.

'Yes, here is fine. There's a well and there's lots of fruit to eat. It's if you tried to leave here that's the problem. Your water would run out long before you got anywhere you could find more.'

'So if we didn't have the vedhana we'd be stuck here for the rest of our lives?'

'If that were true, yours would be shorter than you might think,' Petra said. 'Just hope that the monk returns soon, I'm getting tired of your company already. And I've not forgotten what you did to my lovely home.'

Petra never missed an opportunity to remind him how much she disliked him. How he had been responsible for the destruction of her house and property. How she'd be living a comfortable life if it weren't for him.

All this was music to Tyrant's ears. He could deal with an irascible woman who didn't want him around. What he couldn't deal with as easily was the underlying feeling that accompanied the bluster and vitriol. Petra's actions spoke of entirely opposite sentiments. She fussed around him like a mother hen, attended to his every need. The food she gathered was incomparable to anything Tyrant had previously experienced. The lush sweetness of the unfamiliar fruit was filling him with energy and positive feelings, even towards this tiny woman.

'Watch this,' Petra said, taking a strip of cloth and looping it around the trunk of a ridiculously tall tree with branches only at the very top. She fastened it around her waist and, gripping the tree with her heels, slid the cloth up the trunk, then used it to pull herself up. It was like watching some bizarre creature adapted for the job of climbing unclimbable trees. Tyrant couldn't help but worry about the integrity of the cloth or what might happen if she missed a foothold when she was twenty feet above. 'Watch out below,' she called as she swiped at some enormous green egg-shaped fruit, which came crashing to earth with a great thump. Had Tyrant not been on his toes, he reckoned he'd have had his brains smashed in. Maybe his theories about Petra were wide of the mark and she really was trying to kill him.

The fruit she gathered contained delicious sweet water and a white flesh of unusual texture. The whole thing was delicious. He wondered what price they would fetch in the markets of Gort. Certainly there had never been anything even remotely like them sold anywhere he'd ever visited. It was plentiful here; there were groves and groves of trees all bearing copious amounts of fruit. All he had to do was devise a way of getting it to market.

'This is good,' Tyrant said between mouthfuls.

'It's more than you deserve,' Petra said, passing him another chunk that she'd carved off with her machete. 'Where shall we go when the monk returns to take us away from here?' she asked.

'I don't know and I don't care,' Tyrant said. 'I go where the fancy takes me and I travel light. And alone.'

'I thought we might stick together, at least for a while,' Petra said. 'You're obviously incapable of looking after yourself and I need a companion who can carry stuff.'

'Then get yourself a horse.'

Petra laughed. It was the kind of laugh that Tyrant associated with parents when their precious child said something cute and funny.

***

The monk arrived several days later. Tyrant thought Petra looked disappointed at his arrival, but she greeted him warmly.

The monk, a small man with a completely bald head, expressed no surprise at seeing Tyrant. Petra made any enquiry superfluous by telling him all about the two of them, including the story about the map and her precious house.

'We can all go together if you are agreeable,' the monk said. 'I just need to gather my teapot and tea, then we'll be on our way.'

'Shouldn't we take some fruit with us?' Tyrant asked. 'We could sell it for a good price when we get where we're going.'

'I think you'll find that fruit of all kinds is plentiful in the monastery,' the monk said. 'We gather it in the same way; through the vedhanas we have created in remote areas. It provides our staple food supply, as we have little opportunity for producing our own crops situated where we are.'

Tyrant shrugged and took an armful of the biggest specimens he could select. In his experience, you could never be certain where your next meal might be coming from. Anyway, he had a sneaking fear that despite the monk's air of confidence, there was still the possibility that they all might end up back in the tower. Then at least he'd have something to throw at the crossbowmen to put them off their aim.

The three of them stepped into the vedhana. There were a few moments of constricted breath, a period of darkness, then they stepped out into a much cooler and darker environment.

'This is my home,' the monk said. 'You are both very welcome.' He bowed solemnly, as if this meant a lot to him. Tyrant managed a cursory nod back. Petra had already scuttled off in exploration.

'It's a cave,' she said on her return. 'We're deep underground, I think.'

‘How do we get out?’ Tyrant asked, still clutching his armful of exotic fruit.

The monk didn’t reply.

53

Tyrant was disappointed with his new situation. He had grown used to the feeling of the hot sun on his back and the open air of the desert. Now he felt crushed beneath a mountain of black stone. The life was being squeezed out of him.

Petra, on the other hand, was her usual darting self, full of curiosity and intent on exploration. The bald monk had shown them a place to sleep, where to get food, then lost interest in them. Tyrant took to following her as best he could, still carrying his exotic fruit to ensure that it wasn't stolen.

The monastery was a vast array of huge halls and smaller rooms that served as refectories and sleeping quarters. Everywhere they went there were monks, clad in red or orange, who paid little attention to them beyond a polite bow.

'We have to get out of here,' Tyrant said. 'This place makes me feel trapped.'

'That's because we are trapped.' Petra laughed. 'But it's a nice sort of trapped, don't you agree? We're being provided with food and shelter and they're letting us have the run of the place.'

'It's the same as a prison,' Tyrant said. 'And I speak from considerable experience. They feed and shelter you, some better than others for sure, but the bottom line is that they have you trapped until it becomes time for them to do what it is they want with you. In my case, it has generally been a short stay to allow time to erect a gibbet.'

'I don't think they mean to hang us,' Petra said.

'But they want us here for a reason. There's always something that people want from you.'

'Then we'll find out when they're ready,' Petra said. 'In the meantime, we can at least make the best of it.'

'The best of what? Imprisonment? Not a lot of *best* to be derived from that.'

'Stop moaning. And put down that fruit; it looks like you're obsessed with it. People will think you're crazy walking around like that. Maybe that's why nobody will talk to us. Would you talk to some madman with an armful of fruit and a permanent scowl on his face?'

'Someone might steal it,' Tyrant said.

'They're monks. They have their own fruit. What possible interest could they have in yours?'

'Mine's special. It comes from those big trees that don't grow anywhere else. I reckon this stuff is valuable. If I can get it back to Gort, it'll fetch a good price.'

'If you ever get back to Gort, they'll be waiting for you with a rope. How many soldiers did you kill in your amazing jailbreak? A hundred, at least, from what you told me. They won't forget something like that in a hurry. You're better off here. Put down the fruit, we can go outside and sit for a while.'

'And look at the rock surrounding us on all sides,' Tyrant said.

'Put your name on the fruit if it's so important. Scratch it into the skin with your sword so that everyone will know it's yours.'

Tyrant looked at the precious items in his arms. 'It's OK, I'll just stack them here in this alcove. Try to remember where I put them in case I forget.'

Outside was just a slightly less oppressive version of inside as far as Tyrant was concerned. Petra sat closer to him than he felt was necessary or comfortable. She chattered about the lack of sunlight, the absence of birds and strange insects. Tyrant listened politely, but his mind was set on finding a way out. He had a feeling in the pit of his stomach that told him that this place wasn't as safe as it might seem.

'Listen to that,' Petra said. Tyrant was trying not to let the faint sounds of men chanting make him more irritated than he already was.

'I'd rather not,' Tyrant said. 'In fact, I've decided to go back inside, get my fruit, and then head off out of here. I've a bad feeling about this place and I think it's time to go.'

'Nonsense, you're just being grumpy. Everyone here is really nice and kind. Where else are you going to find a place like this?' Petra asked.

'I don't want a place like this. I preferred it where we were. I like to be able to see the sun in the sky.'

'Admit it. You liked it in the desert because you had me all to yourself. Now you're feeling a bit deprived. Don't worry. I'll not run off with some red-robed hunk.'

Tyrant felt the words searing into his very core. They twisted his stomach into a fiery knot. He opened his mouth to scream, then thought better of it. He framed several withering replies, then refrained from uttering them on the basis that they would be woefully inadequate to express his complete horror at Petra's insinuation. He even considered physical violence. Taking the woman's throat and trying to shake some sense into her seemed the best solution, but he remembered the difficulty he'd had in coming to grips with her in the past. As soon as he made a lunge, she'd be on his back with her machete at his throat.

Tyrant had to face it. Whatever he said or did, Petra would interpret it the wrong way. Her way. So he bit his tongue and listened to the monotonous singing instead.

'Let's go down to the Great Hall and watch the monks at prayer,' Petra said.

Anything was better than sitting there, Tyrant thought, so he stood up and followed her towards the noise.

When the singing stopped and the screams began, he allowed himself a moment of self-congratulation for being right about this place before chasing after Petra as she sped to investigate.

54

Lone watched Malachi as he hunched over the pathetic tangle of twigs and struck spark after spark. Each one fizzled and hissed before being extinguished by the dampness. His groans of disappointment were becoming louder and more frequent with each failure.

The snowstorm had forced them to seek shelter and abandon the search for the boy. This was the best they could find. It was more of an indentation in the rocks than a cave and afforded little protection against the violent gusts that slashed her face with blades of ice. If they didn't manage to light a fire, she feared she would freeze to death overnight. Her clothes were unsuited to this harsh climate and even the addition of Malachi and his cloak was not going to save her.

'The wood is too wet,' Malachi said. 'Even if I do manage to light some shavings, the fire won't catch. I'm going to have to use other methods.'

'Then get on with it.' Lone shivered. 'It has been obvious for the last half hour that what you've been doing is worse than useless.'

Malachi brought out a small silver flask from the recesses of his black cloak. 'This is precious stuff; it took me years to accumulate even this tiny amount. It's not to be used lightly.'

'Then allow me to freeze to death gracefully rather than squander some of your precious concoction.'

In response, he unscrewed the stopper with exaggerated care, as if forgetting that the thing had been in his pocket during the entire bone-shaking journey. A few precious drops were dribbled onto the small pile of twigs, the stopper replaced, and the flask disappeared to be replaced by a parcel of leather bound tightly with twine. As this was laboriously unwrapped, Lone wanted to scream. She was cold, tired and, above all else, frustrated by the way events had unfolded.

She'd done her bit. It was always the way. Malachi, however, had contrived to waste all her efforts by allowing the King to slip away while they embarked on this pointless journey. They should have gone south.

Followed the King and set the demon to work. Instead, her husband had insisted they make their way to this empty wasteland and bring along the stray boy for good measure. More fool her for tagging along like a dutiful wife. Would she never learn? Or were all those centuries of female oppression weighing down too heavily on her?

'Stand back,' Malachi announced with a great deal more imperiousness than the occasion warranted. If she retreated at all, she'd be outside in the blizzard and she wasn't prepared to do that whatever he might say.

He cut a tiny piece from whatever was wrapped inside the leather, held it balanced on the edge of his knife, then re-tied the parcel before putting it back. With the knife poised over the twigs, Malachi began to chant in a deep, untuneful voice.

'Are you sure the incantation is absolutely necessary?' Lone interrupted.

Malachi gave her a hard stare. 'It goes with the process. I've not tried it without and I'm not willing to risk failure just because of your impatience.'

'Perhaps I should light the fire, then. You've had long enough without success. Let me have a go.'

Her provocation was rewarded with an angry flick of the wrist that spilt the shard from the knife onto the wood. A thin column of white smoke rose from where it had been dropped. Seconds passed. The smoke intensified before there was a low whooshing noise and the wood erupted into flames. She could feel the heat on her face as Malachi fed larger pieces to the fire and they too burst into fiery life. 'I told you the incantation wasn't necessary,' she said.

They sat side by side, backs to the stone and facing the entrance. The fire was burning strongly, she was wrapped in Malachi's cloak, and warmth had returned to her bones for the first time since they'd set foot in the wastelands. As if sensing her return to a reasonable humour, Malachi began pressing her for an account of her time away from him.

'Although long winded and tedious beyond description, the snaring of the demon was the easier part. You can't ever know what it's like to walk down a street having to endure the looks that men give to a woman like me. You'll never appreciate what it's like to live in a society where women are considered only in terms of the man who possesses them. All the time I lived there, I wanted to lash out at every male I encountered. Living alone, even in that backwater, was a stupid risk. If that wasn't bad enough, having an intelligent mind made me a prime candidate for hanging as a witch. You know how the King encourages the slaughter of any woman who tries to assert any measure of independence. It only needed some male finger to be pointed in my direction and I would have been hauled to the scaffold and dispatched. They hanged a dozen or so completely innocent women in the time I was there.'

'While ignoring the one genuine exponent of the black arts that lived amongst them?' Malachi laughed.

'If you think it's funny, you can do it next time and I'll spend two years living in comfort.'

'There won't need to be a next time, my dear. You have the demon and the boy will bring us the secret of the device. Once we control that, we will have all the power we shall ever need.'

'You have more faith in the value of that boy than I have,' Lone said.

'He's got great potential; I can feel it in him. He also knows more than he's letting on.'

'Then squeeze the truth out of him and be done with it.'

'There's more to the boy than a bit of tittle-tattle learned from his father.'

'Maybe. But is that a good reason to adopt him as the son you've never had? Are you going to pick up every waif or stray to add to your pretend family?'

Malachi laughed despite her attempt to provoke him. 'Tell me more about the demon. What are his powers?'

'He calls himself Patch, an unlikely name for a demon. He seems quite adept at manifestation, though a bit too unreliable for my peace of mind. Sometimes I think he gets distracted but he may be mischievously trying to upset me. Either way, he needs to be punished and shown who's boss.'

'I'd be careful. There will come a parting of the ways when the binding spell is released. Then he'll be free to exact revenge. Better to tread carefully. Try to reach a harmonious compromise.'

It was Lone's turn to laugh. The idea was ridiculous.

'As for the boy, I'd appreciate it if you let him be,' Malachi continued.

She found that even more amusing than the harmonious compromise suggestion.

'He's all yours. What makes you think I've any interest in him?'

'I've seen how he looks at you.'

'He's a lovesick child, that's all.'

'You shouldn't encourage him, Lone. It's hard enough for a boy of his age without you taking every opportunity to inflame his passion.'

'If he's going to be of any value, he's going to have to become more aware of his feelings. If I amplify them, and I'm not saying that's what I'm doing, surely that can only speed up the process?'

'I know what you're like, dear. It may amuse you to have him drooling at every sight of you but, believe me, it's not helping. Let him go. Please.'

'I can't help it if he's lusting after every female he sees. It's what men do and he's practising at being a man. You know full well that I have no interest in that frantic rubbing together of body parts that obsesses you males.'

'Of that, my love, I am well aware. It would, however, be kinder if that information could be imparted to Ant in as gentle a manner as possible so that he can get on with learning what I have to teach.'

The recollection of the intensity of Ant's longing made her shiver. This was something more than the doe-eyed devotion of an adolescent. There was something underlying the emotion, something very powerful but as yet unformed.

55

Patch had felt that things were beginning to get better. He could feel the binding spell had weakened with time. He was no longer tightly constrained. It was as if the invisible bonds were loosening. It gave him hope that *she* would be forced to let him go sooner rather than later.

He thought about the things he might do as soon as he was free enough. Most of them involved complex variations on generating maximum discomfiture for his mistress; prior to her demise in as painful a manner as could be devised. It wasn't much fun, but it was all the entertainment to be had in this awful situation.

His musings were temporarily interrupted by Cali's arrival. He hadn't had any contact with her for days, and now she seemed very different from the last time she'd turned up. Patch searched for the word to describe her and came up with one that made him very nervous. She seemed happier, and happiness was not a state that a tortured spirit like her ought to be exhibiting, not in his opinion anyway. Demons were created to be morose and should consider phlegmatic to be the pinnacle of positivity.

'Where have you been hiding?' he asked by way of greeting.

'I've been down there. Deep in the earth, where there are some very interesting humans,' Cali said.

'What could possibly be interesting about humans?' Patch asked.

'Compared with my own kind, everything seems interesting. All they ever do is whinge and moan. These humans are full of joy. It's very good to be around them.'

'So that's what I could detect the moment you arrived. Joy. What on earth possessed you to hang around beings exhibiting joy?' Patch laughed at the thought.

'I like it, and so do lots of others like me.'

'There's more of you down there?' Patch asked.

'Lots of us. Hundreds even. We all congregate in this massive hall where the humans sit and produce positive energy. It flows up into the rafters and we can feed on it. Believe me, it's the best feeling you'll ever have.'

'Positive energy indeed. You'll get decomposed by it, there'll be nothing left of you. It's a dangerous addiction; I've seen what can happen to your kind when you get exposed.' Patch had to admit he was intrigued by the thought of so many spirits gathered somewhere close by.

'Positive, negative, good, bad. It's all energy. There's no difference. It's what you do with the energy that makes the difference. You're such a miserable beggar that you could hang about in that roof for a thousand years without developing a single positive thought.'

Patch felt that was as good a compliment as he had heard in a very long time. 'Who are these humans and why do they spend their time like that?'

'I have no idea why they do it. Maybe it's because they can. Why do you do the things that you do?' Cali asked.

'I have to do what I'm told for the time being. That's my problem.'

'Maybe you can find something to help you become free again. There are all sorts of entities down there, and some of them appear to be very powerful. Maybe you can get her to do a swap,' Cali said.

'Then I'd be indebted to something I'd rather not be indebted to,' Patch said. *That might not be strictly true*, he thought. *Arrangements to suit both parties can sometimes be worked out.* Perhaps he should run the risk of his mistress's displeasure and check the place out. She might not miss him if he acted quickly. Nothing of any importance seemed to be happening; all the humans were sitting around in various degrees of misery as usual. 'If I wanted to come with you, how long would it take to get there and back?'

'In what form? Embodied or disembodied?'

'Disembodied for speed, I suppose,' Patch said.

'Then a few seconds, a minute or two at the most. It depends on what you want to do when you get there.'

'I'd want to scope out the situation, see who and what was haunting the place. Maybe have a brief conversation with one or two,' Patch said.

'Knowing your idea of a brief conversation, you'd better budget on being away for an indefinite length of time,' Cali said.

Patch did not appreciate her newfound levity. These were serious considerations. He would have to abandon any manifestations in order to make the trip. The horse would disappear and everything that was loaded on its imaginary back would once more be subject to the laws of gravity. *She* would notice, he had no doubt about that. It was what she was prepared to do about it that Patch had to consider. He knew all too well how uncomfortable she could make things for him and he really needed her to be cooperative for the moment. At least until she had let him go.

He was considering his options when he was summoned to be present with his mistress. *Here we go,* he thought, *she'll be asking more questions that I can't be arsed answering. I feel like making up something really outrageous this time.*

'Patch, I need you to guide us through the caves to where the boy has gone.'

But mistress, I've already told you that it's very dangerous for me to be here, even. Never mind down there, where the worst kind of danger lurks.

'I, for one, am willing to take that risk,' Lone said.

Then unbind me; let me go free as soon as I've done your bidding. That's if there's anything left of me to release. I've surely served you well; there have been at least two previous occasions where I've saved you. This will be the third and will satisfy all the conditions of even the most exacting spell. Agree to that and I'll go. Say the words that will release me automatically on my return. Otherwise, I'll not risk immolation. Why should I? Patch watched the woman hesitate, then she conferred with that awful husband of hers.

'I agree,' she said. 'This mission, successfully executed, will satisfy the terms of your binding.'

Then say the words.

'When you return,' Lone said.

Now. Make it conditional, but make it now.

Lone closed her eyes. Her voice took on an unworldly pitch as she chanted the spell. Patch could feel that the change was being made. *At last*, he thought, *I'm going to be able to make this horrible woman suffer.*

56

'There should have been more markers along the way,' Malachi was saying. 'Are you sure you gave Patch the right instructions?'

Lone sighed. She had a very bad feeling that Patch had either misunderstood or deliberately ignored her again. Either way, they were as good as lost. 'I'll get him back here and sort out what went wrong.' She summoned Patch with all the energy she could muster. After a long wait, she became aware of his presence. She wondered if he had been there all the time and kept her waiting just to anger her further. No matter, she had already decided to inflict the maximum punishment she could on him. 'Manifest yourself. I need you to provide a physical guide for the rest of the way. Get us to the boy as quickly as you can.'

'If you insist. But I can't be in two places at once, mistress. If I'm tied to a physical form here with you, I can't be keeping tabs on what's happening elsewhere. There could be deadly danger around every corner. The whole situation could have gone tits up and you'd be none the wiser.'

'I'll take that chance. Now show yourself and lead the way.'

Lone watched as a patch of darkness became more intense, began to solidify into a recognisable form. It began to lighten from black to light grey. A head was formed, hanging ghostlike in the air, before a body and four legs were attached and the familiar misshapen horse appeared, this time somewhat smaller than before but no less ugly. 'Here I am,' Patch said as a bright yellow light began to shine from the horse's nostrils. 'Follow me.'

Lone sighed with exasperation. But she followed Patch's lead.

'Ask it where we're being taken. Demons can be very pedantic, Lone. You should make sure it understands exactly what you require of it.'

Lone let out another gasp. First the recalcitrant demon, then her nit-picking husband. He always had to be in control of everything and everyone. So much so that she suspected he regularly persuaded people to do things he didn't really want them to do just to prove to himself that he could. He was getting as tiresome as the rest of them. 'Where are we going, exactly?' she asked.

It's called the Great Hall. Everyone will be there. Including the boy.

She passed the information on to Malachi, who opened his mouth then closed it again as if thinking twice about burdening her with more questions. A very wise move, the way she was feeling.

57

The annoyingly peculiar horse plodded its way along the dark passageways, turning this way and that in a seemingly random fashion. Lone sunk deeper into the black mood that was being amplified by the darkness.

What was she doing here? The answer to her own question was easy. No matter how much she tried to pretend this had been her choice, the truth was obvious. The stark realisation that she'd been played and manipulated coursed through her being and sapped every drop of remaining resolve.

Malachi was just as much a victim as she was. Malachi, the smooth arch manipulator himself had been out-thought and out-manoeuvred. Her spirits fell even further as she trudged through the gloom.

She only had herself to blame, of course. Taking it out on Malachi, while automatically soothing, was pointless. It was the boy who had led here them like baby goats in search of their mother.

Her demon, while disappointingly futile, had at least been consistent in its truculence and uncooperative attitude. Thinking of the lost opportunity that the demons in Gort had presented made her want to scream. Any half-decent demon would have granted her enough protection to weather the storm of carnage and madness. Then, with the King gone, she'd have taken control. Restored the things that he'd taken from his subjects. Rebuilt the temple. Summoned the goddess of old to take the cruel King's place.

Instead, she'd been forced to make a mad dash without any careful thought for the consequences, ending up in this gloomy and distant place searching for something that didn't exist. Had she also released the demon prematurely? Once she'd been taken to the boy and then safely delivered from this dreadful place and into the sunlight, the demon would be free. It would feel like a relief for her as well, despite the abject disappointment of toiling so long only to achieve absolutely nothing.

Her thoughts returned to the boy and her behaviour towards him. Was she right to inflame his basic desires as she did? Probably not. But she knew she had placed a hook into his heart that would not be easily removed and, when tugged on, would give her sway with him. It had also revealed something beneath all the teenage lust that she might never have discovered had she not. Malachi thought the boy had potential and that he could be useful once moulded into shape. He'd underestimated the boy's power. They both had.

Only now, as she approached what she feared would be the end of her own journey, Ant's special nature had finally been revealed to her. She suspected that everything they were seeking had been known to the boy all along. The secrets Malachi wished to discover had never been hidden from Ant. He'd known everything right from the start.

Memory of her scolding remarks to Malachi dismissing Ant as an unwelcome distraction made her cringe. She'd been wrong. But was it too late to do anything about her mistake?

Before she could decide how to tell Malachi about their compounded errors, they emerged from the cave system into the light, and Lone saw a strange boy sitting on a rock. Patch let out a loud expletive and vanished completely. 'We need to find the Great Hall. And quickly,' she told the boy. That's where Patch had said they had to be, and there was no point turning back now.

'Would you like me to show you the way?'

'Yes, but hurry. We haven't much time,' Lone said.

The boy rose slowly from his sitting position and began to walk very slowly in the direction of the large building that dominated the landscape. 'Can't you go a bit faster?' she asked.

He stopped and turned around. His eyes had a peculiar quality that she had never before encountered. His gaze made her uncomfortable and she began to wonder if her powers of persuasion had been reduced by all this travel and constantly having to play second fiddle to Malachi. 'Yes, I can go much faster,' the boy replied, but carried on walking at exactly the same pace.

Lone decided to let his insolence go for the time being. If they attempted to push on ahead and find the place themselves, Malachi would somehow manage to get them lost again. Throughout this whole affair, he'd turned out to be worse than useless. Two years apart had taught her the benefits of self-reliance, but didn't seem to have improved Malachi's attitude or abilities one bit. If it weren't for her conjuring a demon to help, they would never have made it this far.

The boy walked delicately up a path that wound through borders of tiny bushes, some with specks of white flowers. They looked completely out of place growing in this sunless terrain out of the cracks between black rocks. Lone shuddered. None of this was natural, which meant that powerful supernatural forces were at work. Whether Malachi was up to taking advantage of them was the big question.

She had her demon and, whatever he might think to the contrary, he was bound to assist her and keep her safe until she was well away from this underground realm. She was prepared for a certain amount of resentment being expressed when Patch realised that his release wasn't automatic when she arrived at the Great Hall as promised, but she was confident he would get over it. After all, if he killed her, he would be trapped forever.

The boy stopped. Lone almost collided with him because she was following so closely. She listened, as he did, to the sounds that were on the air. The faint monkish chanting had given way to more raucous shouts of alarm. There might have been the odd scream of pain amongst them for good measure.

It seemed that they were arriving at an interesting moment.

58

Tyrant hustled through the archway and into the cavernous hall to be met by a terrible sight and an even worse stench. Taking up half the space was a monster ten men high and fifty paces long. It was a gelatinous worm made of grey blubber. Dark eyes were staring at the hundred or so monks that were slowly retreating towards the doorway where Tyrant was standing. It was big, ugly, and stank as if it had been rotting in the ground for years.

The amorphous lump changed as he watched. Appendages were slowly appearing. Shiny scales were replacing the jellied bands of maggoty flesh. Its half-formed face was regenerating features. It seemed to notice him. Tyrant shivered under the implacable gaze, his legs dissolving beneath him. The single eye flickered sideways back to the familiar figures that stood closest to the monstrosity. His heart skipped a beat as he recognised the witch and wondered if this was some new manifestation of the inadequate horse demon she'd been dragging along with her. His answer was in the palpable fear and loathing that she was demonstrating. This wasn't her demon. Far from it. Malachi was held aloft in its grasp.

A monk broke ranks and ran towards him and was enveloped in a cloud of greenish gas that spurted from the monster's half-formed nostrils. The monk let out a piteous scream as he fell to the ground and began writhing in agony, hands clawing at his face. Petra ran forward to help before Tyrant could restrain her. There was a loud popping sound and one of the shiny scales detached itself from the back of the monster and landed a few paces from the monk. The flat bony plate sprouted appendages and eyes that swivelled on the ends of long stalks, turning it into a man-sized spiderlike creature that grasped Petra's leg with one of its claws. She rained blow after blow on it with her sharp knife without piercing its hard shell.

Tyrant brought his sword down hard on its back, splitting it in two. Yellow ooze leaked from its insides as its legs quivered and skittered on the stone. He grabbed Petra's arm and pushed her behind him. More popping noises heralded the arrival of more armoured spiders intent on getting their claws on him and Petra. More sweeps of his sword. Frantic parries. Legs severed; carapaces punctured. Three more dead monsters with body parts scattered wide.

Tyrant was beginning to appreciate the value of his new sword. It felt good in his hand and cut cleanly and effortlessly through anything it was presented with. A wonderful weapon, indeed. But it wasn't going to save him.

The monster was too big, the spiders too numerous. The gas that had felled the monk still lingered and it tore at Tyrant's lungs, making him gasp for air.

Backing away, he found himself close to Malachi, who was being crushed by the monster's gigantic hand. Instinctively, Tyrant brought his sword down with all the strength he could muster and severed the arm at the wrist. This single stroke of his remarkable sword sent Malachi rolling on the ground, still encased in grey blubber. Cut from its host, the hand relaxed enough for Malachi to extricate himself, gasping and wheezing as he fought for breath.

'Let the demon go!' Malachi's first words were directed at his wife, who stood transfixed. She opened her mouth to reply. A puff of gas hit her in the face and she collapsed as if her bones had been turned to dust.

The boy stepped forward. It was the one that they had taken from the gibbet at the castle. He stood in front of the witch's body, shielding her as far as was possible from further attack. His hands were by his side, clenched in obvious effort as he faced down the monster. Tyrant waited for more gas, more spiders, another claw to grab the boy and crush the life out of him. Nothing happened. It was as if time was standing still. Neither the monster nor the boy moved.

'Get Lone,' Malachi gasped. 'Pick her up, Tyrant. Get her out of here. Quickly, it's our only chance.'

'There's nowhere to go,' Tyrant said. 'We're trapped underground with a monster. Even if I could escape, I don't see how it would help you.'

'No time to explain. Take her as far away as you can. Now do it!' Malachi's voice boomed off the walls and ceiling. There was nothing

Tyrant could do but obey. He swept Lone up in his arms and ran back the way he'd come, then braced for the monster's inevitable response.

Reaching the door unscathed, he looked back at the sight of Malachi, Ant, and Petra lined up in front of the colossus. Tiny, weak humans with no prospect of survival. The only surprise was that they hadn't yet been destroyed.

Malachi's instruction rang in his ears as he sped down dark corridors carrying the witch, who remained inert in his arms. Perhaps she was already dead. It didn't matter either way. None of this made any sense. He should have stayed to die with Petra. At least shown he could be relied on for once in his life.

The strange glow drew him towards it. Of course. The device. It had to be the way out of here that Malachi desperately needed him to take.

He dived into the coils of light, felt the constriction in his chest, wondered where he'd end up this time, and hoped it wouldn't be the tower. A jolt of fear accompanied his thought about the tower. Perhaps this thing took you wherever you thought about. Like the depths of the underworld, where eternal fires burned and demons presided. Another bad thought. He needed to imagine somewhere pleasant.

The images in his mind hardened into the reality of hot sun, warm sand, and lush vegetation. After the gloomy confines of the monastery, this was paradise. It was the oasis that he had shared with Petra. The place he wished they'd never left. The prospect of having to stay here with the witch was a different matter, though. As soon as she regained consciousness, she would certainly want to kill him.

Stumbling out of the device, he laid Lone down on the ground and took a breath. He could run over the dunes and hide. Wait for her to come round and hope that she went straight back into the device and disappeared for good. The problem with this plan was a big one. There was no hiding place from the witch. She'd quickly sniff him out if he was anywhere in the vicinity and then he'd be in big trouble.

His only alternative was to jump back into the device and get as far away from her as possible as quickly as he could. She might not even be aware who it was that dumped her here and he'd be in the clear. Knowing her, though, she'd be bound to find out and want to exact revenge. Either way, getting out of the desert was the only option.

‘What have you done?’ she asked.

The sound of her voice propelled him into the device, heart racing. ‘Saving your life,’ he shouted, while trying to keep his thoughts on returning to the monastery. There were three devices that he knew of. One in an inaccessible cave where he could be trapped forever, one in the tower where the guards would skewer him on sight, and the dull, dismal monastery that was about to be destroyed by a huge demonic dragon. Not a great choice.

As the tightness in his chest grew, he saw her stand up and approach the device. In a panic, he dropped to his knees and took a firm hold of the rope that had been used to fashion the vedhana’s pattern.

There was a brief glimpse of Lone’s distorted face, and then blackness came.

The tug of the ropes almost pulled Tyrant’s shoulders out of their sockets. Although they had looked as if they were casually laid out in the pattern and secured with stones, it was as if they had been cemented deeply into the sand. Nevertheless, he arrived at the monastery with the mass of ropes trailing behind him and the hope that Lone couldn’t follow him.

Tyrant felt exultance and disappointment at the same time. He didn’t know whether to laugh or be sad. That quiet oasis would be forever denied to him and with it the opportunity to replenish his supply of big nuts.

He walked quickly back to the Great Hall, fearful of the carnage he would certainly find.

To his surprise, everything was as he had left it. Nobody and nothing had moved since he’d left carrying the witch.

As if galvanised by his return, monks began moving towards the doorway where he stood. Fearful of what was going to happen next, Tyrant ran across to grab Petra and dragged her behind a thick stone pillar. All around him, monks were trying to leave the hall, but it seemed the monster had different ideas.

Two monks were swept to the floor by the monster’s flaming spittle, their screams cut short by the ferocity of the flames that consumed them. Tyrant crouched behind the thick stone. Petra was holding on to him much too tightly, either in an effort of self-preservation or because she wanted to prevent him from engaging the beast.

Tyrant watched as a familiar figure clopped slowly into the hall. There could be no mistaking the twisted figure of Lone's horse, the one she called Patch. The poor thing looked as crestfallen as ever and it was way beyond Tyrant's imagination to come up with an explanation of what possessed it to be confronting such a terrible monster.

He watched as Patch's head moved from side to side in an exaggerated way, as if he was weighing up the creature in front of it. Then he shook his long head, as if in disdain. When he spoke, the powerful voice startled him. All that time they'd spent together in the forest hadn't prepared him for Patch being able to speak. Tyrant knew that he shouldn't have been surprised. But he was.

'What do you call that?' Patch's voice rang out and echoed through the hall. 'A dragon? Is that what it's supposed to be? I've trod in stuff that would make a more lifelike dragon than that. You're pathetic. Now be off with you, back where you came.'

The dragon answered with a stream of flaming spit that engulfed the pathetic horse from head to tail and turned him instantly to ash.

Something stirred deep inside Tyrant that made him shake off Petra's grasp and emerge from relative safety. Demon or not, that poor excuse for a horse had tried to save them and the way it had been instantly destroyed by a bloated lump of evil seemed remarkably unfair. Rage at this injustice flared uncontrollably and overwhelmed his well-practised instincts for preservation. He couldn't stand meekly by without at least attempting some retaliation.

He ran forward. 'Run for it!' he screamed, primarily to Petra, but happy to extend the invitation to everyone else as he hacked away at the monster's flank.

The monks needed no further encouragement, and they dashed towards the exit. Ant, meanwhile, didn't move. He stood motionless in front of the monster, seemingly unperturbed by the smouldering ashes of the once-peculiar horse that lay scattered at his feet.

An acrid stench of burnt flesh assaulted Tyrant's nostrils, which were already nauseated by the disgusting faecal odour of the monster itself. Disappointed by the apparent futility of his attack, which the monster had completely ignored, he retreated to the relative safety of his stone column where Petra took hold of his left arm, gripping it in an overly friendly manner. The expected words of admonition didn't arrive. Instead, she was exhibiting a fierce pride in his foolhardy actions, which worried him almost as much as what the gruesome dragon would do next.

The charred heap of burnt horse began to quiver. This was accompanied by the sound of laughter. It was a disproportionately loud noise, considering its origin. A booming, whole-hearted guffaw that echoed from the ceiling and walls. The scorched remains were shaking in time to the laughter, little shards of charcoal being scattered around by the convulsions. 'Now that's what I call funny,' Patch's voice sounded out between spasms of laughter. 'Trying to burn me. That's not only highly amusing, but it's also very, very stupid. Call yourself a dragon? I'll show you a dragon.'

As Patch's laughter continued unabated, the pile of horse ashes began to grow until it towered over the ugly monster. Recognisable features began to appear. First, a tail with a barbed tip extended backwards through the main arch before it was lost to Tyrant's view. Then legs grew to support a massive frame, which took on a sparkling, jewel-like sheen. Finally, a long head formed with prominent nostrils and two massive eyes that swivelled independently. Tyrant felt the ominous gaze pass over him. There was a shudder of recognition and a momentary connection, which left him in no doubt that Patch, in his new form, knew exactly who he was.

Patch's head rose high on the end of a serpentine neck, overhung the seemingly petrified monster, then flames belched from his nostrils. Even as the searing heat played on the monster's flanks, Tyrant could still hear chuckles beneath the fiery roar. Sheltering behind the stone column to avoid the dreadful heat, he felt Petra clinging to his chest as he tried to shield her with his body.

The monster's agonised screaming continued long after its body had been completely consumed. All that remained as testament to its existence was a dark outline on the stone floor.

Patch stopped raining fire but still carried on laughing. 'There, now don't you agree that's a better dragon than that idiot managed?' His eyes seemed to be fixed in Tyrant's direction, as if he was expecting a reply.

'Marvellous!' Tyrant stood up and clapped his hands together.

‘Tyrant.’ The dragon spoke his name as if he found it amusing. Tyrant immediately regretted his impulse. The sound of his name was more like a death knell than a greeting.

59

Ant was sitting in his usual place in the garden. The sun was warming the top of his head as he felt the gentle tickle of grass beneath his feet. It was his way of checking to see if he was still alive.

The birds were in full song, as if trying to attract Ant's attention to their exuberance. He tried to allow his spirit to soar towards the sky to greet them, but it stubbornly kept returning to the horror of the charnel heap.

Waking or sleeping, the vision of the hanged girl's sightless stare still haunted him. Even the bees that buzzed harmoniously amongst the lavender evoked the sounds of carrion flies feasting on corpses.

In the valley, he could see the ominous stone scar that was Gort. The King's tower rose from the grey mass of the citadel, marking the place where he had been taken for hanging. The feeling of constriction around his throat grew in intensity and he had to keep swallowing in case his air passage became permanently blocked. Waves of fear rolled over him. He allowed himself to fall sideways onto the soft turf, where he held on to his knees and rocked himself gently.

Malachi raised him back to a sitting position, placed a cup of sweet tea at his lips. The potion calmed him; he began to take notice of his surroundings again. The bees sounded friendlier and the birdsong lifted his heart. 'Are they hanging more people today?' he asked.

'I don't know,' Malachi replied.

'Why does he do it?'

'Fear. Since the demons were unleashed, his madness has only increased. Now they are gone, he thinks he can prevent their return by killing his subjects,' Malachi said.

'But he's the king, he needs to fear no one. Surely he can't be so afraid of children that he has them slaughtered.'

'That's the way of this king. Despite his vast armies and impregnable fortress, he lives in fear,' Malachi said.

'Then he's wrong. He should be made to change his ways or…'

'Or he should be removed?' Malachi asked.

'I'd like to show him what it's like to be hanged. That might open his eyes to the unspeakable horror he's creating for ordinary people.'

'Hang him. Then what? Another king who is even more afraid for his own skin. Worse atrocities than ever might be the result,' Malachi said.

'Then get a king who has some compassion and who isn't afraid.'

'That, my boy, is a rare sort of king in my experience,' Malachi said. 'Here, drink the rest of your tea.'

Ant savoured the sweet liquid, felt it warming his gullet and easing the scars that he imagined were there. 'I'm not going to let him get away with it. Someone has to put a stop to this cruelty and madness.'

'And what are you going to do?' Malachi asked.

'I don't exactly know but kill him, obviously.'

'You can find a better use for your talents, Ant.'

'Why should I?'

Malachi swept back his hood to reveal his hawkish features. 'You have the power to create the vedhanas. They can help us make a difference. Together we can control this king, make things better for the world.'

'Better, surely, to get rid of this tyrant and make sure his successor has a heart that can be trusted.'

'That may be more difficult than you can imagine. Trust me, my way is better. I'll teach you what I can, Ant, but then it's your life to lead as you wish.'

Ant put his head in his hands. The hanged girl's face still stared at him in the darkness. He thought of her, of the lively boys who had been destroyed at the King's behest. Of all the horror and suffering he'd experienced.

The King had to die.

60

Lone had discovered a makeshift shelter towards the end of her first day in the desert. By that time, her anger had subsided enough for her to regain control of her body and all that shaking and waving of fists in Tyrant's imagined direction had stopped. She lapsed into a simmering silence, where she comforted herself with visions of how she might make him suffer when she caught up with him. And she *would* catch up with him, if it took the rest of her life to do it.

The tea ration she discovered in the shelter did nothing to reduce her wrath. Her desperation to escape the confines of this small green island in a sea of sand was undiminished. Revenge aside, she had pressing matters to attend to, not least of which was to learn how to create those travelling devices and use them to take over the kingdom. The ability to instantly transport herself to wherever she wanted would give her immense power.

She sent her astral projection soaring high, scanning the farthest horizons for signs of anything but desert. There was nothing as far as she could see. To attempt to walk out of there would be foolhardy in the extreme. It would take weeks of travel through the burning heat before she had any chance of escaping the desert. If she attempted it, she would dry up like a dead leaf and be blown to the four winds.

She had to wait for something to happen. She needed transport, a horse at least, a camel in preference. Something she could load with life-giving water.

Day after day she sat and visualised her greatest need being fulfilled. All her energy was concentrated on this one desire.

There were no wandering herds of beasts of burden, no signs of any life out there, bar skittering lizards and the flies that came in clouds when the sun went down.

Weeks passed. Her desperation increased while her regret for all her mistakes refused to diminish. Hope began to ebb, leaving only the tedium of gathering fruit and eating it, collecting fuel and burning it, drawing water and drinking it.

Sitting high on the crest of a dune, Lone looked out through the unchanging haze that shimmered over the sand. She imagined she could see a solitary horse slowly approaching. She kept her eyes on the mirage as it flicked in and out of view. Very slowly, it grew from a whitish speck in a sea of light brown to a more solid quadruped with unmistakeably equine qualities. Her heart raced with excitement. The image approached. She began to taste freedom. Her mind raced through plans for collecting and storing water. She'd travel north, she thought. In that direction lay the best chance of escaping the implacable desert and returning to civilisation.

By now, the beast was recognisable as a horse and it continued to walk directly towards her. She ran down the hill of sand to greet it, eyes streaming with tears of gratitude and joy. It stopped and waited patiently for her approach.

The familiar shape suddenly registered and her heart missed a beat.

'Patch,' she said.

The misshapen horse pulled back his lips in a ridiculous smirk. 'I couldn't leave this world without telling you that you're trapped here for ever. Think of it as punishment for what you did to me and be grateful things aren't much worse.'

THE END

Printed in Great Britain
by Amazon

72093324R00149